Joseph Schlüter

A General History of Music

Joseph Schlüter

A General History of Music

ISBN/EAN: 9783337087067

Printed in Europe, USA, Canada, Australia, Japan

Cover: Foto ©Thomas Meinert / pixelio.de

More available books at **www.hansebooks.com**

A GENERAL

HISTORY OF MUSIC.

BY

DR. JOSEPH SCHLÜTER.

From the German, by

MRS. ROBERT TUBBS.

"Die Vergangenheit gehört der Gegenwart an und die Schrift dem Leben."
F. C. Dahlmann.

AUTHORIZED TRANSLATION.

LONDON:
RICHARD BENTLEY, NEW BURLINGTON STREET.
Publisher in Ordinary to Her Majesty.
1865.

LONDON: PRINTED BY WILLIAM CLOWES AND SONS, STAMFORD STREET
AND CHARING CROSS.

THE AUTHOR'S PREFACE.

For a Treatise of the History of Music from a general point of view R. G. Kiesewetter has laid the foundation in his admirable work (entirely the result of personal researches), entitled: "History of our Modern, or European, Music."* The task that devolves on those who come after him is, on the one hand, to treat more in detail of the last century than he has done—carefully summing up the results of modern research—, on the other, to condense in a shorter review the period of preparation for " our modern music ;"—in fact, to allot to each period as much time and consideration as its intrinsic worth and interest at the present day shall appear to warrant. Above all, while thus treating of the subject, taken as a whole, it is necessary to unfold the doctrine of

* Leipsic, 1834. Second edition, 1846.

progressive development having an actual inherent sequence, to demonstrate the fact that the Present is not merely connected with the Past by the loose chain of tradition, but grows out of it by reason of its internal structure and formation.

That the latest Histories of Music, which have been presented to the public in the desultory form of 'Lectures,' do not meet the requirements of thoughtful readers has been asserted before now; and we have only to glance at such accounts of concert and operatic performances as are interspersed with historical notices and remarks to be assured that the sources of information accessible to the public at large flow neither freely nor clearly. Whether, and in what degree, the present Work has attained the end desired, I am not qualified to form an opinion; I beg merely to offer this assurance to the reader, that I have steadfastly and carefully kept in view the progressive development of Art, and instead of crowding the pages of this little book with biographical anecdotes cheaply collected, or names and titles of books, have strictly excluded everything superfluous.

As to the style, I have endeavoured to combine

brevity with pleasant reading and warmth of expression. I intended neither to write a compendium for the memory, nor afford facility to those who *skim* a book. Some accompanying remarks are printed in smaller type, so as not to interfere with the proposed general survey of the subject. May this little book, in the absence of a reliable work of greater scope, find favour with those who cherish " divine Cecilia's " Art, and serve as a guide and foundation for future study!

J. SCHLÜTER.

Emmerich on the Rhine.

CONTENTS.

CHAPTER I.
Before the Christian Era 1

CHAPTER II.
Plain Song of the Latin Church. Ambrose, Gregory the Great 10

CHAPTER III.
First attempts in Harmony. Improvements in Musical Notation. Practical arrangement of the same 15

CHAPTER IV.
The Belgian School. Orlandus Lassus 20

CHAPTER V.
Palestrina and Ecclesiastical Music in Italy (the Roman and Venetian Schools) 32

CHAPTER VI.
Origin of the Opera. Influence of the Neapolitan School .. 47

CHAPTER VII.
The Protestant Church Song 68

CHAPTER VIII.

Johann Sebastian Bach (The Sacred Cantata) 78

CHAPTER IX.

George Frederick Handel (The Oratorio) .. 95

CHAPTER X.

The French Opera and Gluck 116

CHAPTER XI.

Foundation and improvement of instrumental music in Germany by Haydn 147

CHAPTER XII.

Mozart (The Opera) 165

CHAPTER XIII.

Zenith of instrumental and ballad composition. Beethoven and Schubert 195

CHAPTER XIV.

The successors of Mozart. The Italian, French, and German Opera 251

CHAPTER XV.

The later musicians of Germany: Spohr, Mendelssohn, Schumann. Present and future 306

HISTORY OF MUSIC.

CHAPTER I.

BEFORE THE CHRISTIAN ERA.

WHEREAS the history of the Arts of Design furnishes reliable information concerning periods of remote antiquity by means of those monuments that have been preserved to posterity, that of Music must perforce commence with the avowal, that she is wholly incompetent to do as much. Even were our knowledge more extensive than it is, an archæology of music, previous to the Christian—or, to go still further back, previous to the Grecian—era, would be of no value or advantage to us. In short, there can be no history of music as an art, where no musical works of art exist.* "There is such a marked

* Zelter, in a letter to Goethe, says of FORKEL—the best known and most esteemed of German music-antiquaries—"He has begun a history of music, and left it off at the very period when its history can be realized by ourselves." He might have said with greater precision: where it begins to have an interest for us.

difference between the music of the East and that of the West, that, even if we knew more, we should find little to suit our ear." We may apply these words of Herder without reservation to the music of the ISRAELITISH nation, notwithstanding Herder himself, by his classical work 'On the Spirit of Hebrew Poetry,' gave rise to a more ideal view of its nature. As among all Oriental nations at the present day, so in the Hebrew music, the rhythmic element greatly preponderated. Song and dance stood in intimate connexion with each other; and, besides loud wind instruments, percussion instruments (viz., kettledrums, cymbals, &c.), which are so powerful in their effects on the untutored feelings, played an important part. Even during the flourishing reigns of David and Solomon, the music taught in the school of the prophets—limited as it was in its use in the service of the temple and sacred lyrics—was unable to rise beyond the showy splendour of the worship of Jehovah, and attain to artistic development. Doubtless, the severe, uncompromising spirit of Monotheism contributed likewise to impede the progress of what is, in its very nature, a liberal art. Mendelssohn's choruses in 'Athalia,' with their trumpet and harp accompaniments, may be taken as a sample (though of course highly idealized) of the sacred festal hymn of the Israelites—the maestro having evidently intended, particularly in the instrumentation, to give an historical colouring to the composition.

Turning from the sacred music of the Hebrews —rather noisy than melodious—, we find it impossible to determine to what extent the development of GRECIAN music was affected by the meagre attempts of the Indians, and, in particular, the Egyptians, in this art; in any case, the first theoretical foundation of a scientific treatment of music among the Greeks was laid somewhere about the sixth century [B.C.], chiefly by the philosopher PYTHAGORAS, and LASOS of Hermione, Pindar's preceptor. But, with the Greeks, music, "the art of the Muses," had altogether a far wider range; for, besides the actual art of melody, it included poetry, dancing, and the drama. In this union, which embraced intellectual, moral, and, in part, physical culture, music was considered, together with gymnastics, the second necessary part of a liberal education, as leading, by means of harmony and rhythmical proportion ($εὐρυθμια$), to the purest elevation of mind, as well as moral restraint. Music was not, as with us, merely an *object* of education, but a *means* thereto.

The actual history of Greek music, omitting the fables of Orpheus and other bards of that remote age, begins with TERPANDER of Lesbos [B.C. circa 670]. Terpander appears to be the real founder of Greek music; he introduced the seven-stringed cithara, which had an octave in compass, in lieu of the ancient (four-stringed) tetrachord; he arranged popular melodies in accordance with the canons of art, and determined with greater precision than heretofore the relative positions of the three most ancient keys or "harmonies" (Doric, Phrygian, Lydian). *Flute-playing*, an art of anterior-Asiatic origin, and peculiar to the worship of Dionysos, was treated in an artistic manner by OLYMPOS the Phrygian, but did not meet with universal acceptance till a later date. Lyre and cithara were the only genuine Hellenic instruments, sacred to the purer worship of Apollo.

Music, as performed on the *Phorminx**—the most ancient of Grecian stringed instruments—, played only a subordinate part in the intoned recital of epic poems (whereby the Homeric are chiefly understood); it was used merely to accent the rhythm. Lyric poetry (subjective Æolian poesy, as well as the solemn Doric chorus), on the contrary, was, from the nature of its metrical structure, peculiarly adapted for the assistance of music; and, consequently, reached its full development as an art when the mechanical powers of music attained to some degree of perfection. Poetry and music were intimately allied in song, in the vocal rhythmic-melodic recitation of the

---

* The phorminx was, in all probability, the earliest stringed instrument of the lyre genus. It was employed to accent the words of the heroic metre, and was therefore dedicated to Apollo.

choruses employed in tragedy; and, to increase the effect of this latter on sentiment and **imagination**, the lyre or cithara, with sounds of octaves, fifths, and fourths, above and below, was employed as accompaniment. Thus, music was the handmaid of poetry, reverently following the bard's inspiration, animating and accenting his words, giving character to the whole, but without independent existence either in lyric or dramatic poetry. According to all testimony, there is not the slightest trace of instrumental music, independent of singing, to be discovered during the best period of Grecian art; as, neither in the days of Homer, do we find singing alluded to apart from instrumental accompaniment. Music and poetry were inseparably united; musical **rhythm** followed the poetical cadence, or **rather, we may** say, this cadence was a musical **one; poets** were, in like manner, musicians. **It was** the same with the Troubadours of the Middle Ages; "song and **story**", words and melody, were *one* undivided art. That the power of wondrous charm which poetry gained by its connexion with music was deeply felt by the poets themselves, is witnessed to by the famous eulogy—one among many—by Pindar **in the first Pythian prize song.** "Even the flaming lightning-dart **is extinguished by the** tones of the lyre, the eagle **slumbers on the** sceptre of Jove, his swift pinions droop on each **side the royal** bird; for the sound has shed a dark mist over his bowed head, and softly closed his eyelids; slumbering, he raises his gently heaving plumage, tamed by the power of melody; yea, even the heart of mighty Ares is rejoiced, seeing the terrible lance rests peacefully on his large temple. But he whom Jove loveth not is terrified, and withdraws himself in fear, when he hears the voices of the Pierides on the earth and boundless ocean; yea, even Typhos, abhorred of the Gods, in Tartarus." As Pindar, in these words, celebrates the conquering might of music over all the nobler powers of nature, so did the Hellenes, in general, consider its lofty and only true aim to be that of imparting to every passionate emotion measure and moderation—the highest mental repose. For it was not to assert its own claims by promoting merely æsthetic enjoyment, but assist, " as an auxiliary given by the Muses against the dissonant currents of the soul," in connexion with noble exalted poesy, in forming the mind, manners, and character.

It was especially the office of Tragedy—in the representation of which the several arts of the Muses met in combined operation—to raise and purify the passions by means of poetry and music (καθαρσις); and this object was doubtless attained till, simultaneously with the decay of national and political life, the several arts threw off their mutual allegiance and the former strict control of the state, and essayed to shine on their own account. The exaggerated dithyrambic choral hymn was wrested from its former noble and suitable relation to the action represented; lyre and flute playing vied in public rivalry for the applause of pleasure-seeking crowds; while to the more thoughtful Greek the mere craft of the *virtuoso* appeared restricted and mean, unless supported by talent and skill of a high order. It was not long before the simplicity and severity which characterized the old music had to make way for novelties which tickled the ear of the multitude, and the aristocracy of *connoisseurs* succumbed to a "certain low *theatrocracy*." Plato, in particular, blames—besides the intermixture of various styles of composition—the sundering of music from poetry, by which the "melody without words presented to the ear" was entirely abandoned to the insecure guidance of the feelings, and thus became more and more diverted from its original lofty ethical intention. Thus, singularly enough, the first appearance of Grecian music as an independent art was the sign of its decay. Proceeding directly from the genuine national life of the people, closely entwined with poetry, religion, and custom, and furnished with such scanty means of harmony, it was unable to soar to the heights of independent art; the soul's art, that which addresses itself to the deep consciousness in man, could not, among a people like the Greeks—prone to the more material contemplation of beauty in its external manifestations—attain the same perfection as sculpture and painting.* That little of Greek music which is supposed to be still preserved in writing is, comparatively, of small value; an acquaintance, founded on trustworthy documents, with the composition of one chorus, would be more important to us than all the learned dissertations on Greek music that have ever been held.

The ROMANS have contributed nothing to the

---

* The manifold attempts to claim for Greek music the possession of harmony (in our sense of the word) are so many failures; for they ignore the very essence of classical, as opposed to *romantic*, art. "Music opened to the Greek no Romantic spirit-world from which is wafted an atmosphere of mysterious awe and enchantment;—rather it brought the Pindaric Ode, the Sophocleian scene, into the full blaze of Hellenic daylight, whose blue heavens beamed with unclouded brightness. If we may be allowed the metaphor, Grecian music bore the same relation to Grecian poetry as polychromy to a Grecian temple or statue. Just as the office of this latter was, in a subordinate capacity, to assist the effect of architectural forms by delicate and judicious tinting, and vaguely indicate—not coarsely mock—the appearance of life in the statue, music was to lend its aid in giving full and distinct utterance to the poet's thoughts—not arrogantly to assert itself to the detriment of his expression. Therefore, it is not to be reckoned a fault in Greek music that it lacked harmony and breadth according to our ideas of music. . . . . Polyphony was, in the very nature of Greek music, an *impossibility*." A. W. AMBROS, History of Music, vol. i., p. 221. Breslau, 1862.

Böckh is quite right when he says that our music would have displeased the Greeks as much as our Gothic architecture. "Tantum abhorret ab antiquitatis indole nostræ harmoniæ ratio, ut eam veteribus displicituram fuisse, si nossent, contendere ausim." (Pindari opera quæ supersunt, p. 253.)

history of music, seeing that in art as in literature they merely followed Greek models, and left the performance of music almost entirely to Greek slaves and freedmen. Only when employed in public purposes of utility and splendour—particularly in military pageants—did they achieve an increase of *material*. During the Empire, especially in the reign of Nero—who appeared in public as a singer and performer—, the art was degraded to the service of fashion and folly, and a mere toy for the gratification of vanity and frivolity.

CHAPTER II.

PLAIN SONG OF THE LATIN CHURCH. AMBROSE. GREGORY THE GREAT.

IN the early days of Christianity, the efforts made to preserve the infant Church from contact with the luxurious and dissolute practices of the heathens, as well as precautions enforced by the persecutions, banished instrumental music from the Christian Liturgy; whereas, to quote Herder's expression, the entire "setting" of it was vocal. The peculiar versification of the Psalms (*parallelismus membrorum*) gave rise to the *antiphonal*, or alternate, chant, which was sung, either by male and female choirs, or by priests and people. It is, however, by no means improbable, that, with the Christian converts, echoes of Greek melodies may have found their way into the Christian Hymn.

Pope SYLVESTER established a singing school at Rome [circa A.D. 330]; and, somewhat later, St. AMBROSE, Archbishop of Milan [A.D. 374—397], rendered signal services to the cause of art by judicious encouragement of, and efforts to popularize, church singing. His endeavours were especially directed to improve the alternate chanting of *antiphony* and *responsory*; to this end, he wrote and composed hymns and spiritual songs himself. The so-called Ambrosian Hymn, *Te Deum laudamus*, is, however, the work of a subsequent author.

GREGORY THE GREAT [Pope A.D. 590—604] endeavoured to reform church singing—which, in the meantime, had become altogether too free and secular in character—and restore it to its pristine simplicity and vigour. To the four *authentic* (primitive) ecclesiastical "modes" or "tones" of Ambrose, which were founded on the Greek tetrachord (Doric, Phrygian, Lydian, and Mixolydian), he added four *plagal* (derivative) *modes* on the fourth note below (*hypo*) the key-note; and thus founded the system of octaves, and the eight ancient ecclesiastical "modes" or keys, calling the several notes after the seven first letters of the Latin alphabet. He collected and placed in his *Antiphonarium* all the best church melodies extant, carefully marked with points (*neumas*, i.e. signs); which *Antiphonarium*, with subsequent additions and variations, is used to this day in the Roman Catholic Church. The *Gregorian* or *Roman* chant introduced by, and called after, him (consisting of a monotonous chant with a strongly-marked cadence) received the appellation of "*canto fermo*" (*cantus firmus*) and "*plain-chant*" (*cantus planus*) by the Italians and French, in contradistinction to the rhythmical variety and movement of secular (particularly *figurate*) melody. In order to preserve this severe style of chanting from any foreign influences, he established a normal school of singing, and entrusted the execution of Church music to the choir that was formed there, by which means the former active participation of the congregation in the singing was almost entirely done away with. While admiring the creative genius of Ambrose and his lively sympathy with the people's spiritual needs, we cannot fail to acknowledge the greater intellectual energy of Gregory, whose talent for criticism and organization has left its impress on several succeeding centuries.

The Gregorian *choir* chant, which now supplanted the Ambrosian *congregational* chant, was speedily diffused over Christian Europe. Its most zealous promoter was Charlemagne, who, true to his saying "I will that Church music be pleasing to the Almighty," reformed the singing in his private chapel, and, with the valuable assistance of the British monk Alcuin, founded numerous normal singing schools on the Roman pattern in France and Germany. A century later, ALFRED the Great did as much for England; he is supposed to be the founder of a professorship of music at Oxford.

Though we are quite ready to admit, from its universal acceptance and the testimony of St. Bernard and others, the great value of **the Gregorian chant *in its day*** (i. e. down to the thirteenth century **and at farthest Palestrina's age**), yet we cannot but think the recent attempts which have been made to restore it in the ritual of the Roman Catholic Church a signal mistake and complete failure. Putting **aside** that the manifold changes it has incurred during the lapse **of ages,** and, above all, **the** necessitated transposition into the **modern system of music** — and consequently **a** different pitch— have enormously shorn it of its peculiar character **and solemnity, it lacks everything that we admire** in music at the present **day— time, rhythm, distinct, heart-stirring *tune***, and, consequently, that quality **which addresses** itself to the feelings of the multitude, **and** induces a spirit **of** devotion. **Just as** learned archæologists discover beauty, which **is** unintelligible to the ordinary comprehension, **in stiff** pottery-pictures **and** antique woodcuts, we hear some **out-and-out** mediævalist extol—with senseless affectation **of** profound **knowledge**—the Gregorian chant as the *ne plus ultra* of all **ecclesiastical** art, the commencement **of whose** decline **a** recent **author*** has connected with the names of **Raphael and Palestrina!** Why should we at the **present day be severer than the Fathers at the Council of Trent?** How shall we undertake to run counter to the education and art-culture **of modern times, just to procure for** a few persons **the satisfaction of imagining themselves back** in the palmy days of **ecclesiastical supremacy, through the** medium of Gothic architecture **and Gregorian chants?†**

F. **Mendelssohn, roused** by foolish panegyric, expresses the same **feeling in a** letter to Zelter, dated from Rome. " I can't help it ; **it** shocks me to hear the most solemn and beautiful words chanted along **to** such unmeaning hurdy-gurdy sounds. They call it 'canto fermo' —Gregorian—that doesn't signify. **If in** former **times things were not** deeply felt, or **could** not be done **better, we can do better now, and there is certainly** nothing of **this monotonous handicraft in the words of the Bible;** there, everything **is vigorous and genuine, and**

---

* F. CLEMENT, Histoire générale de la Musique Religieuse. Paris, 1861.

† NOTE BY THE TRANSLATOR. **If the truth** of the above remarks **be** admitted, how much greater force **do** they acquire when applied **to the** revival of plain Gregorian chant **in** our Anglican liturgy!

besides that, is as well and as naturally expressed as it is possible to be. Why then should it sound like a formula? Is that what they call Church music? Certainly, it has not a *false* expression, for it has no expression *whatever*; but is it **not** downright profanation of the words? Thus, hundreds **of times** during the ceremonies here, I have been quite **savage**; and when people come and say, 'How beautiful it is!' **it sounds** like a bad joke, and yet they mean it seriously!"

CHAPTER III.

First attempts in Harmony. Improvements in Musical Notation. Practical Arrangement of the same.

If, as before stated, it is probable that remnants of old Grecian melodies were preserved in the early Christian hymns, the uniform movement of the chant introduced by Gregory was entirely opposed to the delicate metrical division which distinguished Greek rhythm. In one respect only it resembled Greek (as indeed all ancient) music, viz.—in its *unisonal* character, i.e., the concentration of *all* the voices on the *same* note; that wherein it differed from the former, was at least no improvement on it. The antique theory was only fully superseded when a new element was introduced, viz.—*harmony,* which is the root and principle of modern music. Kiesewetter's opinion, that the Grecian system, which Hucbald and Guido still adhered to, was an obstacle to the free development of music, and that "the new music only flourished in proportion as it began to relinquish the old Greek system which had been forced upon it," is perfectly correct.

With the tenth century commenced the first attempts to introduce *polyphony* instead of *unisony* in singing—i.e., the simultaneous sounding of several voices on different notes. But before music attained the undoubted possession of a genuine art of harmony, it had to undergo a long and rigorous training, during which it did not escape manifold errors. Reared in the bosom of the Church, and taught its first utterance in the liturgical Latin, it now likewise obtained this first, purely theoretical, cultivation in the cloister—almost the sole abode of learning in the Middle Ages.

HUCBALD, a Flemish monk [840—930], made the first attempt in two part song by adding to the principal voice an accompaniment of progressive fourths and fifths. This "*concentum concorditer dissonum*" he called *diaphony*, and the accompaniment *discantus* or ordinary *organum*—which latter appellation clearly denotes the presence of organ music, which took rise in the eighth, and became generally extended during the ninth century, though still in a very primitive condition. From the combination of simultaneous sounds in chords, and their results, he deduced the theory of harmonized melody—however uncouth and disagreeable his sequences of fourths and fifths appear to us.

The following period, including the Benedictine monk GUIDO OF AREZZO (famed as "inventor musicæ"), who lived in the early part of the eleventh century, in reality added nothing to the resources of harmony. Though unacquainted with musical notation (which consists of dots placed on and between several parallel lines), he paved the way for it, and made it practicable. It is here necessary to explain, that the *neumas* (small crooks and strokes of various shapes and positions) were formerly placed on and between two lines drawn horizontally above the text: in order to designate more clearly the higher or lower pitch of the notes, Guido spread them over four lines. So little satisfactory, however, did this reform appear even to himself, that he recommended the Gregorian characters as the more convenient method of notation. His chief merit was the invention of an improved, purely practical, method of singing, which addressed itself to the memory. In order to insure correct intonation, he made use of the syllables with which the first lines of a well-known Latin hymn commenced: *ut* (C), *re* (D), *mi* (E), *fa* (F), *sol* (G), *la* (A); this was called Guido's solmisation or *Solfa*. The syllable *si* (B), for the seventh note, was added at a much later period; and, thus completed, both the Italians and French still employ this nomenclature, of which the range has been considerably enlarged by the additions in use for the major and minor keys.

FRANCO OF COLOGNE, a presbyter, invented a method of notation which completely answered the requirements of the age in which he lived (the end of the twelfth or beginning of the thirteenth century); he not only denoted with greater precision than heretofore the higher and lower pitch of the notes by their position, but also determined their duration or value by the shape (*figura*). Prosody, as well as music—which followed its rhythm—, was, till then, distinguished merely by *longs* and *breves;* Franco assumed four periods of duration, viz., very long, long, short, half short,—to which he gave the corresponding nomenclature of *maxima, longa, brevis, semibrevis* (the latter our semibreve). He thus founded the system of musical time, or *mensuration,* and the distinction which afterwards came into general use between *choral music* and *figurate* or *mensurable music.*

In the fourteenth century, MARCHETTUS OF PADUA and a Frenchman JOHANNES DE MURIS (Jean de Meurs) carried his theory still further; they also established the first correct principles in the use of consonances and dissonances.

But in order to understand how awkward and clumsy were the first *practical* attempts in the art of harmony compared with secular melody (already enjoying a considerable amount of cultivation), we have only to turn to the recently discovered productions of the Trouvère ADAM DE

LA HALE ("le boiteux d'Arras"). He composed three part songs and Motets; but his plays (*jeux*), of which both words and music were his own composition, evince—for that period (the latter half of the thirteenth century)—a surprising degree of facility and grace, both in rhythm and melody.

CHAPTER IV.

THE BELGIAN SCHOOL. ORLANDUS LASSUS.

WHILE secular melody, as yet left to the natural taste of the people—the Troubadours, Minstrels, and "Minne singers"—, had, as we have seen, attained considerable perfection, the labours of the learned, on the contrary, were, till the sixteenth century, solely directed to an extended cultivation of harmony, in which the Low Countries took the lead.* The remarkable intellectual energy and penetration which distinguished them, the "patientia laboris" lauded by Erasmus, as well as the wealth and prosperity enjoyed by the nation at the period of which we are treating, eminently fitted the Belgians for devoting themselves wholly and exclusively to the task of working the recently acquired harmonic material. Delighted to have found in

* *Ueber die Verdienste der Niederländer, im* 14., 15., *und* 16. *Jahrhundert, um die Tonkunst,* von R. G. KIESEWETTER. Amsterdam, 1829.

music a concrete variety reducible to certain laws, they applied themselves to the study of polyphony and interweaving of parts (*counterpoint*) with such intense ardour, that they took little account of melodious expression, and seemed quite to divert the art from its real aim and object. It is therefore not to be wondered at—when the very considerable difficulties which at that time attended the construction of polyphonous pieces are taken into consideration—that an art exercised in so formal and restricted a manner frequently degenerated into barren artificialness, and that Beauty was lost in erudition and formalism. The intricacies and subtilties of simple, double, three or more part counterpoint, appear stiff and strange to us; nevertheless, they were the needful preparatory exercises on newly trodden ground. The harsh, unpliant harmonic forms had to undergo a thorough intellectual elaboration before genuine vitality and expression could be breathed into them; and never would modern music have developed its powers so freely and so happily, had not the Belgians undertaken this severe mental labour with energy and zeal. The influence of the (so-called) Belgian school spread far and wide, and was so universally acknowledged, that the Belgians occupied the most distinguished and influential places in Italy, France, and Germany.

The oldest known master and teacher of

counterpoint was GUILLAUME DUFAY, who was chapel-master and tenor singer in the papal chapel from 1380 to 1432. His compositions are chiefly for four parts, or voices, and usually have a chorale or secular tune for their *motif*; though devoid of expression, melody, or invention, they display considerable advance, viz.—correct harmony.

The more elaborate, *fugued*, style was founded by JOHANNES OCKENHEIM [Ockeghem; born between 1420—1430, died circa 1513]. He has been called, though the epithet is scarcely appropriate, the Sebastian Bach of the fifteenth century. His name marks the period when polyphony, which now formed an integral part of vocal music—especially in the Church—, " caused the parts or voices to carry out a theme without regard to expression or beauty, to separate and join again; likewise formed and resolved dissonances, and executed a musical theme consisting of a few notes moved backwards and forwards in different relative positions."[*] The increasing taste for artificial devices turned the progress of art into a yet narrower channel; its enigmatical canons, quaint conceits and calculations, far outstripped all other crudities of mediæval art; though, at the same time, it must be admitted, that the unremitting thoughtful search for esoteric rules established

[*] CARRIERE, *Aesthetik*.

the practice of the art of harmony on a firm basis, and provided a safe starting-point for feeling and imagination. The papal chapel still possesses seven masses of Ockenheim.

Ockenheim's celebrated pupil, the gifted and accomplished JOSQUIN DES PRÉS [born circa 1440, died when chapel-master to the Emperor Maximilian, circa 1515], was one of the first who seriously endeavoured to raise abstract technical skill—which hitherto had almost entirely absorbed the attention of musicians—to higher æsthetic significance, and make it a vehicle of sympathetic expression. Although even he occasionally surpassed others in artificialness, and sometimes—particularly in sequences of chords—attempted quaint and even grotesque combinations, his best works (chiefly four and five part Masses and Motets) are, according to Rochlitz,* "easier to comprehend, less spun out, less laden with contrapuntal artifices." Though he bestowed extraordinary pains on the elaboration and finish of his works, they were not merely the result of difficult and abstruse calculation; he understood well how to employ wit and humour in the treatment of his art. Thus, while chapel-master to Lewis XII. of France, wishing to remind the king of his promise to bestow on him a prebend, he composed two motets on the words "*Memor*

* *Für Freunde der Tonkunst*, vol. iv., p. 49. Vier Bände. Leipzig, 1824-1832.

esto verbi tui" and "*Portio mea non est in terra viventium*", and caused them to be performed before the Court. He had previously written a mass on the *solfa* syllables *la sol fa re mi*, in allusion to a nobleman whom he had vainly besought to intercede with the king in his behalf, and who had always put him off with the answer, "Laisse faire moy." Yet he was by no means wanting in thorough appreciation of sacred melody and expression, and there are several of his Motets and Masses, which, in their careful treatment, foreshadow the grandeur and simplicity which afterwards characterized Church music. While allowing free play to his varied and humorous tendencies, his principal efforts were directed to the production of noble, dignified, and simple forms in composition; he was thorough master of the resources of his art in all its branches. "Perfectly versed in all styles of art, enormously productive, yet remarkable for carefulness of execution (for which Glarean praises him while contrasting him with his somewhat older contemporary, Jacob Hobrecht), attempting bold flights, yet always intelligible, at once learned and pleasing, everywhere graceful, he was the universal favourite of the age, welcomed everywhere, ruling without a rival."* Josquin, called by Luther "master of notes, while others were

---

* Heimsoeth, in Aschbach's *Kirchenlexicon*, vol. iii., p. 841.

mastered by notes", closes the series of musical calculators, and opens that of real composers.

Though Josquin had exercised his art for a considerable space of time in Italy and France, his own country was the scene of his principal labours; but the most remarkable Belgian composers who succeeded him — Jean Mouton, Clemens non Papa, Arcadelt, Goudimel, Willaert, his pupils, and others—were employed almost entirely in foreign countries. The invention of music-printing with moveable types (by Ottavio Petrucci in 1502) was of important service to them in the speedy and extensive diffusion of their works; and, till after the middle of the sixteenth century, the Belgians enjoyed undisputed supremacy throughout Europe. At Rome, after Josquin had introduced the art of counterpoint into the papal chapel, the Belgians were preferred before the Italians; besides these, however, the French and Spaniards could boast excellent composers in Carpentras and Morales. A noble and deep conception of this latter is a Motet for six voices: *Lamentabatur Jacobus* ("una maraviglia dell' arte"), which still retains its place in the performances of the Sistine chapel. The "nuova musica" was not much exercised by the Italians themselves, with the exception of the Florentine Costanzo Festa (distinguished as the forerunner of Palestrina), who still survives in a noble and simple *Te Deum*. [He died in 1545].

Thus, the Belgians—especially since the papal chapel-master GOUDIMEL established a music-school at Rome in 1540—held nearly all the musical appointments; which monopoly, however, was broken up by Animuccia, Palestrina, and Nanini—Italians educated in Goudimel's school.

ADRIAN WILLAERT [born at Bruges circa 1490] contributed in a far greater degree to the progress of art than even Goudimel at Rome; he was likewise a pupil of Josquin, and chapel-master at St. Mark's, Venice, from 1527 till his death [1563]. The style of composition usual with his predecessors was a four part *canon* constructed on a given melody; Willaert wrote his Motets for five, six, and seven voices; whereby he did not aim at greater intricacy, but, on the contrary, distinguished the parts from each other, and, instead of closely interweaving the phrases in sacred melody (as had previously been the custom), disengaged them freely from each other. To this end—according to the testimony of his pupil ZARLINO [1517-1593], highly esteemed for his additions to the science of harmony—he first arranged sacred songs, and particularly psalms, for two or three separate choirs (*a coro spezzato*); —thereby reviving the ancient antiphonal song enriched with all the improvements of recent art. By alternating the full and divided choir, he attained the grandest effects—for an actual instrumental accompaniment was not as yet in use.

Heimsoeth* graphically records the splendour of public life at Venice, "where a peculiarly vivid interest in the common weal, and the intimate relation between the ecclesiastical and national *fête* resulting therefrom, found its common meeting-ground in the State Church of St. Mark, and created a perpetual demand for musical productions of a grand and solemn character, inasmuch as the attractions of the art were required, both within and without the Church, to enhance the brilliancy of the celebration."

But the importance of Willaert's great influence will not be justly appreciated unless taken in connection with the so-called Venetian school which he founded, and which continued to develop his style. His pupil and successor in office, CYPRIAN DE RORE—surnamed "il divino" by the Italians, and considered even equal to Orlando Lasso by the Belgians—, was born at Mechlin in 1516; he succeeded in popularizing the art of polyphony in the Madrigal (or secular love-ditty, analogous in form to the Motet), whereby he exercised no unimportant influence on secular melody.

The last great master among the Belgians, and, after Palestrina, the greatest of the sixteenth century, was *ORLANDUS LASSUS* [born 1520 at Mons in Hainault, died 1595 at

---

* See HEIMSOETH, etc., p. 844.

Munich].* After holding distinguished situations at Rome and Naples, he visited France and England, then passed a considerable time in modest retirement in his native country, whence, at the invitation of Duke Albert V. of Bavaria, he repaired to Munich in 1557 ; here he resided as chapel-master till his death, employed in improving the style of Church music.

That he furthered the development of German music, may be seen by referring to his pupil Eccard; on the other hand, his works reveal the influence of the land in which he passed the larger and more famous portion of his life, and after a short sojourn in other countries came to look upon as a second home. He did not rest satisfied with the mere ingenious embroidery of parts on a given melody, though his general mode of treatment was more closely allied to the formal mannerism of that style, than Palestrina's. "He is the brilliant master of the North, great and sublime in sacred composition, of inexhaustible invention, displaying much breadth, variety, and depth in his treatment; he delights in full and powerful harmonies, yet after all—owing to an existence passed in journeys as well as service at Court, and occupied at the same time with both sacred and secular music—he came short of that

* *Biographische Notiz über Roland de Lattre bekannt unter dem Namen Orland de Lassus. Aus dem Französischen des H. Delmotte übersetzt und mit Anmerkungen herausgegeben von S. W. Dehn Berlin, 1837.*

lofty, solemn tone which pervades the works of the great master of the South—Palestrina, who, with advancing years, restricted himself more and more to Church music."* And besides vigour, depth, and sublimity, the works of Lassus reveal a loving and gentle spirit, whose purity, piety, and simplicity of expression in the Motet " *Gustate et videte quam suavis sit Dominus timentibus eum et confidentibus ei* " (sung on the feast of Corpus Domini at Munich) excited universal admiration.

His compositions in print and manuscript (altogether upwards of two thousand in number) form a choice collection. They are, for the most part, at Munich; and consist of Motets in four to eight parts, of which many are composed on secular themes; Motets, principally in five or six parts—though some in more or less—; Hymns, Psalms, Magnificats, Lamentations (of Jeremiah, to which he added the composition of the "Lessons on Job"), Responsories, Litanies, &c. Of these the *Motets*—a branch of composition in which he was considered to have excelled—and the *Seven penitential Psalms* in five parts, were most highly esteemed; concerning this latter composition, Thibaut repeats a story without foundation, viz., that Charles IX. of France ordered them for his own use, "in order to obtain rest to his soul after the massacre of St. Bartholomew". But, apart from these noble and multi-

* HEIMSOETH.

farious productions, he would have rendered his name everlastingly famous by his admirable improvements in musical art, such as the introduction of the chromatic element—thereby introducing greater variety in modulation—, the mensuration of time by reducing a number of different kinds and their signs to two principal kinds—equal and unequal, with the manner of denoting the measure, as: *allegro, adagio,* &c. His generation admired in him, as well as Palestrina, a "Prince of Music," the Pope created him Knight of the Golden Spur in 1574, and—even in Italy—on the title-page of one of his Masses, beneath his likeness, these words were placed: "*Hic est Lassus, qui lassum recreat orbem.*" Unconcerned as to fame, the "gentle, peaceful man" (so Eccard portrays him) lived for his art alone, and a contemporary (the admirable historian Thuanus or de Thou) aptly says of him, that the flattering expressions of the great, as well as a European reputation, were not so much *enjoyed* as *endured* by him.

Kiesewetter concludes his description of this period in these words: "Lassus shed lustre on, and at the same time closed, the great epoch of Belgian ascendancy, which, during the space of two hundred years, had given to the world nearly three hundred musicians of marvellous science for the times in which they lived, many of whom were excellent composers." The musical " Decline and Fall" of the Netherlands, which began with Lassus' death, is not (as Fétis thought) so much to be ascribed to the political disturbances of the sixteenth century, and wars of the two succeeding ones, as to the fact that the contrapuntal art peculiar to the Belgians, after having gained its best and last triumphs in Italy, and afterwards Germany, was, in the nature of things, forced to give way to the melodious and beautiful style which appeared with the seventeenth century, and, in particular, to a genus of music, surpassing every other, which was beginning to assert itself: —the Opera.

CHAPTER V.

PALESTRINA AND ECCLESIASTICAL MUSIC IN ITALY (THE ROMAN AND VENETIAN SCHOOLS).

WILLAERT, and in particular Orlandus Lassus, had, with the intuition of genius, understood the requirements of the age and country in which they lived; and, embodying the same in their own art-conceptions, added new lustre to the Belgian name. In Rome, on the contrary, at that time the chief seat of Belgian art, the exclusive study of technical skill had frozen it to a mere formula, which, in itself lifeless, was unable to stand its ground against the newly-awakened taste of the nation.

So early as the tenth century, and from that time down, improvements resulting from the progressive development of harmony were adopted in the practice of ecclesiastical music—especially in the papal chapel. From the latter half of the thirteenth century—particularly after the return of the Pope from Avignon (1377)—the Gregorian chant became more and more overladen with contrapuntal embellishments which rendered the prescribed Church-song difficult of recognition in its borrowed garb. From increasing disregard both of meaning and connection in the text, the ancient simple Church-song was threatened with complete annihilation; it became so complicated and overcharged, that it degenerated into a confused jumble of sound. Still more common was it for musicians—entirely losing sight of the real intention of ecclesiastical music—to take melodies from secular songs for the themes of their Masses and Motets; and, making no secret of this, to call them by their profane titles; as for instance: *L'homme armé, Adieu mes amours, Baisez moy, Venere bella, Chiare, fresche e dolce acque*, &c. The Church could no longer behold with indifference these aberrations of an art depraved and degraded almost to a craft; wherefore, at the Council of Trent (in 1562), a thorough and complete reformation of ecclesiastical music was brought under consideration. The just reproofs of the Council, which seriously threatened the entire existence of *figurate music*, roused the creative genius of Palestrina, who raised music to an independent national existence, and made it rank as one of the fine arts, along with sculpture and painting;—these last having already reached their zenith in Leonardo da Vinci, Raphael, Correggio, Titian, and Michel Angelo.

Giovanni Pierluigi da *PALESTRINA* was

(according to Baini*) born at Palestrina in 1524, and educated in the severe school of Goudimel, whose peculiarities were exaggerated to weakness by the majority of his pupils,—the master being thus held responsible for their follies, and made to appear the representative of a scholastic doctrine totally devoid of life. Palestrina grasped the essential doctrines of the school, without adopting its mannerism. He did not bid defiance to established rules, but moved within their limits with so much freedom and easy grace, as to suggest the idea of having struck out an entirely new path.

Of his hitherto known compositions, the *Lamentations*, and especially the *Improperie* (tender reproaches of the Lord to his ungrateful people), which were performed on Good Friday 1560, during the Adoration of the Cross, captivated all hearts by their sublime simplicity and gentle piety of expression;—for music of such purity, solemnity, and majesty had never yet been heard in the Church. The 'Improperie' have been repeated yearly ever since, down to the present time: in our day, Goethe and Mendelssohn have recorded in touching words the deep impression this music produced on them. His next work of importance was (in 1562) a six-part Mass (*super ut, re, mi, fa, sol, la*), in which the "*Crucifixus*

---

* G. BAINI; *Memorie storico-critiche della vita e delle opere di Giov. Pierl. da Palestrina.* 2 *volumi, Roma,* 1828.

etiam pro nobis" for four high voices, was particularly admired.

But beyond Rome, the compositions of the master were as yet unknown; and, consequently, of so little account in the deliberations of the Council of Trent, that the Fathers, in the first blush of indignation, and almost shame, that an art so licentious should have been so long tolerated in the house of God, insisted upon the abolition of all Church music except the ancient Gregorian chant. At length, in accordance with the earnest remonstrance of the Emperor Ferdinand I. and the Roman Cardinals, who repeatedly cited Palestrina's compositions, it was agreed that practical measures should be taken in order to ascertain whether the declared abuses of the four (or more) part *figurate* melody lay in the nature of the art, or only in the carelessness of composers; and to let the final decision rest upon a new composition of Palestrina's, on a grander scale than he had hitherto attempted.

Young Palestrina was therefore to write a Mass—as a specimen—in which, above all, distinct intelligibility of the words was required, and have it performed before a commission of eight cardinals—of whom St. Carlo Borromeo was one. Thus, all eyes were directed to him, at a time when the very existence of the art was at stake. With the enthusiasm of the artist—with the pious trustful confidence expressed in the motto of his first Mass "*Illumina oculos meos*," Palestrina applied himself to this noble task. Instead of only one, he wrote three six-part Masses, of which the third — written for soprano, alto, two tenors, and two basses — excited such universal admiration on its public performance [19th June, 1565] that the Pope himself (Pius IV.) exclaimed in raptures: "It is John who gives us here, in this earthly Jerusalem, a foretaste of that new song, which the holy Apostle John realized in the heavenly Jerusalem long since, in prophetic trance." Palestrina afterwards entitled his prize Mass '*Missa Papae Marcelli*', in grateful memory of his former illustrious patron, Marcellus II.

Several provincial synods followed the example of the Council of Trent; among them, one at Milan in the same year (1565, over which Cardinal Carlo Borromeo presided), one at Cambray (also in 1565), at Constance, and Augsburg (both in 1567), Namur, and Mechlin (in 1570), and others; all of which set to work in earnest to reform the loose practices of the composers of Church music.

Palestrina's versatility and eminent genius powerfully furthered the improved tendency of the age. It is true that, previously, he had occasionally made use of secular themes in his compositions; but the best period of his productions is characterized by the invariable connexion of the sacred text with its ancient proper Church tune. By transposing the ecclesiastical melody (*canto fermo*) from the tenor to the soprano (thus rendering it more intelligible to the ear), he created that glorious thing—choir-song, with its refined harmony,—that noble and sublime music of which his works are incomparable models, and the papal chapel is the oracle. Of his very numerous works (Masses, Motets, Hymns, Litanies, &c.) scarcely one half has been printed; besides those already alluded to, and a few others, the following are still performed at Rome—principally during the Holy Week: a brilliant Mass for the Assumption of the Virgin—"*Assumpta est Maria in Cœlum*," an incomparably sublime Offertory on Holy Thursday—"*Fratres ego enim accepi*," that masterpiece of Motets—"*Surge illuminare Jerusalem*," and a "*Stabat Mater*" for two choirs.

Palestrina died in the arms of St. Filippo Neri, on the 2nd of February 1594, and was buried in St. Peter's, to the pious strains of his "*Libera me Domine*." On his tomb is the following noble epitaph: *Joannes Petrus Aloysius Prænestinus Musicæ Princeps*.

Essentially choral, as all Church music should be, Palestrina's music is the very opposite of the "melting mood;" it is characterized by an entire absence of *contrast* and local *colouring*. The harmony is one of gentle repose, where "the voices do not seek for individual display, but emerge from the full choir to return again and mutually contribute to its soft, clear sound. There is not the least trace of *dramatic* movement—not even when several choirs respond to each other; unruffled serenity broods over the entire composition, which, nevertheless, is not devoid of occasional warm and decided touches—disposed, however, in such a manner that the even rhythmical measure is only partially varied, and the general **equilibrium** left undisturbed. Human voices, combined either in choirs **or** harmonized *soli*, are the sole interpreters of this music; no attempt **at** individual expression is permitted, the religious element alone prevails, and the expression consists above all in this:—that no individual pre-eminence shall disturb and weaken the ideal atmosphere of the entire work."* The studied effects obtained by an abundant use of *chromatic* passages, of dissonances, and violent contrasts—so congenial to the modern ear—are not to be found in these pure harmonies. "He is," Thibaut† says of Palestrina, "so completely master of the ancient ecclesiastical modes, and of the treatment of the simple tonic chord in composition, that repose and enjoyment are to be found in his works, in a greater degree, perhaps, than in those of any other master."

The enthusiastic Baini, with refined analysis, distinguished ten different styles in Palestrina's productions (he might, as Winterfeld aptly remarks, have assumed as many styles as there are compositions); yet on us—accustomed as we are to a tenderer and **more** marked expression in melody—his works, on first hearing, are apt to produce an impression of uniformity, and even rigidity. At any **rate**, this "musica dall' altro mondo" will scarcely fulfil the expectations of those who esteem it adapted to revive Church sympathy and hearty devotion in our own day; and for this reason: that modern choirs rarely attain to that correctness and precision (so difficult where there is an almost continual interchange of the parts or voices) which are indispensable to the *true* appreciation of these magnificent conceptions, and which Palestrina would **be** justified in expecting of his own choir—specially trained for the purpose. But *when* this **perfection is** attained, our spirits are held in thrall by the **ineffable sublimity and** overwhelming majesty of these heavenly **strains.** For **this** reason, Palestrina's choruses should **only** be produced in **the Church** when the execution is perfectly irreproachable, and never in the remotest degree suggesting the idea of a **mere** art-performance. Kiesewetter's advice (valuable as coming from one whose opinion can be safely relied on), concerning Palestrina's

---

* Vischer. *Aesthetik.* Vol. iii., p. 1135.
† *Ueber Reinheit der Tonkunst.* P. 54.

compositions, is: "not to perform them to a modern audience without careful selection and examination, as it can **never be our intention to** bring Church music back to the simplicity of Palestrina's **time."**

The choir **of the Sistine chapel,** by the inheritance of long-cherished tradition, **is the** most perfect, and, consequently, most effective, **exponent of Palestrina's music.** Modern travellers, like Jacobi and **Mendelssohn, cannot sufficiently** admire the wonderful blending of **the voices,** the prolonged tones gradually merging from **one note and chord to another,** softly swelling, decreasing, and **finally dying out almost** inaudibly. "They understand," said the latter (in the letter to Zelter about the execution of the 'Improperie' above referred to), "how to bring out and place each delicate trait in the most favourable light, without giving it undue prominence; one chord gently melts into another. The ceremony, at the same time, is solemn and imposing; deep silence prevails in the chapel, only **broken by** the re-echoing Greek "Holy," sung with unvarying sweetness and expression." Paër was (in 1805) so impressed with the "perfect musical piety" of the composition and performance, that he exclaimed: "This is indeed divine music, such as I **have long** sought for and my imagination was **never able to realize, but which** I knew *must* exist!"

Unquestionably, **this powerful impression is (according to** Krause),* **in great** measure, **due to the sublimity and beauty** of the place of worship, **as also** to the Liturgy of the Roman Catholic Church—in itself one **of the** greatest religious works of art; unquestionably, this music **can** only exercise full sway over minds who receive the doctrines of that Church with a believing heart. But, also, those whose intellect and feeling rise superior to the distinctions of creeds are most deeply and powerfully impressed by the sacred music of Palestrina and of those composers who resemble him; for **his compositions, like** all genuine music, soar—as far as religious considerations are concerned—sublime above words and creeds of this world to the regions of everlasting Truth. Our great composers would doubtless be able, if they could attune their feelings to the task, to write *alla Palestrina;*—for we learn from the **Treatise on** Purity in Music,† that Cherubini achieved as much in **a grand eight-**

---

* *Darstellungen aus der Geschichte der* **Musik.**

† *Ueber Reinheit der Tonkunst.* Thibaut. Second edition. Heidelberg, 1826. Fourth edition, edited by Bähr. Heidelberg, 1861.

part *Credo*. Just as modern architects have revived the Gothic architecture of the Middle Ages, and Thorwaldsen and Canova Grecian statuary, our great musicians might follow their example in this purest branch of musical art. Under any circumstances, however, the immortal models of Palestrina and his contemporaries will always remain far superior to any mere reproductive imitations; for every peculiar genus of art is the result of innate, genuine inspiration, and the spontaneous growth of the age which produces it.

Palestrina and his fellow-pupil under Goudimel, M. Giov. Nanini [died 1607], founded, and jointly presided over, a music-school which faithfully continued Palestrina's style. Among Palestrina's successors, Baini mentions, as admirable in their Motets (songs set to a sacred text [*mot*] with its ancient traditional Church tune): Nanini—more given to tenderness of expression than his great predecessor—, and Tommaso Ludovico da Vittoria [born 1560], who, according to Thibaut, "combined Spanish warmth with spiritual meekness." Next to Vittoria [went to Munich circa 1594] deserves mention: Felice Anerio, Palestrina's successor in office, of whose works a "*Te Deum*," an eight-part "*Ave Regina*," and a mass "*Dixit Maria*," are known to posterity.

But Nanini's pupil, Gregorio Allegri [born at Rome in 1590, died there in 1652], surpassed them all in his five and four part *Miserere* with a conclusion for nine voices. Against Leop. Mozart's, Spohr's, and Adam's depreciation (continually urged and reiterated) of this magnificent composition, the fact speaks for itself, that the young W. A. Mozart, after a second hearing, secretly wrote it **down, and carried it** away like treasure trove. Its association with the ceremonies of the Sistine chapel (which cannot fail to strike even the most jaded as well as the most unimpressionable listener) may have **promoted its** wide-world fame—its intrinsic **merit is,** nevertheless, beyond question. *Figurate* embellishments are rarely employed in this melodious and expressive composition. Like the approach of impending fate, from time to time resounds, between the four and five part phrases, the same mournful monotonous psalmody; till in the last verse, " Tunc imponent super **altare tuum vitulos,"** the full glory of the nine-part harmony **bursts** forth like eternal and glorious redemption, obliterating **the remembrance of** earthly **sorrows.** Besides Allegri's *Miserere*, one by **Baini** (in Mendelssohn's opinion vapid and tame), and another by Tommaso BAI [died 1714], composed in imitation of Allegri, are performed annually at Rome during the Holy Week, when a judicious gradation of effect is obtained, by crowning the performance of Baini's work on Wednesday, and Bai's on Holy Thursday, with **that of Allegri on Good Friday.***

* NOTE BY THE TRANSLATOR. This order was not observed when we were at Rome (in 1862). A *Miserere* by a modern composer was performed in the Sistine chapel on Good Friday, which by no means equalled that of Allegri, sung in the Choir chapel of St. Peter's on the day previous.

The musicians of the following period departed from the noble simplicity and solemnity which distinguished their predecessors, and introduced greater intricacy into their compositions. Palestrina wrote almost exclusively for from four to eight voices; it now became the fashion to write for several choirs consisting of 12, 16, 24, and even 36 and 48 parts—a style of composition in which Orazio BENEVOLI [chapel-master of St. Peter's at Rome from 1646 till his death in 1672], his successor in office BERNABEI [died 1690], and PITONI [died 1743] achieved celebrity. Of this latter (styled the Palestrina of the eighteenth century) a six-part 'Dies iræ,' composed in the true Palestrina spirit, is highly spoken of. It is understood, as a matter of course, that in all these compositions for a number of parts, or rather choirs, the full and divided choir was employed alternately, and only in such passages as required a more powerful expression were the choirs united in one full chorus.

Contemporary with the Roman, rose and flourished the Venetian school, in which the treatment of choir-composition received a more important characteristic development than elsewhere. Its strong proclivity for full-voiced songs and choruses corresponds, in some measure, to the broad, flowing outline and brilliant colouring which distinguished the Venetian school of painting, and culminated in Titian [died 1576]. The greatest master in this style of composition was GIOVANNI GABRIELI [born circa 1540, died 1612], nephew and pupil of the learned contrapuntist Andrea Gabrieli; he applied himself to the improvement of composition for combined choirs—a style for which Willaert had displayed considerable preference—with careful reference to the words furnished by the text.* Of his compositions, which (according to Winterfeld) are highly effective, and combine breadth of harmony with completeness of form, the following deserve mention: Songs for prayer and praise, for the most part selected from verses in the Psalms, in six, seven, and ten parts; Magnificats for two and three choirs; Hymns for the Mass, also for three choirs (he never wrote a complete Mass); Responsories for Christmas and Easter day.—It is worthy of notice that, besides pieces chiefly for two and three choirs which were executed by voices alone (*a capella*), he has left some which are furnished with instrumental preludes and accompaniments. For example: he arranged an "*In ecclesiis benedicite Domino, Alleluia*" for two choirs with three cornets, one fiddle, and two trombones; a "*Surrexit Christus*" for three voices and an orchestra of two cornets, two violins, and four trombones, with preludes and interludes, as well as choruses and solo songs accompanied by different instru-

* *Johannes Gabrieli und sein Zeitalter.* Dargestellt von WINTERFELD. Zwei Theile. Berlin, 1834.

ments—all in the utmost variety. Gabrieli was organist of St. Mark's; and, like Seb. Bach, his professional skill on a full-toned instrument like the organ doubtless suggested a florid style of harmony, and the grand effects to be derived from instrumental combinations. It may not be out of place to mention here that it was at Venice —always famous for skilful organists—that BERNHARD THE GERMAN invented the pedal-board [1470], an improvement which added greatly to the resources of *organ-playing*, as well as to the art of harmony in general.

The masters of the succeeding period: Lotti Caldara, Marcello—Venetians by birth and education—are usually included in the Venetian school; they belong, however,—especially Marcello—rather to the new period ushered in by the Neapolitan school. ANTONIO LOTTI [born circa 1660, died 1740], although adopting the new style in his operas, retained the old severe style of Church music in his best sacred compositions—which, however, were relieved by a touch of sweetness. A difference may, notwithstanding, be observed between his compositions *a capella*, and those in the new *stile concertante*. "Those of his more generally known works consist of some *Crucifixus* for a number of voices, which, however, must not be taken as specimens of the style of his Masses; thus, I have before me a Mass written partly for four, partly for five and six voices (by doubling the treble and counter tenor parts), in which—besides passages similar to the above-mentioned '*Crucifixus*,' such as the "*Qui tollis*" and "*Miserere nobis*," as well as the "*Domine Deus agnus dei*," where the treble performs a Gregorian '*Magnificat*' tune—such anomalies occur as for instance: a "*Domine Deus*" in which a soprano and violin vie with each other in endless runs and flourishes—the whole accompanied by two violins *concertante*, two viols, and a bass-viol, to which a hautboy and trumpet are occasionally added."*

Antonio CALDARA [born circa 1674, died at Vienna, chapel-master to Charles VI., in 1763] was considered to have excelled in the *fugue*; he succeeded admirably in uniting Italian sweetness with German science and religious expression—especially in his Masses *a capella*. On the other hand, the modern element of individual local expression enters largely into the compositions of the aristocratic *dilettante* Benedetto MARCELLO [1680—1739]. Even so late as 1802, a new edition of his principal work: *Parafrasi sopra i* 50 *primi salmi per* 1, 2, 3 *e* 4 *voci con basso continuo* (Paraphrases on the 50 Psalms of David), was published at Cherubini's suggestion. The Italians reverence the 'Salmi' as a classical production, whereas Spohr and others consider them

---

* HEIMSOETH, p. 859, and elsewhere.

poor, monotonous, and tedious. At any rate, they are historically important; for this composition—written in the comparatively loose form of a cantata—had so much influence on the development of the lyric opera, that it has been well remarked that Gluck began where Marcello left off.

The actual development of the Venetian, as a separate school of art, ends with its greatest master and representative G. Gabrieli, whose style of composition was continued by his GERMAN pupils, HEINRICH SCHÜTZ and HANS LEO HASSLER (both to be mentioned hereafter), who with some modifications—according to the different objects for which they worked—developed his style yet further. The German JACOBUS GALLUS from Krain (properly Hänl or Handl, 1550—1591), the contemporary of G. Gabrieli, Palestrina, and Orlandus Lassus, should also be classed with the Italian masters. His works contain specimens of all the styles of composition that had hitherto been invented. A Motet written in 24 parts, for four six-part choirs, proves him to have been an adept in elaborate composition for a large number of parts;—that he did not affect this style may be inferred from the fact, that the greater part of his other compositions, as, for instance, the celebrated Motets: "*Ecce quomodo moritur justus,*" and "*Media vita in morte sumus,*" are worthy to be ranked with the best compositions of Palestrina.

CHAPTER VI.

ORIGIN OF THE OPERA. INFLUENCE OF THE NEAPOLITAN SCHOOL.

THE Venetian school, during its most flourishing period under G. Gabrieli, unquestionably enjoyed a wide-spread influence, especially in Germany, where that influence continued through a lengthened period. The importance of the Venetian school, however, as regards our own epoch, is not to be compared with that of the Roman, and still less with that of the Neapolitan school; in Italy, indeed, it held latterly only a middle place between the two. It is with the Neapolitan school, though its earliest productions are now rarely sought after and indeed scarcely known, that the History of Modern Music commences—in so far as that music speaks the language of the feelings, emotions, and passions. From that school the art of music received an entirely new impulse and direction, which had its origin in popular melody; for secular music, formerly homeless, had taken root and flourished, unshackled by ecclesiastical influences, in the genial soil of Naples. Thus we are led, by the progress of Art, from Rome and Venice to the bright and joyous city of Naples, then to Florence, the seat of learning and the fine arts, and, ultimately, back to Naples.

Willaert and his pupils, especially Zarlino (as well as Palestrina and Orl. Lassus, whom we are accustomed to think of only as singers "of the long robe"), had already applied the art of polyphony to secular melody in the Madrigal (a species of song treating of love or pastoral scenes). This style of composition, "in which a lively air with strongly-marked rhythm (then somewhat rare) was accompanied by a simple counterpoint of several—three, four, and up to seven—voices,"* was speedily diffused throughout Italy, and especially cherished at Naples, even by the mass of the people, in the light and easy form of the *Villanelle* or *Villote alla Napolitana*. LUCA MARENZIO [born circa 1550, "*il più dolce cigno*"] and GESUALDO DI VENOSA [1588—1612] are the most celebrated and prolific Madrigal writers.

The transition from the lyrical poetry of polyphonous song to the "drama with chorus" (still customary in our day) was a very natural one; for the choruses of the then prevalent pas-

---

* KIESEWETTER.

toral plays (for example Tasso's 'Aminta,' Guarini's 'Pastor Fido,' and others), which connected the several scenes and acts and formed the conclusion, were in their tenor and substance essentially lyrical. But that the same polyphonous form should be employed also for dialogue and monologue—though it had never been nor was objected to in Church music (Palestrina's 'Improperie' for instance)—could not fail to appear not only unsuitable, but ridiculous, on the stage. Let the reader, for instance, picture to himself the situation of two lovers who were to address each other by means of choruses placed behind, and sometimes even actually on, the stage. Another attempt to adapt Madrigal music to dramatic monologue by assigning to this latter the highest, and to instruments the remaining, parts of the Madrigal, was not much more successful. Thus, the only form of art which had hitherto been acknowledged—ecclesiastical polyphonous song—, was found wholly inadequate for the expression of individual feeling. It was therefore requisite to discover some other and better mode of expression; at the same time, there was an unwillingness to relinquish the old, approved methods.

That which musicians would never have dared to attempt, was undertaken by a society of literati established at Florence in 1580. The primary object of this association was the revival of Greek art (inclusive of music) at its best period; and, in accordance with this theory, nothing less than an entire reconstruction of contemporary musical art was insisted on. In order to comprehend this tendency in the present day, when the study of the classics is becoming of less and less importance, we must bear in mind that the antiquarian lore of those days, rejoicing in the ardour of youth, disdained to minister only to learned pedantry; on the contrary, its endeavours had an immediate practical bearing on Art and Literature. National Poetry—though for a time held in restraint by a too servile imitation of antique forms—, Statuary, and Painting forsook the monopolizing service of the Church; nor was the art of Music able to resist the spirit of the *Renaissance* (revival of classic antiquity) which was everywhere successfully making head against ecclesiastical domination.

As opposed to the art of polyphony, whose very existence was contrary to Greek theories of art, the society which had been formed at the same place (and about the same period) as the Platonic Academy founded by Cosmo de' Medici, laid down as its primary axiom :—distinct individuality of expression, and clear intelligibility of the words to be sung. At length, after a number of failures, the attempts to revive Greek Tragedy gave birth to the *recitative*—the foundation of the modern vocal drama, and answering to the intoned recitation of the ancients. The recitative, being a kind of compromise between speaking and singing, was, therefore, aptly denominated "*musica parlante*," (*speaking music*.)

The first production of importance in the new "*stile rappresentativo*," or "*recitativo*," was Jacopo Peri's 'Eurydice,' of which Rinuccini furnished the poem. It was performed at Florence on the occasion of the nuptials of Henry IV. of France with Mary of Medicis [February 6th, 1600], and speedily achieved renown. In spite, or rather in consequence, of the increasing expenditure which afterwards attended the performance of "music dramas" ("*dramme per musica*") at the Italian Courts on gala days, the result fell short of the expectation of its founders. The musical recitation, which, in accordance with the rules laid down by antiquarians, plumed itself on "a noble contempt for melody," could not fail to strike a music-loving people as insipid and tame, and to incite gifted and ambitious musicians to fresh efforts.

The inventive genius of Claudio Monteverde [born at Cremona circa 1566, died at Venice 1650]—to whom Kiesewetter assigns a special epoch—considerably improved the Opera, which was as yet, on the whole, sufficiently unmusical. So far from adhering to the prescribed rule concerning antique models, which required that the actual musical form be almost entirely sacrificed to distinct enunciation of the words, he ventured to assert his art on an equal footing with poetry, by rendering the recitative more susceptible of melody, variety, and expresssion, and giving to the instrumental accompaniment a wider and more independent range. It was especially in this last particular that his innovations incurred violent censure. For his mode of employing the instruments connected with vocal performance in various characteristic ways, and of introducing dissonances when the expression required was one of passion or excitement, made it clearly evident that his sole aim and object was by no means comprised in the endeavour to equal the much-vaunted models of antiquity. Characteristic hereof is his attempt to represent musically and dramatically an episode from Tasso's 'Jerusalem Delivered' ('Tancred and Chlorinda'), in a kind of cantata; whereas, in the narrow zeal of imitating Greek Tragedy, national poetry had hitherto been almost entirely neglected by musicians. In this particular, Monteverde's views are all the more remarkable, because Tasso's poem, which if rendered into prose would be scarcely tolerable, seems, on the other hand, not to require the assistance of music to give it effect. Tasso's tender and melodious poem has rarely— and then only in a greatly altered form—been made use of in the subsequent Italian Opera, whose range of subjects was almost entirely limited to ancient mythology and history. With

Monteverde, the *musical* element of dramatic representation began to usurp the place of the *poetical*—previously so anxiously cherished—; and, although his Operas ("*favole in musica*") do not contain the remotest indications of that mighty spirit of melody which before long was completely to supersede the sister art of poetry, it is none the less certain that the musical drama was thenceforth deflected from its original tendency—a circumstance which contributed in no small degree to the progress of modern music.

The Church compositions of Viadana and Carissimi, which were in like manner based on the new theory of individual expression, had a more important, though indirect, share in forming the flowing melodious opera style than all the Opera compositions that had hitherto appeared. Ludovico VIADANA, a monk [in the early part of the seventeenth century], was the first who in sacred music disengaged melody from the restraints of contrapuntal laws, by treating the harmony, which hitherto had engaged supreme consideration, merely as the ground-work of a tune complete and entire in itself. His principal productions were what he styled *Sacred Concerts* (*concerti ecclesiastici* or *sacri*), " a style of composition in which *Cantilene* were executed by one, two, three, or more voices, and required an instrumental accompaniment—generally speaking, the organ—to complete the harmony."* A *basso continuo* for the organ (*basso per organo*) formed the ground-work, to which it was the province of the organist to add chords as fitness and taste should suggest. The organist was therefore expected to be versed in the art of playing harmonies to an *unfigured* bass; subsequently, the further development of the art of harmony necessitated the use of *figured* basses, and, in consequence, the practice of *Thorough Bass*. "In these sacred songs of Viadana, we find songs for each of the four voices; some for one, for two, for three, or for four voices, in all possible combinations; occasionally, some of the parts are doubled; there are also four-part songs interrupted by *soli* (for example, a "*Diei solemnia fulget dies*" for an introductory tenor solo followed by a chorus; or a "*Dic Maria quid vidisti*," repeated four times as a chorus with *soli*, or four voices in succession, interpolated); there are also, for the sake of variety, songs with instruments, for ex.—a three-part *Bone Jesu* for tenor and two trombones, a four-part song, "*Repleatur cor meum laude tua*," for alto, tenor, and (*si placet*) two trombones. These compositions, as such, are of no great value. But the whole arrangement is very appropriate for Church singing, and favourable to the development of a well-defined melody

* KIESEWETTER.

concentrated in one and the self-same part, and of organ accompaniment in its best form. It is true that, in former times, there were complete songs in three and four parts, but those were invariably in the form of a *canon* or *fugue*, and devoid of accompaniment."* Herein was established the precedence of melody over harmony; the cohesion of all the parts or voices in the construction of musical pieces fell away; the contrapuntal theory of composition had to make room for inventions of a purely melodious character— for a simple, tuneful style, as distinct from harmonic treatment. The "varied, graceful style" (so much admired by Prætorius) of "Viadana's Concerts" found numerous imitators both among Italian and German composers.

Giacomo CARISSIMI [born at Venice in 1600], during a life nearly coextensive with the century, contributed still further to the development of genuine melody. He it was who, more than any previous composer, gave to individual feeling and expression that prominence which caused it thenceforth—even in sacred music—to become the chief aim and object of the musician. He was so eminently successful in the treatment of the independent forms in monody—the *recitative* and *arioso*—, that his works served as models for the now rapidly rising Opera.

Its musical development once thoroughly se-

* HEIMSOETH.

cured, the Opera made quick progress, especially when the performances began to take place in public (about the middle of the seventeenth century). The *impresari*, in order to compensate for the necessarily diminished splendour of public representations, endeavoured to substitute the delectation of the ear for that of the eye, while increasing public favour encouraged composers to improve upon the recitative and *arioso* till they achieved the *aria* (air). The natural result of these causes, working conjointly, was that an entirely new direction was given to the Opera. The *vocal Opera*, supported by the co-operation of the great singing-schools, and formed by the Neapolitan school, and especially by the elder Scarlatti and his pupils, ere long became a national institution.

With Carissimi's pupil, ALESSANDRO SCARLATTI [born at Trapani 1659, died at Naples 1725]—so much admired for the fertility and versatility of his genius—, begins the actual history of the modern Opera. The improvement of opera melody (deplored as a "relapse into Paganism" by R. Wagner) is chiefly due to him; he fixed the forms of the Italian Opera of the last century in all its most important details. More especially is the Opera indebted to him for a fuller and freer instrumentation, as well in those portions of the performance where it is employed without singing (viz., introductions and *intermezzi*), as in the recitative, which, since then, has usually been accompanied or *obligato*. He moulded the *aria* into the graceful, finished form it has since retained, by dividing it into three parts, viz., *principal phrase, middle phrase*, and *da capo* (repetition of the first part with fresh and more florid ornamentations). In his numerous sacred compositions (Masses, Motets, Oratorios, Cantatas), Scarlatti adhered to the old, severe style. Among these, the most celebrated are a *Miserere* composed for the Papal chapel in 1680, and a fugue for two choruses: *Tu es Petrus*, which is still sung on Easter day on the occasion of the Pope's entrance into church.

Scarlatti's pupil, Francesco DURANTE [born at Naples 1693, died there 1755], did not himself write for the theatre, but the most celebrated composers of Italian Opera—Duni, Terradeglias, Piccini, Jomelli, and a number of others—were educated in his school. In Church compositions Durante adopted the modern style, though without detriment to the dignity befitting sacred music; he had a partiality for the vocal system founded on ancient Church tunes, and employed it successfully. Other pupils of Scarlatti's school, deserving of mention, are FRANCESCO FEO, whose Mass for two choirs is described as not only brilliant, but grand and vigorous in character, and Alessandro STRADELLA, famed for his romantic history. Of yet greater note—likewise in sacred music—was Durante's contemporary, LEONARDO LEO [born at Naples 1694, died there 1745], also a pupil of Scarlatti's and of the Roman school under Pitoni. His *chef-d'œuvre* in the old style (*a capella*) is a grand eight-part *Miserere*, " which was for Naples, what Allegri's was for Rome one hundred years before."* Graceful and dignified as are his compositions in the old vocal style, he is on the other hand—especially in Oratorio (*La morte d'Abelle*)—an ardent promoter of the concerted style with recitative, of the *aria* (though of a solemn cast), and of full-toned orchestral accompaniment; he has (observes Reichardt) " carried the epoch of the grand style in music into that of the graceful style."

The novelties which obtained after Leo's time brought about a radical change in Church music, which lost in dignity, solemnity, and sublimity, in proportion as the more or less florid style of solo singing, borrowed from the Opera and instrumental music, supplanted the chorus and organ. On the other hand, it is worthy of notice that the last celebrated composers of Church music exclusively, viz., Viadana, Carissimi, and Durante, were singularly influential in furthering the improvement of the Opera.

Among the most celebrated of Leo's Operas was 'ced *Olympiade*,' in which occurs the duet "*Nei giorni*

* Compare HEINSE. *Hildegard von Hohenthal*, vol. i., p. 149-154.

tuoi felici," and the air, "*Nò so donde viene.*" In the brilliant series of Italian Opera composers formed in the school of Durante and Leo, we distinguish the following : PERGOLESE, DUNI, TERRADEGLIAS, JOMELLI [1714—1774], TRAETTA, CICCIO DI MAJO, GALUPPI, GUGLIELMI, and, especially, Niccolo PICCINI [born at Bari 1728, died at Passy, near Paris, 1800] and Gasparo SACCHINI [born at Naples 1735, died at Paris 1786], who made beauty of form and vocal perfection their almost exclusive study. After the custom had obtained of employing a peculiar class of voices whose chief excellence lay in an almost inconceivable degree of technical skill, the style of the Opera degenerated into weakness and affectation, and little more was required of opera composers than a series of brilliant *bravura* airs (generally from twenty to thirty in number) loosely hung on to the recitative ;—as to the few duets, trios, and *pièces d'ensemble*, which entered into these compositions, they were not in the least appreciated by the general public.

The compositions of Joseph Adolf HASSE [born at Bergedorf near Hamburg 1699, died at Venice 1783], who was called by the Italians "*il caro*" or "*divino Sassone*," are of a higher class than those we have just alluded to ; indeed, Hasse may be considered as the chief representative of the most brilliant period of Italian Opera. "No other master has equalled him in his correct and genuine appreciation and rendering of the general outline and features of the Italian school at that period."* A pupil of the venerable Scarlatti, and, in 1771, a rival of the young Mozart (at that time fifteen years of age), his life and works comprise the entire history and development of the early Italian Opera. His prophecy concerning Mozart, "That boy will cause us all to be forgotten" (" *Questo ragazzo ci farà dimenticar tutti*"), was only too speedily to be fulfilled.

METASTASIO [1698—1782], almost contemporary with Hasse, represents the poetical, as the latter does the musical, element of the Italian *Opera seria*. A musician (principally vocal) by education, he has never been surpassed as a lyric dramatic poet; his language is admirably adapted for singing, while his verses breathe a tender lyrical expression. On the other hand, there is a sameness of dramatic invention in his very numerous productions; he wrote, as composers desired, solely *for the music*, and we must not—like the too severe A. W. Von Schlegel—expect to find in him the dignity of a tragic poet. Riehl aptly contrasts him with the French stage poet Scribe, in whose works the subjects, and sudden — often inconsequent—dramatic effect predominates; whereas, in Metastasio, the subject-matter

---

* W. H. RIEHL. Compare his admirable portraiture of Hasse, the "*Dresden Royal Opera composer*," in the *Musikalische Charakterköpfe*, vol. i.

adapts itself easily to the musical *plastique*. In Italy, Da Ponte is, perhaps, the only genuine stage poet who may be considered his equal. His merits and defects are very justly and fairly weighed and canvassed by Arteaga.*

Originally called into existence by the Opera, instrumental music—more especially fiddle-playing—emerged by degrees from the subordinate office of accompaniment and introduction to the singing into an independent sphere of musical art. After CORELLI [1653—1713]—who excelled in graceful and sweet-toned execution—and his pupil GEMINIANI, came the gifted TARTINI [1692—1770, "*il maestro delle nazioni*"], who brought technical skill on the violin to the utmost perfection—especially in the management of the bow. As a proof of his marvellous powers of execution, we may cite his "*devilish*" grotesque *Devil's Sonata* ("*Trille du diable*")—a piece that has recently been re-edited, and performed at concerts. "One cannot understand how such a piece can be executed by four fingers only—it is like listening to three or four violins playing at once." From his school at Padua proceeded the great *virtuosi* NARDINI and PUGNANI, who, in their turn, produced excellent pupils in LOZZI and VIOTTI.

Vocalists of artistic and historical celebrity were: the *soprani* SENESINO and BERNACCHI

* *Le Revoluzioni del teatro musicale Italiano.* Venezia, 1785.

(pupils of Pistocchi), Caffarelli (whose voice earned him a dukedom), Carlo Broschi, surnamed Farinelli (pupil of Porpora, and the all-powerful favourite of Philip V. and Ferdinand VI. of Spain); also Pacchiarotti, Marchesi, Crescentini, Velluti, and the female singers: Vittoria Tesi, Faustina Bordoni (Hasse's wife), Francesca Cuzzoni, Francesca Gabrieli. Lastly, deserving of mention are the famous Cremona fiddle-makers — the Amati, Guarneri, Straduari, whose instruments fetch large sums at the present day.

Notwithstanding the efforts of those who contributed to the brilliancy of the Italian Opera, its splendour—based as it was on the immediate gratification of the senses—was destined to fade away rapidly. "The spirit of the ancient legends of gods and heroes was not in the least understood or appreciated—the taste of the age was too debased; they were employed merely as a convenient garb for the expression of modern sentimentality as well as to adorn and beautify the same.* In addition to this, the Opera was entirely adapted to the individual capacities of the singers (all Hasse's for instance, above a hundred in number, are arranged with reference to his wife Faustina's powers); its existence was therefore necessarily an ephemeral one, owing to changes in the performers as well as the decrease

* F. Chrysander. *Händel*, vol. i., p. 82.

of the extraordinary vocal execution above referred to, for which, indeed, it served only as a scaffolding. How many are at the present day acquainted with even the names of those once famous compositions for which W. Heinse in his art-novel 'Hildegard von Hohenthal' (companion to 'Ardinghello,' a work treating of the arts of design, and especially of Italian painting) expressed such exceeding enthusiasm? "Probably many beautiful thoughts, both in melody and expression, have perished with the innumerable operas (now consigned to oblivion) of the two first centuries of this branch of art; but the musical drama could not prosper in such a soil."*

A few Church compositions alone escaped universal oblivion; and these are less remarkable for religious depth and power than for a soft, tender expression, and pleasing facility, both in execution and effect, which rendered them acceptable to the worldly tendency of that age. Of the gentle and melancholy EMANUELE D' ASTORGA [born 1680] a *Stabat Mater* has obtained celebrity. Equal, if not superior, to it is one by PERGOLESE [1710—1736] for two female voices with quartet accompaniment,—the last pious strain of the early departing *maestro*. Klopstock has written a German text for it, and it has of late been performed in Germany with considerable success. That Pergolese could also write with

* VISCHER. *Aesthetik.* Vol. iii., p. 1139.

fire and spirit is evident from his Masses, his 113th Psalm for five voices, and other compositions. Of Astorga, whose memory has been revived by Fr. Rochlitz,* and by Riehl,† little else is known. Of his *Stabat* writes the latter: "Astorga vacillates between the modern manner of dramatizing the sacred text, and the old mystical style of contemplation, as we find it in Palestrina's school—soaring sublime in evenly progressing musical lyric above the varied signification and expression of the words of the text." JOMELLI's Church compositions, including even his *Requiem* and *Miserere* (the latter set to Italian words: "*Pietà, Signore*"), are of inferior value. Mozart says of him: "This man has a certain line in which he excels (the opera), so that we cannot hope to supplant him in that which he understands so thoroughly well. But he should never have attempted to go out of his province and write, for instance, Church music in the old style." Of HASSE, a grand and noble *Te Deum*, as well as a *Requiem* (according to Krause, superior even to Mozart's), are still annually performed in the Catholic Court Church at Dresden. On the other hand, the light Italian style and opera air appear without disguise or reticence in his Masses and Oratorios.

If, as must be avowed, the Catholic Church

* *Für Freunde der Tonkunst.* Vol. ii., p. 87-101
† *Musikalische Charakterköpfe.* Vol. i.

music of the eighteenth century approached somewhat too closely to that of the Opera, so that between an *Opera seria* and a solemn Mass little or no difference can be discerned, yet in the masters of the early Neapolitan school, Church music " could always be distinctly recognized from profane music, and retained its dignity notwithstanding the introduction of new and showy styles."* Though, indeed, it cannot be denied that the modern tendency degenerated latterly into narrow egotism and vain display, yet it would be unfair—not to say bigoted—to regard this tendency as inimical to the Church; and, while extolling a soulless and unartistic reaction, to insist with puritanical rigour on the exclusion of all concerted music from the Church. One should rather (to use O. Jahn's† admirable expression) regard it as the natural consequence of the revival of art, that an ardent desire was manifested to express devotional feelings with all the force and reality of genuine sentiment free from conventional restraints, and "to consecrate all the resources of an art which was developing itself so splendidly, in the same manner as had been the case with the arts of design. This new impulse and direction was followed up with the zeal of a newly-awakened artistic effort— one which, of its kind, was as sincere as the simple pious faith which thought to consecrate

* KIESEWETTER. † *Mozart*, vol. i., p. 441.

its best endeavours by devoting them to the Church."

Thus, on the whole, the music of the Church and that of the Opera progressed amicably hand in hand, mutually influencing each other; the improvement and extension of the new forms benefited both, and their history is henceforward inseparable. The Italian *Oratorio*, in particular, which, from the first, took the same course as the Opera, was, in the eighteenth century, only a kind of sacred Opera, the object of which was to indemnify lovers of music for the privations of Lent. It was not till the great German masters, Seb. Bach and Handel, had taken the Oratorio in hand, that it acquired its ultimate and distinctive character. Altogether, the relation of art in general, and music in particular, to the Church was a totally different one in Italy to what it was in Protestant Germany; in the former it was free, and more or less superior to ecclesiastical restraint, in the latter (particularly during the early Lutheran period) it was almost exclusively ecclesiastical. The great intellectual movement of the sixteenth century, brought about by the study of classic antiquity, led, in Italy, to freedom in art—in Germany to freedom in matters of faith. The gay, artistic Italian temperament was utterly at variance with the intellectual energy and purely spiritual worship brought in by the Reformation—which was, in truth, unfavourable to art; and thus it also came to pass that Giordano Bruno's and Savonarola's attempts at reform met with scant appreciation, and obtained no hold on the general sympathy.

CHAPTER VII.

THE PROTESTANT CHURCH SONG.*

IN Germany, the only branch of music worthy of being called national was Church music, which, through the agency of LUTHER and his musical friends, Walther and Senfl, was imbued with a strongly-marked *Protestant* tendency. What Ambrose had been to the Latin, Luther was to the German Church song, which, as well as everything pertaining to the Church, he endeavoured to popularize to the utmost. Instead of the hitherto purely liturgical choir song of the Roman Church (which he called a dismal ass's bray), he instituted the German *chorale*, taking for his models the sacred songs of the Hussites or Bohemian and Moravian Brothers. Concerning these latter, says Herder: "Many of them express simplicity and devotion, piety and brotherly com-

* K. v. WINTERFELD. "*Der Evangelische Kirchengesang und sein Verhältniss zur Kunst des Tonsatzes.*" 3 Theile, Leipzig, 1843-47.

munion in a manner we cannot hope to emulate, because we have it not." Musically educated, and so enthusiastically partial to the art that he "ranked it next in importance to theology," Luther's chief aim, while arranging the new Church song, was to ensure that "the words be worthily expressed, not babbled or drawled," and above all that the "*masses join in the singing* and pay devout attention."

The chorale of the Protestant Church was, in the main, a combination of the Gregorian tune with the modern principle of harmony. A metrical song in the language of the country (whatever that might happen to be) furnished the words, while the tune of these songs was the Gregorian style combined with a simple counterpoint according to the music of the period. It was, however, only by degrees that the song resulting from this combination which obtained in the service of the new churches, assumed a marked, complete, and, above all, *popular* character. At first, metrical songs in the mother-tongue were collected for the use of the congregation. As to the music, it was either taken from popular tunes of old church hymns, or else easy secular melodies were adapted for use in churches.

In the LUTHERAN Church, Luther appears as a poet—translating old (biblical, Roman and Bohemian) songs, arranging German, and writing original ones,—among others his famous hymn:

"Our God is a tower of strength."* He caused these songs to be set for a number of voices, and the congregation had to join in the leading melody.—The FRENCH CALVINIST Church song was of inferior importance as compared with the German Lutheran. It was confined principally to the melodies of the Psalms versified in the mother tongue by Marot and Beza (of which the airs were chiefly borrowed from secular songs); these were set very simply in four parts by GOUDIMEL [already mentioned; he died a Huguenot, at Lyons, in 1572]. Of similar origin were the three part musical pieces of Goudimel's contemporary, CLEMENS NON PAPA, as well as the tunes on the SOUTER LIEDEKENS—a Flemish translation of the Psalms with doctrinal songs and songs of praise annexed. ZWINGLI maintained the severely matter-of-fact view that singing, or even music, in church was superfluous, disturbing to devotion, yea sinful. He is said to have *sung* the proposal to the Zurich Council for abolishing church singing.

It was the Church song, as arranged by Luther, that alone met with general acceptance, and received artistic development. The adversaries of Protestantism have even gone so far as to assert that, together with Luther's translation of the Bible, it was the principal cause of the rapid spread of that religion. People literally *sang*

* "*Ein' feste Burg ist unser Gott.*"

themselves into the new doctrine, and it was said that many were by this means induced to embrace it, who "formerly could not bear the name of Luther."*

The first Lutheran hymn-book appeared at Wittenberg, in 1524, and was called 'an Attempt at an Arrangement of a German Mass;' it contained, besides several songs retained from the old Church, eight by Luther—all arranged for four-part singing by his friend WALTHER. The Protestant Church song was, in fact, originally intended for part singing; and, in order to bring about the desired participation of the congregation, this latter was to join in the tune, which was generally placed in the tenor part. Musicians were too much accustomed to harmony to dispense with it altogether, and the organ was not in use as an accompaniment till fully one hundred years later. The chorale did not take the simpler form of a tune for one voice, with an accompaniment

---

* Luther, however, could appreciate the more artistic form of the Motet—admirably treated by his friend Ludwig SENFL—as performed by a choir; for he admires the lovely miracle of such "music polished and adorned by art, of which it is above all things strange and wonderful that a simple tune or tenor (as musicians are wont to call it) is sung by one voice, and along with it three, four, or five other voices sing likewise, and wondrously and variously decorate and adorn the same, and lead, as it were, a heavenly dance, where they meet, and sweetly and smilingly embrace, so that he who understands and feels this music cannot refrain from wondering mightily, and thinks there can be nothing in the world more wonderful than such singing adorned by a number of voices."

of the other voices, till the seventeenth century, when the melody was transferred from the tenor (where it was frequently scarcely to be recognized by reason of the surrounding voices) to the treble, and, in accordance with this arrangement, the hymn-books contained merely the tune and the words. LUCAS OSIANDER's work, entitled " Fifty Spiritual Songs and Psalms set in counterpoint for four voices, in such wise that a Christian congregation may join in the singing throughout," was chiefly instrumental in bringing about a change which tended in so great a measure to secure the participation of the people in the singing. "I know very well," says he, in the dedication to the schoolmasters of Würtemberg (January 1st, 1586), "that composers are in the habit of assigning the chorale to the tenor. But, if this be done, the chorale cannot be distinguished from among the other parts; the common people cannot tell what psalm it is, nor join in the singing. For this reason, I have placed the chorale in the treble, so that it shall be recognized distinctly, and every lay member can sing too." The same views are set forth by one who was considered the greatest organist of his time—HANS LEO HASSLER [born at Nuremberg 1564, died 1618]—in the preface to his book entitled: "Church Songs, Psalms, and Spiritual Songs, set to common melodies *simpliciter* in four parts," (1608), in which he has "endeavoured so to harmonize the best known church tunes that the chorale shall be distinctly heard throughout the treble, and at the same time the congregation can join in and sing too."

The greatest master in this style of polyphonous Church song was JOHANNES *ECCARD* [born at Mühlhausen in Thüringen 1533, died chapel-master at Berlin 1611], pupil of Orlandus Lassus. His principal works are: '*Spiritual Songs* set to a chorale or common church tune, and composed for five voices' (in two parts, Konigsberg, 1597),* and '*Prussian Festival Songs* for the whole year, for five, six, and up to eight, voices' (1598). More especially in this latter work did he achieve a truly artistic amalgamation of solo and polyphonous, congregational and choir singing, as well as of the Song and the Motet—in Winterfeld's estimation a " vigorous, expressive *ensemble*, singularly delicate and ingenious in the detail, yet, notwithstanding this care and finish, fully intelligible to the people, and addressing itself to their sympathies." The Protestant chorale or congregational hymn, supported by harmony either of the choir or organ (which soon after came into universal use), attained its utmost perfection through

---

* The first part contains one hymn for Advent, six for Christmas, three for the Epiphany, Passion Week, Easter, and Whitsuntide each; two for the Feast of the Trinity, besides a *Magnificat* and *Te Deum*: the second part consists of twenty-nine songs for general use, viz. (so called) Catechism Songs, Psalms, &c.

Eccard, with whom its historical epoch may be said to close.

It must not, however, be supposed that in the seventeenth century there were not many admirable composers of church music. Joh. STOBÄUS and HEINRICH ALBERT (pupils of Eccard's so-called Prussian school of music) are worthy of notice. These, as well as the Berlin and Saxon composers, Joh. CRÜGER, Joh. Georg EBELING, Joachim NEANDER, Georg NEUMARK, wrote chiefly for the sacred poetry of their contemporaries—Simon Dach, Paul Gerhard, and others. A number of their melodies have found their way into the congregational Church song, and many authors of chorale melodies are now quite forgotten—those who are held to be the composers, being, very frequently, merely the contrapuntists who arranged the harmonies to these melodies.

During that sceptical period, the eighteenth century—when organists were accustomed to play trivial minuet tunes for introductions, *intermezzi*, and *finali*, during divine service, and poets arranged "refined" songs and airs, not adapted for popular use, for sacred songs—, chorale music necessarily declined; for it had its root and origin solely in religious feeling and the universal love of singing, which created a demand for that kind of music. The chorale gradually gave place to choir and solo singing, so that the musical *connoisseur*, Mattheson, affirms that, in his day, the chorale was only tolerated for the sake of the ignorant and weak.

Though, in modern Protestant chorale books, the character of the old tunes has, on the whole, greatly deteriorated, yet the Protestant Church possesses in her oldest and best chorales the only genuine Church music which thoroughly answers to the grand idea of catholicity — a universal song, in which both words and melody have equal power and effect; whereas in the song of the Roman liturgy the *text*, and in choir song (with or without accompaniment) the *music* usually predominates.

The next important branch of Protestant Church song, and which we find carried to perfection in the works of Seb. Bach, was founded on the choir singing taken from Italian models. Michael Prätorius, [1571—1621], and particularly Heinrich Schütz (pupil of the celebrated Johannes Gabrieli), were the first who attempted this style. Prätorius endeavoured to combine both old and new styles—the chorale and *concerto* —and to establish a kind of compromise between the two; but Schütz boldly adopted the new style.

Heinrich Schütz [born at Köstritz on the Elster, 1585—exactly one hundred years before Seb. Bach—died, chapel-master, at Dresden, 1672] introduced, in a considerable number of productions, the new forms of song, viz., the recitative and air, duet and trio, as well as an independent, if not continuous, instrumental accompaniment into German music. Besides his '*Sacred Concerts* for 1—5 voices,' and the partially accompanied songs of the '*Symphoniæ Sacræ*,' he also attempted the Oratorio style—thereby laying the foundation of that branch of art in Germany. These pieces deserve notice, and are as follows: '*History of our Lord's Resurrection*,' '*The Seven Words* of our dear Saviour and Redeemer Jesus Christ, which he spoke on the Tree of the Holy Cross; set to music most touchingly,' and '*The Passion* according to the four Evangelists;' this latter he considered his *chef-d'œuvre*. Schütz's only secular piece was his opera '*Daphne*,' the first in Germany, and performed [1627] on the occasion of a princely wedding at Torgau. It was composed to Opitz's translation of Rinuccini's poem, and is a first and only attempt; but on that account all the more remarkable. Thus, we find in Schütz an artist of great and varied powers, who, though almost forgotten at the present day, was by his contemporaries not inaptly called the "father of German music."

The succeeding period, during which neither congregational nor choir singing made any advance, and the Hamburg Opera alone flourished for a short space, was, for Germany, a transition period — conservative merely as concerns the *methods* of art, and preparatory to the appearance of Bach and Handel. Both these creative geniuses—each in his different line—brought Protestant music to the utmost perfection; at the same time they mark the epoch when "a new nation made its appearance, and took first rank in the History of Music."

CHAPTER VIII.

Johann Sebastian Bach (The Sacred Cantata).

JOHANN SEBASTIAN BACH, who, in continuation of the foregoing remarks, comes next under our notice, was born at Eisenach (Luther's birthplace) on the 12th of March, 1685.* After having been [since 1704] organist at Arnstadt, Mühlhausen, Weimar, and Köthen, successively, he was appointed [1723] precentor at the Thomas' School, Leipsic, which office he held till his death [July 28th, 1750]. One incident of a singularly uneventful life deserves notice,—his encounter [1717] with the French organist royal, Marchand, whom he vanquished without an effort, seeing that, instead of appearing at the hour appointed for the contest with Bach, Marchand "took the express, and vanished from Dresden at break of day!" Bach occasionally visited Dresden with his eldest son Friedemann, in order to (what

* *Ueber Joh. Seb. Bach's Leben, Kunst und Kunstwerke*, von J. W. FORKEL. Leipzig, 1802. New edition, 1855.

"*thoughtful*" musicians in these days would think very ill of him for doing) hear the Italian operas of Hasse and others. In his latter years, shortly before he became blind [1747], Frederick the Great sent for him. At that time, his son Emanuel was accompanyist (on the clavichord) to the royal flute-player—by no means a perfect timist. The king was "wonderfully struck" with the bold artistic performance of the elder Bach.

In accordance with the even tenour of a life solely and earnestly devoted to the study of his art, and in marked contrast to other great masters of the period (especially Handel, Hasse, and Gluck), the field of Bach's energies was restricted to his own country— nay, to only a limited portion of that country—, and was almost exclusively employed in the service of his Church. True it is, he did not particularly affect congregational singing, and the greater part of the chorale songs collected from his Cantatas have never been completely adopted by the Church, nor were they intended to lead the congregational song. His grand individuality stands so entirely aloof from the comprehension and sympathy of the average, that, down to the present day, he is the least *popular* of any composer. But in all his works—in the Preludes and Fugues for organ, in his Motets, Cantatas, and 'Passions'—we find the old Church tune rendered in a very characteristic and original manner. In this respect, Bach (who has been called the "musical embodiment of contemplative Lutheranism") displays a remarkable affinity to the greatest composer of the Mother Church—Palestrina—, who in like manner almost always based his compositions on the Gregorian chant. And as this latter composed entirely for the Sistine choir, so did the Leipsic precentor work solely and immediately for Divine service and his choir at the Thomas' School. Both these gifted men also resemble each other in the simple Christian tenour of their lives; both worked principally for the Church; but Bach not so exclusively, and with greater individuality of expression—as well in detail, as with regard to instrumental accompaniment.

All Bach's numerous sacred vocal compositions —his Motets, Cantatas and "Passions"—are the result of this tendency of his genius, always employed on the musical treatment of the chorale and its text. The *Cantatas* for all the Sundays and holidays in the year, of which there is said to have been five entire series (answering to as many years), above three hundred altogether, are even more remarkable than his *Motets* for one and two choirs without instrumental accompaniment. A part of the latter is now lost. It is related that Mozart spent several hours of his brief visit to Leipsic in studying them. While closely adhering to the Liturgy, Bach displays in the treatment of the text (which was on each occasion, by previous understanding, made to correspond with the sermon) a truly marvellous wealth of grand, and original musical invention. Besides an introductory chorus, each Cantata contains several recitatives and airs or duets (though these latter but seldom) and a concluding chorale. But the *cantus firmus* of the chorale forms the ground-work of all the pieces equally, and is skilfully varied and arranged so as to correspond to the sense of the words. "Although delighting in the utmost variety of form, he never loses sight of the religious feeling embodied in the text. The treble or bass, &c. sing the usual Church song, while the remaining voices add their solemn, joyful, or plaintive strains."* Besides the organ, the stringed quartet, flutes, hautboys, and trumpets are employed in the accompaniment.

Robert Franz has recently published a very successful pianoforte edition of several of the Cantatas. It is all the more valuable to us, because not only several of the instruments (as for example the *violoncello piccolo* and the *corni da caccia*) are no longer in use, but the constant *obligato* treatment of the others (particularly of the trumpets) would probably throw great difficulties in the way of a perfotmance of these pieces in the

* HEIMSOETH. Vol. iii., p. 861.

G

original form. It is only some of the texts that are antiquated; their *naïve* mysticism no longer suits our taste and feeling. But with regard even to this objection, the following words of S. Bagge (in his detailed and profound criticism of the 'Passion according to St. Matthew' on the occasion of its performance at Vienna)* are applicable. "The words may savour ever so much of 'pietism,' the principal thing to bear in mind is, that the music penetrates and ennobles both words and sentiment, and endows them with the utmost sublimity of expression. We are therefore led to overlook the actual words, just as in an opera of Mozart, or in Fidelio, or a song of Schubert's, we forgive the weakness of the poetry." The so-called *Christmas Oratorio* may be described as a Cantata in a more florid and detailed style—a cheerful idyllic piece as contrasted with the '*Passions musik.*'

But his principal sacred composition in this style is the grand double-choired 'Passion' according to St. Matthew (chapters xxvi. and xxvii.), called the *Matthäuspassion*. It was performed for the first time in St. Thomas's Church, Leipsic, at vespers on Good Friday, 1729, and consisted of two distinct parts, between which was preached the midnight sermon.

* *Deutsche Musikzeitung.* Jahrg. 1862. No. 17.

"The orchestra is divided into two choruses—the Sionites and the Faithful—which are placed on different sides. The Sionites are assembled to follow the sufferings of the Just One; they call on their companions in the faith to do likewise. Between the choruses is heard the well-known chorale, whose words contain the mystery of salvation—"Oh, Thou guileless Lamb of God."* The solemn service thus opened, there follows the narrative, word for word, according to St. Matthew, in the course of which Gospel personages speak in character, the choruses coming in between; thus forming part of the service. The chorus of the People (*turba*) represents the law and the crowd—bigoted, intolerant, cold, discontented; while sympathizing, peaceful, and loving, the disciples of Jesus and their followers are scattered among the coarse, unfeeling populace. They are in the minority, and do not come forward prominently till the end of the first part, when all is lost; but they remain faithful to the last, and follow their Lord to the grave, trusting in the victory of their faith."† At suitable periods of the narrative, simple and touching reflections are introduced—sometimes in the form of an air or duet (with or without the addition of chorus), at others in the religious choral hymn of the Church, suitably arranged—all in such a simple, heartfelt manner, that the people can follow it with sympathy and join in the chorales, so that the result is a really solemn religious service for the entire congregation.

The choruses are the finest of all; both the grand lyrical ones of the imaginary crowd (at the beginning and end of the first, and particularly the end of the second part), as well as those which represent the Jewish people—dramatic, excited, fanatic, cruel. The most imposing of all is the mighty chorus: "Have thunders and lightnings both vanished in clouds?"‡ the sublimity of which astounded even Oulibicheff, who seldom admires any music but Mozart's. It was encored at the first performance of the 'Passion' at Vienna (Good Friday, April 15th, 1862). Songs written for solo voices are always the most transient part of any great work; but in this one of Bach's there is very little one would wish to see omitted. The whole of the accompanied recitatives are very remarkable; among the airs we distinguish one for treble: "Re-

---

* "*O Lamm Gottes unschuldig.*"
† ZELTER. Preface to the book of the first Berlin performance.
‡ "*Sind Blitze und Donner in Wolken verschwunden.*"

pentance and sorrow,"* and, above all, another for counter-tenor with violin solo: "My God, have mercy!"† They **have** a melody and beauty such as we should hardly expect to find in the learned fugue writer. But it is in the treatment of the Evangelist's words that Bach's great originality proclaims itself. No subsequent composer can ever hope to emulate his unaffected piety of expression. Even in the ordinary *secco* recitative, Bach's wonderful skill shines forth; it is quite impossible to imagine a more judicious and appropriate rendering of the text. Another point worthy of observation—as affording a strong contrast to the increasing tendency to dramatize in the modern Oratorio—is that Bach passes over without emphasis points that would furnish opportunity **for** "dramatic effect," but which do not strictly belong to the main subject—as, for example, the death of Judas the traitor.

The orchestra is everywhere employed with careful reference to the meaning of the words; double orchestra for the full choruses, and single orchestra for the rest. Many of the airs and accompanied recitatives have *obligato* instruments; the words of Christ **have** nothing but a quartet accompaniment, while the harpsichord (*cembalo*) is used for the chords of the *secco* recitative. The accompaniment, generally speaking very subdued, rises with the force and dignity of the words. When Jesus speaks—always, as we have said, to **a** quartet accompaniment of treble chords—it is as if the Holy Saviour were represented encompassed by a halo of glory. **Worthy of notice,** also, is the charming *obligato* management of the wood instruments, particularly in the air "I will watch with Jesus"‡ (hautboy), **and** the recitative "Golgotha, alas!"§ (clarionet.) **Dramatic pre-eminence of** the whole orchestra by itself is, of course, **out of the** question. It is only on one occasion—the death of Christ—, when the voices cease, that it comes forward on its own account—a **dramatic** personality, as it were.

The poem which embodies the words of the Evangelist is by Friedrich HENRICI, surnamed Picander [1700—1764]. It bears traces of an unpoetical age; yet has, as Böhm‖ very justly remarks, "with

* "*Buss und Reu'*."
† "*Erbarme dich,* **mein Gott**."
‡ "*Ich will bei meinem Jesus wachen.*"
§ "*Ach Golgatha.*"
‖ *Das Oratorium. Eine historische Studie* von F. M. BÖHME. Leipzig, 1861.

all its affectation and exaggeration, on the whole, expressed the sentiment of genuine Gospel faith with more truth and accuracy than all the bald, formal rhymes that appeared subsequently."

After exactly one hundred years' rest and oblivion, Mendelssohn revived this noble and sublime composition. It was performed, under his auspices, by the Berlin *Singakademie* on Good Friday (March 12th, 1829), and again by general desire on March 21st—Bach's birthday. The solemn season of Passion Week was well chosen for the public performance of this work; for the deeply religious spirit in which it is written requires, in order to be felt and appreciated, a corresponding devout frame of mind in the listener—one which can scarcely be realized at any other season, except in church. Even Berlioz—a Frenchman—said, after one of the Berlin performances of the 'Passionsmusik,' "it was not a concert, but Divine service he had been attending."

Of the smaller, and probably earlier, *Johannespassion*, Fr. Rochlitz[*] has prepared an "accurate index, interspersed with a few observations." He considers as the climax of the work, and what cannot be sufficiently admired, "the actual biblical and historical—consequently the descriptive element, as apart from that of expression, viz., the recitatives and the numerous greater or smaller choruses that are interwoven with them." Besides a manuscript 'Passion' according to St. Luke, of doubtful authenticity, two other '*Passionsmusik*' are said to have existed.

Bach, although a pious Protestant, did not withhold his talents from the Roman Catholic Church—a proof that he was free from any sectarian spirit. Still less was he a bigoted or intolerant man; but one fully capable of realizing the essence and true spirit of Christianity, apart from the formal dogmatism of different creeds. The finest of his Masses is the so-called *Grand* or *High Mass* in B minor (*a* 8 *voci reali e* 4 *ripiene*). Of modern compositions of this kind, it is perhaps the only one which has successfully combined the

[*] *Für Freunde der Tonkunst.* Vol. iv. p. 435—448.

purity and dignity of Church feeling with originality of invention and the unrestricted employment of all the resources of art (chorus and solo, orchestra and organ). More especially in the *Credo*, the *Sanctus*, and *Osanna*, has the grand choral polyphony once more splendidly asserted its claims to be, of all others, the form which is most admirably adapted to express the fervour and solemnity of religious feeling. The 'High Mass' has, on account of its marvellous polyphonous structure, been described as a Gothic cathedral in music;—in like manner, the early Italian Opera may be likened to the florid Renaissance architecture, while Gluck's would answer to the chaste and severe Grecian temple.

As to Bach's instrumental works, we shall, as a matter of course, assign the priority to those which (according to Beethoven) represent him as the "patriarch of harmony," viz.—his compositions for the *Organ*, consisting in the profound and masterly treatment of the chorale in a series of preludes and variations, as well as pieces in the less severe form of the Fantasia with Fugue. "It was (says K. M. von Weber)[*] his perfect command of the organ that determined the bent of his genius. The grandiose character of this noble instrument reminds one strongly of Bach; while the magnificence of his works, in point of har-

---

[*] *Hinterl. Schriften.* Vol. iii., p. 67.

mony, is due to the ingenuity and acuteness of intellect which enabled him to combine the most seemingly contradictory lines of harmony to a perfect whole. This freedom in the flow of different parts, while the utmost smoothness is maintained throughout, forced him to invent new aids to the execution of his pieces. Hence it arose that *pianoforte-playing*, in particular, enjoys the advantages of a system of *fingering*, which was first promulgated by his son Emanuel. Its peculiarity consisted in the adoption of the thumb in playing; whereas, before his time, the four fingers only were usually employed." Both as organist and composer for the organ, Bach stands unrivalled in the annals of art. Not only did he surpass all his predecessors: Joh. Jacob FROBERGER [born 1637], FRESCOBALDI'S pupil, SCHEIDT, KERL, PACHELBEL, and J. A. REINECKE, in boldness of execution and grandeur of conception, he has never been equalled by his successors: Joh. Christian KITTEL [1732—1809], his best pupil, and the pupils of this latter: M. G. FISCHER, HÄSSLER, UMBREIT, and Joh. Christian RINK [1770—1846]—the patriarch of modern organists.

Bach's *pianoforte* works are, at the present day, highly esteemed rather than actually known. The *Well-tempered Clavichord*,* of which the

* " *Das wohltemperirte Klavier.* ('2 *Mal* 24 *Präludien und Fugen durch alle Tonarten.*')"

first edition appeared in 1800 (fifty years after the composer's death), forms no exception to this rule. Indeed, the generality of pianoforte musicians are of opinion that this music is no longer adapted to our taste—is, in short, too formal in style, as well as devoid of feeling and expression. But the fact is, that very few performers can play these pieces, particularly the fugues, correctly and fluently, and, what is of still more consequence, in the true Bach spirit. Even those who have mastered the difficulties of Mozart and Beethoven will hesitate to attempt these *colossi*. The best preparation for this (Bach's greatest pianoforte work) are the small and great (*English*) *Suites*—a "series" of, generally speaking, dance tunes in every variety of time, rhythm, and expression, but all in the same key, and—unlike the more modern Sonata—unconnected with each other. The *Prelude*, also called *Ouverture* or *Entrée*, is usually succeeded by the gentle German *Allemande*, the lively French *Courante*, the *Sarabande* full of Spanish *grandezza*, and the excited Italian *Gigue*. Other forms of the dance tune are the stately *Menuetto*, the *Gavotte*, *Bourrée*, *Pavane*, *Passecaille*, *Chaconne*, &c. "Bach was the first who embodied artistic feeling in this kind of casual form; he displayed so much originality of invention, both of melody and harmony, in the '*Suites Anglaises*,' that the brightness and animation, as well as the admirable keeping and dignity of these pieces, will always cause them to be regarded as models of style."* Even those who look upon these graceful pieces in rhythmical dance measure merely as a kind of "*étude*" will derive considerable enjoyment from their vivacious, stirring movement.— Bach's '*Suites*' for orchestra are, on the whole, inferior to them, and only historically valuable.

The *Invenzioni*—small model pieces for the cultivation of skill and taste—are chiefly important as studies. The original title-page explains their object: "A complete Guide, to show lovers of the pianoforte a clear method of playing correctly in two parts; and also how to obtain good '*inventiones*,' and to carry them out properly; above all, to acquire a '*cantabile*' style of playing, and a good foretaste of composition."—The grander compositions for concert performances are, besides the (30) '*Goldberg Variations*,' the *Chromatic Fantasia*—a model of ingenious and, at the same time, easy-flowing modulations—, the *Concert in the Italian style*, and the concerts for one and several pianofortes after the violin concerts of VIVALDI [died 1743].—Bach's last production was the *Art of the Fugue*,† which was engraved by himself and his son. The four-part arrangement

---

* F. HAND. *Aesthetik der Tonkunst*. Zwei Theile. Jena, 1837, 1841. Vol. ii., p. 364.

† '*Kunst der Fuge*.' Compare M. HAUPTMANN. *Erläuterungen zu J. S. Bach's 'Kunst der Fuge*.'

of the chorale, "When in deep distress"* (in the Appendix), was composed only a few days before his death.

The commonly-received opinion is that these compositions, as well as Bach's music in general, are out of date, dry, too learned, too studied, unintelligible—in short, destitute of melody; whereas, on the contrary, it is only too rich and massive for our ear (unaccustomed to genuine polyphony); the melody, so to speak, predominating throughout. On this head we will quote Forkel's† admirable words. "In Bach's fugues we find all those conditions fulfilled which, generally speaking, are only required in the freer styles of composition. An admirable theme, leading into an equally admirable tune originating in the theme from beginning to end; the remaining parts are *not mere accompaniment*, but each is an independent tune in itself, harmonizing with the rest; the progression of the whole piece is easy, free, and flowing; inexhaustible richness of modulation is combined with irreproachable purity of harmony; and, lastly, an ideal atmosphere envelopes the whole, so that the performer or listener almost fancies the sounds are metamorphosed into spirits." While many a great musician has produced some, more or less, inferior works, there are, among Bach's compositions, some that appear

---

* "*Wenn wir in höchsten Nöthen sein.*"
† *Ueber Joh. Seb. Bach's Leben*, &c., p. 23.

singular to us, but certainly none that are weak. Bach's music is contrapuntal in conception, grand, and peculiar; it is, therefore, no wonder that it cannot be relished by boarding-school misses and young ladies who strum "Arrangements," etc.; but it is downright intellectual music for "men, and such women as are capable of appreciating a right good man."* We are here reminded of the highly cultivated artist, grown grey in the exercise of manifold branches of art—Angelica Romberg, who was actually moved to tears when listening to a Prelude of Bach's. Nothing, indeed, would tend so effectually to improve and form the taste, and especially to raise the tone of pianoforte-playing—greatly deteriorated since it has become a fashionable female accomplishment—and composition, as a constant recurrence to the venerable Bach.† On the other hand, it would, of course, be worse than ignoring him altogether, to restrict one's self entirely to his music, and to affect indifference to the superior charm, beauty, and sweetness of more modern music.

To resume: Bach's historical fame rests on his sacred music—especially the 'Passions,' and his organ compositions. What Palestrina had been to the Roman Catholic, Bach was to the

---

* GOETHE.

† Compare ROCHLITZ. "*Vom Geschmack an Seb. Bach's Compositionen, besonders für das Klavier.*" *Für Freunde der Tonkunst.* Vol. ii., p. 205-230.

Protestant Church, whereas his sons on the other hand, particularly Phillipp Emanuel—who in another line did so much for the advancement of art—, the original, but unfortunate Friedemann, as well as the polished "Londoner" or "Milanese," Joh. Christian, directed their efforts wholly to secular music. Phil. Emanuel admitted that he "was forced to adopt a style of his own, as he never could have equalled his father in his own particular province." A number of musicians—contemporary as well as subsequent—adopted Bach's manner in their Church compositions, as for instance: Telemann at Hamburg, Stölzel at Gotha, Homilius, Doles, Schicht, and others. They have all left several annual series of Church music, 'Passions,' &c. But, sublime above them all stands Sebastian Bach—a monument of severe German art, and that, at a time when a totally different style (the Italian) was gaining ground around him.

Fr. Rochlitz* distinguishes, from among the crowd of those who called themselves Bach's disciples, the following as worthy a place in the History of Art: the organists Joh. Caspar Vogler and Joh. Ludwig Krebs—of whom the first somewhat approached Bach in manual skill, and the latter in conception and feeling—also Gottfr. Aug. Homilius ("Bach popularized")

---

* *Fer Freunde der Tonkunst.* Vol. iv., p. 165.

and Joh. Phil. KIRNBERGER, the famous thorough-bass master, and Court musician to the Princess Amalia of Prussia. The theories set forth in his writings ('The Art of correct Composition'* and 'True Principles of Harmony'†) are deduced from the compositions of Bach.—"Handel had neither time nor inclination to form pupils. Smith was only his faithful amanuensis." (Compare Rochlitz' admirable parallel between Bach and Handel.)‡

In 1843, a simple monument was, by Mendelssohn's instigation, erected to the memory (for a long time almost forgotten) of the *maestro*, close to his old official abode. A revised edition, with notes, of all his works has been published in two parts or volumes by the LEIPZIG BACH SOCIETY (founded in 1850, the centenary of his death). It has already reached the twelfth annual series. According to the example set by Mendelssohn, Marx, Mosewius, and others, separate "Bach Societies" have been organized for the express practice of Bach's great vocal pieces, in Berlin, Breslau, and other cities. The concert performances of Clara WIECK (afterwards SCHUMANN), LISZT, and their disciples, as, for instance, HANS VON BÜLOW and others, have done a great

---

* '*Kunst des reinen Satzes.*'

† '*Wahre Grundsätze zum Gebrauche der Harmonie.*'

‡ *Fur Freunde der Tonkunst.* Vol. iv., p. 153-164, reprinted with some omissions in Brendel's History of Music, p. 212-215.

deal towards reviving the taste for a portion of Bach's pianoforte works.* That "the present generation is able and willing to study Sebastian Bach" may, according to that acute observer, Riehl, confidently be taken as a favourable sign of musical improvement. May his bolder prophecy, concerning Bach, be fulfilled: "He was born for the schools and *connoisseurs* in the eighteenth, but for the nation in the nineteenth, century!"

* NOTE BY THE TRANSLATOR. Recently, in England, Hallé has introduced the works of Seb. Bach in his "Pianoforte Recitals."

CHAPTER IX.

GEORGE FREDERICK HANDEL (THE ORATORIO).

GEORGE FREDERICK HANDEL, Bach's great contemporary, was born February 23rd, 1685, at Halle, in Saxony, where his father (then upwards of sixty years of age) practised as a surgeon.* The boy being destined for the law, the father used every endeavour to repress the early manifestations of musical genius in his son. In defiance, however, of paternal injunctions, the child contrived to play the harpsichord in secret. In his seventh year, at the instance and with the support of the Duke of Weissenfels — who happened to hear him play on the organ—he was placed under the tuition of the celebrated Zachau, organist at Halle. For the space of seven years

---

* *G. F. Händel*, von FRIEDRICH CHRYSANDER. Zwei Bände, Leipzig, 1858, 1860. *Handel, his Life, Personal and Professional*, by MRS. BRAY. *Studies on Handel*, by H. F. CHORLEY. *Handel's Pedigree*, by K. E. FORSTEMANN. *The Life of Handel*, by V. SCHŒLCHER.

he worked unremittingly both at execution and harmony, at the end of which period his master frankly admitted he could teach him nothing more. His father's death occurring shortly afterwards, Handel sought a wider field for the exercise of his talents. Already [in 1698] acquainted with the musical attractions—especially the Italian Opera—of Berlin, he was possessed with the desire of seeing more of the world. Accordingly, he turned his steps to Hamburg [1703], and was, in the first instance, engaged at the theatre as second violinist. While there, several of his Operas ('Almira,' 'Nero,' and others), were produced on the stage with considerable success.

At the time of Handel's arrival in Hamburg, the German Opera, founded there in 1678, was no longer in its prime, though Keiser, its best representative, was still in full activity. Whereas, at the German Courts the Italian Opera alone was in vogue, at Hamburg, which boasted the largest of the city theatres (so numerous at that time), operas by German musicians were brought on the stage, and (their existence depending entirely on the support and sympathy of the audience) in the German language. In order to conciliate, as far as possible, the theological prejudices of the age, the first attempts were made with subjects taken from the Old Testament (for example, Adam and Eve, Cain and Abel, &c.); but soon, operas were always taken from secular subjects, after French and Italian models. Since the year 1690, the operas of STEFFANI [1655—1730], translated into German, were in great favour. (He was chapel-master at Hanover, and famous also for his chamber duets). But REINHOLD KEISER [1673—1739]—considered by Hasse equal even to Al. Scarlatti—gave to the Hamburg stage a marked pre-eminence by his (circa) 120 melodramas, written (subsequently to 1696) expressly for that theatre.

Without endorsing Lindner's* opinion that he was the "Mozart of the first epoch of German dramatic music," we have no hesitation in affirming that he is the first German dramatic composer *previous* to Mozart — particularly excelling in the air and accompanied recitative. "Whatever he said, especially in the love-scenes, was so naturally and gracefully expressed, and fell on the ear in so rich, flowing, and melodious a manner, that one is even more tempted to love than admire."† MATTHESON [1681—1764], the opera singer and composer (in after years, author of a considerable series of theoretical and analytical works), as also TELEMANN [1681—1767], the imitator of Lully—fertile in production, poor in invention, but of great technical ability, are quite inferior as compared to Keiser. After 1718, when Keiser retired from the stage for a considerable time, the Hamburg Opera deteriorated greatly. Music from different composers was pieced together to make an opera, or when Italian operas were performed, the airs were sung in Italian and the rest in German—perhaps for lack of performers who could sing in Italian.

The German Opera thus totally bankrupt, the Italian Opera ("under high patronage") reigned sole and supreme, and was supported, in an almost greater degree than heretofore, by such extravagant admiration and expenditure as was utterly fatal to any independent efforts. The great German masters, Handel, Hasse, and Graun, wrote for Italy and the Italian Opera in London, Dresden, and Berlin; and even Gluck only met with full appreciation in France—after having, like Handel, devoted his talents, during the greater part of his life, to the Italian Opera.

Handel's melodramas (as was afterwards the case with his operas in London) having been banished the stage by unworthy intrigues, the undaunted musician—with some money scraped together by pianoforte teaching—set out [in the early part of 1707] for Italy. (He refused the

* *Die erste stehende deutsche Oper.* Dargestellt von E. O. LINDNER. Berlin, 1855.

† MATTHESON.

heir apparent of Tuscany's offer to accompany him thither free of expense.) It was the true instinct of genius that impelled him to visit that country—the cradle of art—, although the desire to "mature himself and gain experience"* was probably not so distinctly held in view by Handel as it was afterwards by Goethe. Handel was welcomed in all the great cities with all possible honours, not only by the easily excited people —who greeted him in the theatres with shouts of " *Caro Sassone* "—, but by fellow-artists, such as Lotti, Al. Scarlatti and his son Domenico (the celebrated harpsichord performer and composer), Corelli, &c. Thus encouraged, Handel remained in Italy upwards of three years. Of all musicians anterior to Mozart undoubtedly the most *universal*, he, like this latter, knew how to fall in with the prevailing taste while retaining his own artistic individuality, and, consequently, never failed of success.

Thus, for Florence and Venice he wrote the Operas 'Rodrigo' and 'Agrippina;' for Rome (besides other sacred compositions) the Oratorios 'La Resurrezione' and 'Il trionfo del tempo e del disinganno;' while for Naples he composed secular Cantatas with instrumental accompaniment; among others, the pastoral play 'Aci, Galatea e Polifemo'—"the *musical*, as 'Pastor

---

* CHRYSANDER.

fido' was the *poetical*, essence of Arcadian feeling."* Both of these last-named works he afterwards set to English words ('Acis and Galatea,' 1720, "The triumph of time and truth," 1737); in like manner, he was wont to take the best pieces of his earlier sacred and secular compositions, and (often with very trifling alterations) incorporate them in his later operas and oratorios.

In 1710, Handel was appointed to succeed Steffani at Hanover; and in the autumn of that year he paid a visit to London—where, since Purcell's death, the Italian Opera was all the fashion. His Opera 'Rinaldo' (composed within a fortnight) was performed there in the early part of 1711, on which occasion the airs "*Cara sposa*" and "*Lascia ch'io pianga*" created immense sensation.

<small>In London, where, however, excellent musicians were not wanting, Handel met with no rival, whether as a performer or composer. England (according to Chrysander) could formerly boast an epoch of first-rate musical excellence; but that was, at the period of which we are treating, a thing of the past. The most remarkable English composer who may be regarded as Handel's predecessor was Henry PURCELL [1658—1695]. Similar to H. Schütz in Germany, he was the representative of national music as distinguished from that so largely imported from France and Italy—yet he was unable to establish an English style or school of music. English music, properly speaking, had long since reached its zenith in the glorious reign of Queen Elizabeth—so prosperous for art as well as for the nation. TALLIS [born circa 1520, died 1585] and his celebrated</small>

---

* CHRYSANDER.

pupil, William BIRD [born circa 1545, died 1623], were excellent organists as well as composers. In style, they somewhat resemble the early Italian—in particular the Venetian—school, and their *chants* are to this day heard in English cathedrals and churches. Admirable composers, both of sacred and secular music (in the Anthem, Motet, and Madrigal), were also: Thomas MORLEY [died circa 1604], John DOWLAND [born in 1562], John BENNET [flourished circa 1599], Orlando GIBBONS [1583—1625], Pelham HUMPHREYS [1647—1674], John BLOW [1648—1708], and others ; all of whom have bequeathed us many charming pieces breathing a sweetness of melody and tenderness of expression that justly entitle them to the affectionate remembrance of posterity. Among subsequent composers, Dr. ARNE [1710—1778], ARNOLD, STORACE, DIBDIN (famous for his sea-songs), and, more recently still, CALCOTT, HORSLEY, BISHOP and GLOVER, are of historical importance.*

After a second leave of absence [1712], Handel never returned to his official duties at Hanover. His composition in commemoration of the Peace of Utrecht [1713], called the *Utrecht Te Deum* and *Jubilate* (to be, however, distinguished from the greatly superior *Dettingen Te Deum* of thirty years later), procured him a grant of £200 *per annum* from Queen Anne; and he succeeded in conciliating his late master the Elector of Hanover, on his arrival in England as George I. [1714], by his *Water Music*—composed on the occasion of a royal pleasure party on the Thames. When travelling in the King's suite in Germany [1716], Handel took the opportunity of visiting Hamburg and Halle. It is probable that it was

* NOTE BY THE TRANSLATOR. Those who desire further information concerning English music and English musicians are referred to HOGARTH's *Musical History*, Chapters II. (p. 50), V., VI., VIII., XIV., XV., XXI., XXII., XXIII.

during his stay at Hamburg he composed a German *Passionsmusik* after Brockes' poem ('The sufferings and death of Jesus Christ for the sins of the world, described in verse after the four Evangelists by B. H. Brockes') —a subject which has been treated both previously and subsequently by his former fellow-musicians at Hamburg—Keiser, Telemann, and Mattheson.

From 1717 to 1720, Handel resided in the capacity of chapel-master to the Duke of Chandos at Cannons; and, during this period, composed the famous *Chandos Anthems* (twelve in number). In these compositions, as well as in the (four) Coronation and Funeral Anthems of a later date, his manner of interspersing choruses with solo songs, and two and three part solo pieces with instrumental accompaniments, reminds one strongly of the grand Oratorios he composed long afterwards; for which reason, Chrysander classes them with these in regard to form and matter, and even considers them as the preparation and studies for these latter. "The word 'Anthem' (*Ant-hymn*) originally referred to some portion of the church service, and has only this in common with its present relation to the choir song, that it follows on the chorale, or liturgical chant of the officiating priest. Now, we understand it to apply to that genus of composition which in the main combines the Motet and Cantata. As the cantos of an epic refer to one grand centre of heroic deeds and actions, so does this series of songs of praise and thanksgiving form a united whole, and thus becomes almost an oratorio." Undoubtedly, it is neither by accident nor without a significance of its own that Handel's first English Oratorio, *Esther*, followed [1720] immediately on the Chandos Anthems; though it must be admitted that the very operatic style of this Oratorio, as well as *Athaliah* and *Deborah* [1733] (even when remodelled in 1732), has little in common with his subsequent grand productions. Thus we see Handel, when free to follow the instincts of his genius and his own inclination, making the first attempts in his own peculiar province of Oratorio composition—one which he probably little thought he should have to relinquish for twenty years when appointed to the management of the new Italian Opera founded by subscription of the nobility.

But Handel, a man of gigantic proportions both of mind and body, could not adapt his fine, manly nature to the caprices of actors and singers (Cuzzoni, Duristanti, Senesino, &c.); and it is only to be wondered that it did not come to an open rupture before his insisting, but without avail, on the dismissal of the arrogant *soprano*, Senesino. The nobility opened a new Opera house, for which Farinelli and Faustina, with their composers in ordinary, Porpora and Hasse, were in turn engaged—a combination which Handel, with far inferior resources, was wholly unable to compete with. Unsuccessful with two theatres (Haymarket and Covent Garden), nearly ruined in pocket, and completely prostrated both in body and mind, Handel was fain to retire altogether from the Opera [1736].

Handel's Operas—like all those of the period—have lost their value for our generation; but the advantage which the great musician himself derived from his long and (so far as public success was concerned) disastrous connexion with the Opera, is not to be lightly esteemed. Very striking is Chrysander's parallel between the Operas of Handel and the Comedies of Shakespeare. That writer is of opinion that Comedy and Opera were in both instances the best possible schooling "these great artists could have undergone, in order to give shape and consistency to their creations, and by a complete mastery of the forms of art, to free themselves from the *constraining influence of those forms*. Had they restricted themselves solely to Tragedy and Oratorio, they had never effected this in so remarkable a degree.—As with Shakespeare Comedy preceded Tragedy, so with Handel did the Oratorio succeed to the Opera—in both instances the lighter and less congenial style was the foundation of nobler and grander productions."

Tortured by gout, and almost on the verge of

insanity, Handel sought and obtained relief from the baths of Aix-la-Chapelle [1737]. Struck with admiration by his wonderful performance on the organ, devotees exclaimed: "Saint Cecilia has restored him to health that he may sing her praises!" Truly and splendidly did Handel afterwards fulfil this saying in a series of immortal master-pieces. Very significant is the transition from Opera to Oratorio which we mark in '*Alexander's Feast,*' composed to Dryden's Ode in honour of Saint Cecilia [1736]. "In the person of Timotheus, the singer who

'Could swell the soul to rage, or kindle soft desire,'

this highly imaginative poem portrays the power of music in old Grecian times, and closes with a reference to the sublimer influence of Christian music, personified in Saint Cecilia.

' Let old Timotheus yield the prize,
Or both divide the crown ;
He raised a mortal to the skies,
She drew an angel down.'

In these words the poet concludes, by revealing the happy union of both the Grecian and Christian element in music. Handel's work has shed new lustre on this graceful conception of the power of music, and enriched it with an ideal colouring."* This admirable composition, which so wonderfully and accurately portrays sensations of the most varied character, can be compared with nothing

* CHRYSANDER.

in Handel's works but his rendering of Milton's exquisite poem, ' *L'Allegro ed il Pensieroso'* —an ideal representation of the play of conflicting passions and their final reconcilement and harmony in the third part, entitled ' *Il Moderato.*'

After producing a few more mythological subjects ('*Semele*' after Congreve's dramatic poem, and '*The Choice of Hercules*'), no longer in the form of Opera, but rather as Oratorio dramas—studies, as it were, for the great works that were to follow —, Handel, for the remainder of his life, turned his attention exclusively (with what success we all know) to the Oratorio proper (biblical in theme). As his earlier sacred compositions were usually written for some special state occasion, so, in like manner, are his Oratorios (owing to previous dramatic experience) adorned with all imaginable richness and splendour. "The broad, grand foundation of chorus which underlays the whole work, and in which all the resources of counterpoint are employed with marvellous skill and learning, yet without detriment to the distinct, popular character of the chorus, is always forcible and expressive, as are also the solo parts, however brilliant and florid.* He has hit the exact medium between the solemnity of the sacred text

---

* We cannot entirely concur in the above remarks. Handel (according to Chrysander) actually transferred the "air" from the Opera to the Oratorio; wherefore, it is obvious that those written chiefly with a view to display the vocal attainments so cherished at

and the requirements of dramatic effect, and thereby created a genuine Oratorio style, worthy of imitation for ages to come."*

In 1738, *ISRAEL IN EGYPT*, the grandest of Old Testament oratorios—the nation itself being the centre of interest—, was given to the world. Handel is grand beyond description when he represents the people rising to arms, giving battle, and celebrating their triumph. He does indeed (to use Mozart's expression) peal forth like a thunder-clap in the mighty choruses: "He led them through," "The horse and his rider," and a number of others; and to what shall we liken them, as well as the noble duet for two basses, "The Lord is a man of war," for sublimity and colossal grandeur? on the other hand, to what compare the wonderful instrumental imagery of the Plagues of Egypt? As Krüger† admirably expresses it: "The first part of 'Israel in Egypt' is narrated with the plainness of an epic; the second describes a series of grand lyrical effusions, breaking forth into songs of triumph; while the powerful dramatic movement surging throughout gives an air of reality to the whole work."

that period, will be rejected by good taste, and omitted in public performances. On the whole, therefore, both in the Oratorios and Anthems, the solos are inferior to the choruses; but even " if he does scribble now and then, according to the fashion of the day, there is always something in it." (Mozart.)

* HEIMSOETH. Vol. iii., p. 860.
† *Deutsche Musikzeitung.* Vol. iii., p. 170.

After 1740, were produced: '*Saul*,' the '*Messiah*,' '*Samson*,' '*Belsazer*,' '*Susanna*,' '*Joseph*,' '*Judas Maccabæus*,' '*Joshua*,' '*Solomon*,' '*Theodora*,' and, finally, [1751] '*Jephtha*'—written by Smith from Handel's dictation (for—like Bach—the great musician was stone blind during his latter years). Of all these oratorios (with the exception of the incomparable '*Messiah*') '*Samson*,' and '*Judas Maccabæus*' are the finest and most generally popular. In *SAMSON* the thrilling pathos of Milton's poem is softened, while the effect is immeasurably heightened, by the addition of Handel's music,—the whole representing a work of art which (sixteen for the most part antiquated airs and one duet with recitative having been suppressed in MOSEL's tolerably successful remodelling of the text) will survive all changes of time and fashion. As is evident from the immense number of airs, it is no longer the struggles of a nation, but the tragic fate of a hero, that in this Oratorio challenges our sympathy—the character of the entire work being decidedly dramatic. Powerful as are the choruses of Israelites and Philistines, it is the lamentations of Samson and his followers which pierce our very soul, while in the final scene the feelings of the survivors are brought before us in the noble *Dead March* from '*Saul*,'* leading into the chorus "Glorious hero, may thy grave peace and mercy

---

* The Funeral March in '*Saul*' is introduced likewise in '*Samson*.'

ever have"—closing, as it were, in one grand final chord.

In *JUDAS MACCABAEUS* [August 11th, 1746] it is the nation, the affairs of the nation, and its great religious wars, which once more rivet attention. Whereas in Samson the prevailing sentiment was one of deep pathos, so many and varied emotions are here called forth, that it were hard to say whether mourning for the illustrious dead, pious trust in God, martial strains, or, finally, the triumphant return of the warrior ("See, the conquering hero comes"),* is most deeply and truthfully expressed, so marvellously are the different moods—heroic, elegiac, and idyllic—contrasted with, and adapted to, each other. Most of the other Oratorios ('Saul,' 'Joshua,' 'Jephtha,' &c.), in like manner, commemorate the Deliverers of a nation from oppression and bondage. Whether triumphant or succumbing, his heroes proclaim that noble love of liberty of which Handel was the devoted apostle in the land of his adoption—England, the happy and the free.

But the work in which, of all others, Handel's epic-dramatic treatment somewhat approaches the epic-lyric style of Bach, while at the same time it brings out the distinguishing characteristics of both in the fullest light, is the *MESSIAH*†—the

---

* Taken from the oratorio 'Joshua.'

† Compare ROCHLITZ. *Für Freunde der Tonkunst.* Vol. i., p. 227—280.

Oratorio which, at first [April 12th, 1741] rejected in London, and afterwards enthusiastically received at Dublin, became the corner-stone of Handel's fame. The design of the work is itself sublime, universal—it is "a veritable Christian epos in music."* The first part treats of the promised salvation of mankind through Christ; the second and most important part of the work sets forth the Life, Sufferings, and Resurrection of our Lord, in a succession of sublime images, to which is appended (in the third part) the contemplation of "Things that shall be hereafter"—Death, Resurrection, Judgment, and Life eternal. Thus, what other composers have treated in separate works (for example Bach's 'Passion,' his Christmas Oratorio, Spohr's 'Last Judgment,' Schneider's ditto†), Handel combined in ONE grand *trilogy*—himself selecting the plain, unadorned words of Holy Writ for his incomparable theme.—Here again we find the chorus prominent. Taking up from the narrating single voices the solemn themes of sin and suffering, consolation and hope, atonement and salvation, the mighty chorus pours forth the deep sympathies, as it were, of the whole human race. Thus the chorus "Unto us a Child is born," the world-famed HALLELUJAH chorus (during which, in England, the audience remain standing), the elaborate con-

* HERDER.   † '*Das Weltgericht.*'

cluding chorus "Worthy is the Lamb," &c., are the most striking portions of this wonderful masterpiece. The pathos and touching simplicity of the *airs*: "Comfort ye my people," "He shall feed his flock," "He was despised," "I know that my Redeemer liveth," and others, complete the lofty spiritual tone of this matchless—truly *sacred*—Oratorio.

And, whereas Handel completed this grandest achievement of sacred musical art in the short space of twenty-one days, his successor in the *poetical*, "who translated his work from music into poetry"*—Klopstock—laboured many years [1748—1773] at his sacred epic poem, and, after all, only succeeded in producing a now almost forgotten poem of very unequal merit.

The 'Messiah' (so highly prized in England) has not hitherto obtained so great popularity in Germany as 'Samson' and 'Judas Maccabæus;'—indeed, were it not for Mozart's judicious revision of the score, it is probable that it would long have remained unknown in this country. Thibaut † is therefore prejudiced and unreasonable when he inveighs against a fuller instrumentation of Handel's oratorios (more especially against Mozart's), and talks of "polishing" and "adorning" to suit modern taste. The great

* GERVINUS.
† *Ueber Reinheit der Tonkunst*, p. 136-142 of the 2nd edition.

improvements that have taken place in the art of instrumentation, as well as the absence of the masterly organ-playing with which Handel accompanied the performances in England, have necessitated further additions to the scores of his oratorios. Let us not therefore be captious, but gladly and thankfully avail ourselves of the modern revisions (consisting of abridgments and fuller instrumentation) of Handel's works (the 'Messiah,' 'Judas Maccabæus,' 'Alexander's Feast,' the sweet, elegiac, idyll, 'Acis and Galatea,' by Mozart; 'Israel in Egypt,' by Lindpaintner; 'Samson,' by Mosel and Ferd. Hiller). At the same time we are quite willing to believe with Thibaut, that where the only indications in the score are *organ, loud*— "a power and volume of sound was heard when Handel presided at the organ such as hundreds of fiddles and flutes cannot make up for now-a-days."

Handel died, as he had prayed he might, on Good Friday [April 14th, 1759], and was buried in Westminster Abbey. One hundred years afterwards (July 1st, 1859), "his admirers in England and Germany" raised a bronze statue (admirably executed by Heidel of Berlin) to his memory in the market-place of Halle. The LEIPSIC HANDEL SOCIETY is now engaged in raising a "*monumentum ære perennius*" to the great master's memory in the form of a splendid edition of all his works. It has already reached the nineteenth volume. A complete edition of Handel's works (in 50 folio volumes) was published in London, 1786.

Fewer even than Bach's were Handel's successors and imitators. English—*national*—music had almost ceased to exist, and, before J. A. Hiller's and Mozart's time, Handel's works were quite unknown in Germany. Such sacred music as appeared during the latter half of the last century, is characterized by a soft, tender, and—above all, *vocally*—pleasing expression. This period is designated the HASSE-GRAUN, because Hasse was its master and leader, and Graun in his 'Death of Jesus'* (after Ramler) has produced the best work of the then prevailing style. The Roman Catholic Court chapel at Dresden possesses a large number of HASSE's compositions (Masses, Psalms and Hymns) written to Latin texts. Of those annually performed at Dresden, the most celebrated are the *Te Deum* and the great 'Requiem.' Hasse also wrote a quantity of Italian Oratorios — Metastasio furnishing the texts. Krause† calls him the Correggio of Church music, "equally great, whether in sublime and solemn, joyful and exulting passages, or when depicting rapturous devotion and the depth and purity of sacred affection. Hasse's Church style

---

* '*Tod Jesu.*'

† *Darstellungen aus der Geschichte der Musik.* Göttingen 1827, p. 194.

forms a complete, and, at the same time, beautiful, contrast to Palestrina's; both are, taken in connection with the Church music of Bach and Handel, as it were, expressly adapted to complete the entire cycle of sacred music." Hasse's Church style is remarkable for profound unity and artistic finish, as well as for freshness and naturalness of expression; KARL HEINRICH *GRAUN* [born in Saxony 1701, died, chapel-master to Frederick the Great at Berlin, 1759], on the other hand, sought to combine Italian and German style in Church music. Thus, his famous Cantata 'The Death of Jesus' consists, strictly speaking, of two very unequal portions; the airs (out of all proportion long) and other solo songs are quite in the Italian taste, while the choruses are noble and devotional, "learned, yet intelligible; all the parts are interwoven with consummate art, yet they are natural and flowing."* When we bear in mind that even in many of Handel's works, as well as those of other masters, the airs are frequently of so formal a character as to be unattractive—nay displeasing—to us, we are inclined to consider the 'Death of Jesus,' as a composition of genuine piety, and worthy of remembrance—one which, though of inferior originality, is yet deservedly popular, and while it reflects the somewhat sentimental tendency of

* ROCHLITZ. *Für Freunde der Tonkunst*, vol. iv., p. 203.

contemporary literature, is, on the whole, of noble and dignified proportions. "Intense spirituality, as well as deep—much less thrilling—pathos, were not in his nature; nor has he made any pretensions to these great gifts, or sought to display them in his compositions."*

Even J. S. Bach's son, EMANUEL, adopted the style of the period—the Hasse-Graun—in his Church compositions:—the sublime '*Holy*' (for double-choir), and the Oratorio '*Israel in the Desert;*' while, with admirable taste, he carefully avoided the least approach to operatic style.

We ought further to mention Joh. Gottlieb NAUMANN [born 1741, died at Dresden 1801], a highly meritorious German musician of the Italian school, though two biographers† have vainly endeavoured to rescue his name from oblivion. His principal sacred composition was the Cantata 'The Lord's Prayer'‡ (after Klopstock's paraphrase). The same subject has recently been set by Spohr (op. 104) as a double-choir for male voices. Several of his masses still hold a place in the repertory of the Chapel-royal at Dresden; they are not without a considerable admixture of secular feeling. Naumann marks

* ROCHLITZ. *Für Freunde der Tonkunst*, vol. iv., p. 204.
† J. NAUMANN (son of the composer). *Naumann's Biographie, Künstler und Familienleben*. Dresden, 1841.
FR. ROCHLITZ. *Für Freunde der Tonkunst*, vol. iii., p. 3—74.
‡ '*Das Vater unser.*'

the final close of this period, as well as that of sacred music in the last century in general; whatever else has been produced—contemporary and subsequent—is, with very few exceptions, nothing but a repetition of what has been before, and of no historical importance. The mechanical assiduity of organists and precentors (worthy musical *master-singers*) and the characterless skill of Court composers (always ready to obey their Highness's commands, whether in Opera, Oratorio or Mass) were the combined causes which tended more and more to depreciate sacred music, and to remove the Oratorio further and further from the plain Bible words and solemn Church style; till, at length, Haydn and Mozart—though without adopting the old severe Church style—restored genuine devotional feeling to sacred composition.

CHAPTER X.

THE FRENCH OPERA AND GLUCK.

THE melodious Opera of Italy, having succeeded in throwing Church music into shade, achieved complete victory over all branches and styles of music. The French Opera alone maintained a species of rivalry—though in a comparatively subordinate capacity; for the French—always intent on novelty—had adopted the yet immature Italian Opera, and transcribed and transposed it so entirely to their own satisfaction, that they persuaded themselves they had achieved something quite new and original, and accordingly cared little or nothing for anything else.

As early as 1645 (Monteverde's period), the Cardinal Minister Mazarin ("*qui chercha tous les moyens d'amuser Louis XIV*") sent for an Italian Opera company to Paris. The success of the Italians inspired the French with a desire to make a similar attempt, and before long, melodramas in French, set to music in imitation of Italian models, made their appearance. The first attempt ("*la première comèdie française*") is said to have been a pastoral play entitled '*La Pastorale*' [1659], composed by CAMBERT to a poem by the Abbé Perrin, and was succeeded by several others. But it was an Italian—Jean Baptiste LULLY [1633—1687] who gained esteem and popularity—especially at Court—by his operettas. A native of Florence, he was, when twelve years of age, brought to Paris by the Duke of Guise, and, being employed in the Palace as a scullion, soon attracted attention by his droll manner and his skill on the violin. The king placed him in his private band ("*Les vingt-quatre violons*"), and soon after appointed him to the leadership of an orchestra established expressly for him and called "*Les petits violons*." Not long after, Lully appeared as dramatic composer for the Court-revels (*Ballets comiques*); these had been customary before his arrival, and were tricked out with singing, dancing and every imaginable device—Molière frequently supplying the text. Ambitious, and a favourite of fortune (having married Cambert's daughter), he supplanted every rival, and in 1673 obtained the sole patent for the Opera performances at the *Palais Royal* theatre. By means of fuller instrumentation and judicious interspersions of chorus and ballet, Lully, in conjunction with his *libretto* poet QUINAULT, so cleverly adapted Italian music to the French taste, that his operas (*Tragédies lyriques*, or *Tragédies mises en musique*), and those of his successor Rameau, held the stage for more than a century. Laden with riches and honours, Lully died in Paris, March 22nd, 1687.

Notwithstanding this apparently brilliant success, Lully's merit as a musician is, after all, but mediocre. Avoiding the clearly defined forms of air, duet, and *ensemble*, he merely endeavoured to give effect to the words, and great prominence to the pathetic element. In imitation of the early Italian declamatory Opera, and in conformity with his own indolent propensities, he bestowed pains chiefly on the recitative proper (rhythmical speech, or singing like speaking)—to which end he had merely to render the declamatory accent in a manner suitable to the French language. As a matter of course, the absence of a well defined musical form gave to the whole an arbitrary and unstable character; for the time was for ever changing from equal to unequal, just as correct intonation required. In order to avoid the tedious monotony (likened to the ecclesiastical chant) of these phrases—never forming a melody—he introduced, at suitable intervals, short pieces for several parts, as well as choruses and dances.* This

* A curious parallel is drawn by Riehl, in his '*Culturstudien aus drei Jahrhunderten*,' between R. Wagner's idiosyncrasy in dramatic composition, and this primary formation of the Lully Opera. Though seemingly harsh—if not unjust—, his opinion is fully borne out by Wagner's latest productions ('*Die Nibelungen*' and '*Tristan und Isolde*.') "Lully is, so to speak, no 'scholar.' *Construction* is

manner of introducing chorus and ballet during the plot, whereas the Italian Opera only admitted the former at the close of, and the latter between, the acts, was, and still is, peculiar to the **French Opera**; and, regarded in this light, Lully may lay claim to be its founder. A salient point in Lully's operas were the *Overtures* in two parts or movements; whereas the earlier Italian performances were, for the most part, preceded by a flourish of trumpets and a short *ritornello*.

Lully's successor JEAN PHILIPPE *RAMEAU* [born at Dijon, October 25th, 1683, died at Paris September 12th, 1764] was undoubtedly a more

hardly to be found in his works. **His** dry harmonies **might serve** principally to show us how *not* to harmonize. **On the other hand,** GLUCK's **historical importance cannot be fully appreciated** without a previous acquaintance **with Lully's works.** He is the Wagner of the eighteenth century. His **Alceste is, as he himself** calls it, '*une tragédie mise en musique*,'—not **an opera;** for it cannot be divided **into airs, duets,** *ensembles*, **&c., but** only into *scenes*. Lully does not *sing*, he *recites*. The whole opera is one continued *obligato* recitative, interrupted only by scraps of tunes and a few choruses. **I am now** referring to Lully, though I might be thought to allude to **Wagner—it** will do for either. The interpolated marches and dances **alone are music,** and have become popular in Lully and Wagner. Lully **is frequently** amazingly **grand** in dramatic effect — so is Wagner; **then he falls back** into tedious recitative dialogue—so does Wagner. **The choruses are** distinguished by a simplicity, solemnity, and **dignity** which, **even in harmonic** details, remind one occasionally of the sublime **church** hymns of the earlier Italian masters. This is no trifling merit, and one which cannot be denied **to some of** Wagner's choruses. Lully sacrifices the **musical** structure to dramatic expression; he has the *germs* of *tune*, **but no tune.** Lully or Wagner? The common expression 'set to music' is strongly suggestive; but **he to** whom the **faculty of** 'setting' is denied,

thorough-going musician **than the** former. He endeavoured to improve the recitative Opera by employing a richer **and** more varied style of harmony. His taste, however, was not sufficiently elevated to secure him from the reproach of over-ornamentation and artificialness. Jean **Jacques Rousseau,** in particular (who extended his doctrine **of nature** and simplicity even to music), blamed **him severely** for neglecting genuine natural tune for far-fetched harmonies. Rousseau objected to his compositions **on the score that** music, being originally a melodious **art,** "**is a child of nature,** and has a language of its own for expressing emotional transports, which cannot be learnt from thorough-bass rules." But his strictures fell un-

talks of 'writing' music. Thus painters who cannot paint produce 'poems' in pictures, and poets destitute of the poetical faculty employ 'word-painting.' In Lully the result is, therefore, a work incongruous, disconnected, incomplete, which must have left a confused and tedious impression, were it not for carefully-studied contrasts and splendour of stage effect, to achieve which, the composer literally moved heaven and earth for his audience, as was the case in 'Alceste' (and likewise 'Tannhäuser'). Lully and Wagner, taken as musicians, are weak; as musical poets they are better, but best of all as stage managers. Gluck eschewed the looseness of form which characterizes Lully's operas, at the same time he strongly advocated truthfulness of dramatic delineation. Gluck, in the form of his pieces, resembles the best style of Italian music much more nearly than Lully, and Wagner resembles Lully rather than Gluck. If our musicians only studied history more diligently, they would learn that, after all, it is no such great proof of progress to go back to a form of opera composition similar to Lully's, seeing that during the century that has intervened, Gluck's manner and style has been admirably developed. Too much progress sometimes leads to reaction."

heeded by the Parisian public, who thought Rameau's operas, especially 'Castor and Pollux,' quite unsurpassed. Italy alone could furnish them a new and better style.

In 1752, an Italian Opera company, called by the French "*Les Bouffons*," arrived in Paris, where they created immense sensation, both for and against themselves, by their small comic operas—among which was PERGOLESE'S '*La serva Padrona*' (lately performed with great success in a French translation). Two adverse parties, "Nationals" and "Italians" (*bouffonistes* and *anti-bouffonistes*) arose (as was the case twenty years later with regard to Gluck and Piccini), and stood up with great warmth for the merits of French and Italian music respectively. Rousseau, whose views exactly suited the "Italian" party, was, of course, enlisted on their side, and (though he had once written a French melodrama called '*Le Devin du Village*') endeavoured even to demonstrate that the French language was radically unmusical, and therefore there could be no such a thing as French music.

As the Italian comic opera was at this period acquiring considerable importance, we will add a short account of its rise and progress hitherto.* In its infancy, it formed the *intermezzo* between the acts of an opera *seria*, and—similar to the Greek sylvan drama which followed the tragic trilogy—was frequently a parody on the piece which preceded it; though, more frequently still (as for example Pergolese's '*Serva Padrona*'), it was not a satire on any

---

* Chiefly from JAHN. *Mozart*, vol. i., p. 343—359.

particular subject, but designed to heighten the ideal artistic effect of the opera *seria* by the interposed contrast of broad comedy. Having acquired a more complete form on the boards of the small theatres (*teatrini*), the opera *buffa*, as it was now called—generally a two-act piece—, obtained a footing in large theatres, and the very circumstance that for a long time it enjoyed less consideration and fewer advantages than the opera *seria*, was highly favourable to its free and natural development. External splendour and the consummate vocalisation which prevailed at that time were the portion of the more dignified elder sister; but the restriction to simpler forms of song and voices of a more natural calibre, endowed the younger with the means of genuine and characteristic rendering of actual life. " The bass—despised and set aside in the opera *seria*—became the corner-stone of the opera *buffa*, and the *basso buffo* (facetious, elderly gentleman, droll or stupid menial) sustained the principal comic part." The tenor usually represented the sentimental lover; while the *Prima* and *Seconda donna* were the mistress and abigail, or confidant. But the salient characteristic of the opera *buffa* consisted in the *ensembles* and *finali* which brought the dramatic element—thrown quite in the back-ground in the opera *seria*—into full relief. The best masters of this new branch of art were LAGROSCINO ("*le dieu du genre bouffon*"), GALUPPI, and N. *PICCINI*, who surpassed the two former. This gifted composer simplified the form of the *aria* by omitting the *da capo*; he also improved and varied the instrumental accompaniment, and, above all, gave life and brilliancy to the *finali* by a richer and more expressive arrangement of the voices. " His ' *Cecchina*,' or ' *La buona figliuola* ' [1761] seems to mark the time when the opera *buffa* was recognized as a special branch of art—just as Pergolese's *Serva Padrona* marks the *intermezzo* period." Perfected by PAESIELLO, and especially CIMAROSA, the *opera buffa* became the genuine, national musical comedy, which has been admirably cultivated by the Italian composers of the last century down to Rossini and Donizetti in our own. GOLDONI and CASTI were the best writers of the comic opera *libretto*. Goethe admired the *Matrimonio segreto* (Cimarosa) and *Re Teodoro* (Paesiello) of the latter, and remarks at the same time that " the material which is to be embroidered on should not be too close in texture."

The " Nationals " at length gained their point, and the " Bouffons " quitted Paris at the end of two years [1754]; but Italian music continued. No one with the slightest pretension to ear could help admitting—whether in envy or admiration—the peculiar charm of graceful, well-constructed melody. From the strife of opposing tastes—the Italian and French—arose, as it were to reconcile and amalgamate them, the light *piquante French Operette*. So soon as the very year in which the "Bouffons" were expelled from Paris, "*la première comédie à ariettes:*" '*Les Troqueurs*,' by ANTOINE D'AUVERGNE appeared on the stage. To this composer succeeded DUNI [1709—1775], PHILIDOR [1726—1795], and MONSIGNY [1729—1817]—superior to the two first, and the forerunner of Grétry; he was styled "*le véritable créateur de l'opéra comique français.*" Besides '*Le Déserteur*' and '*Félix ou l'Enfant trouvé*,' by Monsigny—pieces much admired by Napoleon and occasionally produced on the French stage—, his charming dramatic idyll '*Rose et Colas*' ("*un vrai chef-d'œuvre de grace naïve*") has been performed of late. The Parisian public of 1862, who thronged to the performance of this piece, was indeed surprised to find the music of 1764 so grateful to its ear. Though by no means lacking in dramatic energy and comic effects, tenderness and sweetness of melody are the prevailing characteristics of Monsigny's works. "*La sensibilité*," says Fétis, "*fut son génie, car il lui dut une multitude de mélodies touchantes, qui rendront, en tout temps, ses ouvrages*

dignes de l'attention des musiciens instruits."
Bernhard Romberg's sister Angelica describes the
'*Déserteur*' as exquisite "both in the subject-
matter and the music," and that at its first performance in Paris, in 1769, the ladies sobbed and
cried "*Oh mon Dieu, mon Dieu!*" We gather
also from other testimony that merriment and
humour are by no means the sole end and aim of
the French Operetta of those days; and the best
composers—particularly Grétry—did not neglect
to turn the nobler emotions to account, and, by a
judicious admixture of sentiment, gave an ideal
colouring to their slight pieces. In the contemporaneous German melodrama, the sentimental
element—in conformity with the taste of the
period—preponderated.

GRÉTRY [born at Liège, February 11th,
1741, died at Paris, September 24th, 1813] is regarded as the greatest master of the French
Operetta. An admirer of Pergolese and Piccini,
he adapted the Italian melody, supported by very
meagre accompaniment, to the national taste, and
combined recitative and song with such consummate art, that his pieces (among which '*Richard
Cœur-de-Lion*' and '*Zémire et Azor*' are reckoned
the best) were, and still are, supreme favourites
with the public. Harmony was, however, his weak
point; of which his three-volumed apologetic
'*Mémoires ou Essais sur la Musique*' affords
ample demonstration. The graceful, though

somewhat frivolous, D'ALAYRAC [1753—1809], whose merry, *naïve* operettas: '*Nina,*' and '*Les deux Savoyards*' were naturalized in Germany, followed closely in Grétry's steps. BERTON [1766—1844], of learned and refined taste, was more original, particularly in his instrumentation and *ensembles*. The remarkable aptitude for expressing deep emotional feeling which he displayed in '*Montano et Stéphanie*' and '*Le Délire*' did not, however, unfit him for the light merriment and joyous spirit of the operetta (vide '*Ponce de Léon,*' '*Aline, reine de Golconde,*' '*Les Maris garçons,*' &c.). GOSSEC [1773—1829] soon forsook comic opera for independent instrumental composition, of which, in France, he is the founder. His symphonies and quartets were written at the same time as Haydn's. CATEL [1773—1830], who wrote also for the *Opera seria* ('*Sémiramis*'), and was, in his day, a theorist of some note, is the author of '*Les Aubergistes de qualité*'—much admired by K. Maria von Weber, who describes him as having united playful French wit to Italian comic spirit and true feeling.

The last composer of legitimate Operetta is NICOLO ISOUARD [born at Malta 1777, died at Paris 1818, commonly called Nicolo de Malte]— a pleasing unaffected writer, fully deserving of popular favour, which he shared with young Boieldieu. That he is a composer of some merit may be inferred from the fact that his '*Cendrillon*' and '*Joconde ou les Coureurs d'aventures*' have held the stage in Germany even to our own generation; though it is only the "*romances*" (ballads) which occur in these operas that we esteem now-a-days, as, indeed, is the case with the later French comic opera; for in Auber's '*Fra Diavolo*,' and '*Le Maçon*,' in Boieldieu's '*La Dame blanche*,' Adam's '*Postillon de Lonjumeau*,' &c., the song (*chanson*)—to use a somewhat *thread-bare* expression—is the "silver cord" shining through the whole tissue.

With Méhul and Boieldieu, who succeeded Isouard, expired the charming hybrid between opera and vaudeville, which, during the first twenty years of its best period, so entirely engrossed French musical talent, that the Lully and Rameau opera style was of a sudden completely neglected. Shortly after Grétry appeared Gluck, who gave to the latter branch of art an artistic perfection, which afterwards found a worthy exponent in Spontini. While the French *Grand Opéra*—with the exception of the incomparable Rameau—was dependent on foreigners or naturalized Frenchmen (Lully, Gluck, Spontini, Cherubini, Meyerbeer—Wagner did *not* attain that honour) for composers, the *opéra comique*, on the other hand—as likewise in drama the comedy—, is the genuine "*genre national, le véritable berceau et la vraie gloire de la musique française.*"*

---

* A. ADAM. *Derniers Souvenirs d'un Musicien*, p. 114.

CHRISTOPH WILLIBALD Chevalier* *GLUCK*, the regenerator of the Opera (and whose name may be said to mark a period in this branch of art), was born at Weidenwang in the Palatinate, July 2nd, 1714.† We shall pass over the larger portion of his artist-life [1741—1762], as the Italian operas which he wrote for the Milan, Venice, and London stages cannot lay claim to superior excellence, and, indeed, were afterwards condemned by himself. After the year 1748, Gluck withdrew from the restlessness of public life, and resided quietly at Vienna, where he employed his leisure in digesting and arranging the treasures of art-experience he had collected in his travels, and prepared himself by deep study and reflection for fresh creative efforts. It is true, that both previous to, as well as contemporary with, Gluck, a

* Gluck was a Knight of the papal order of the Golden Spur, as were also Mozart, Dittersdorf, and other musicians. "It is a characteristic feature, that Gluck laid great stress on his rank. He resembled Klopstock in this particular, who held 'that the artist's calling should meet with due recognition and honour.'" (Jahn *Mozart*, vol. i., p. 205.) On the other hand, Gluck (like Leopold Mozart, who recommended his son to wear his Order on suitable occasions) showed his knowledge of the world in not rejecting outward distinctions when he appeared in the select circles of Paris and Vienna.

† *Gluck und die Oper* von A B. MARX. Zwei Bünde. Berlin, 1863.

Ch. W. Ritter von Gluck. Ein biographisch-ästhetischer Versuch von A. SCHMID. Leipzig, 1854.

Compare JAHN (*Mozart*, vol. ii., p. 220—257), and HEINSE (*Hildegard von Hohenthal*).

change in the Opera form, as it then stood, had been, and still was, strongly advocated, and that Metastasio had expressed himself greatly dissatisfied with the degenerate state of "poor Italian music" which was gradually withdrawing its allegiance from poetry; but where was to be found the creative genius that should venture to oppose the prevailing tendency by his *works*, not words? Gluck alone was equal to the task. Like his own 'Iphigenia,' "seeking with her soul the land of Greece," he achieved in 'Orpheus,' 'Alceste,' and the two 'Iphigenias' (classical operas in a two-fold sense), that which the Florentines of two centuries before had vainly sought — a revival of classic tragedy, but in a new art—that of music. These compositions of Gluck—real tragedies — are far superior to their modern texts; they are, in truth, the genuine offspring of a poetical spirit, and not alone in their rendering of the words, faithfully reproduce the plastic repose and beauty which we admire in antique sculpture and the Sophocleian drama.

Gluck's first attempt, somewhat timid and constrained, to introduce his innovations with regard to truthfulness of dramatic expression, was the opera of '*Orfeo ed Euridice*' [Oct. 15th, 1764], in which he was ably supported by the poet CALZABIGI, who wrote the text. As yet, evidently fearful of offering too much offence to the degenerate taste of the age, he has, in this work, retained several points which are in opposition to his severe principles of art; indeed, in its general plan, it does not differ materially from the usual Italian Opera of the period. The principal part was written for a *contralto*, and the only solo parts in addition were two trebles: that of Eurydice, and the inevitable Cupid, whose apparition somewhat recalls the formal allegorical style of the Court revels of those days. The effect of the whole piece, which consists only of a few emotional passages very similar to each other, is, consequently, not intensely impressive; but it contains several striking points, particularly the well-known scene of Orpheus in the infernal regions in the second act. Gluck's treatment of the chorus, which in the old Italian Opera had made way more and more for solo singing, is masterly in the extreme. Solo and chorus are combined in a manner highly productive of dramatic action, and mutually tend to increase the effect of both. So exquisite is the scene where Orpheus' increasingly plaintive strains at length silence the "*No, No!*" of the chorus, and afterwards draw the unwillingly yielding chorus to sing his praises, till at the words "*Al vincitor*" the gates of Elysium are opened to him, that (like the enthusiastic Heinse) we are carried away by the scene, not even heeding the music that works the enchantment, so truthful and natural is the picture. "After all, there are many veins of precious ore in this opera, but it cannot lay claim to downright originality throughout. It is a compound of his own and foreign forms. It succeeded, however, in arousing the antiquated indolent spirit."* The sentimental J. J. Rousseau expressed himself still more favourably: "What I more particularly admire in Gluck is not so much the remarkable amount of beauty his works display, as his discretion and moderation. As regards what are called the proprieties of art, I know of nothing so perfect as the scene of Orpheus in the Elysian fields. Pure, unalloyed happiness is portrayed throughout with such evenness of expression, that neither song nor dance tune interfere with the fixed measure of enjoyment one derives throughout this scene."

The opera of '*Alceste*' [1767] was a great improvement as regards dramatic interest (of which the addition of male voices is of itself characteristic), and marks the actual period of Gluck's reforms. The dedication of this work to the Grand Duke Leopold of Tuscany "gave him an opportunity of stating his views, which were opposed to the prevailing style, with the consciousness that became him—clear and correct as far as his artistic feeling went, but erroneous when he (or his collaborators) philosophized on the aim and object of music."†

* HEINSE. † MARX.

"When I undertook," writes Gluck, "to set this opera to music, it was with the intention of freeing it from all those abuses which, partly through misplaced vanity on the singers', and a too yielding spirit on the musicians', part, had, during a lengthened period, disfigured the Italian Opera to such an extent, that what ought to have been grand and touching, degenerated into the most tedious and absurd drama. I wished to confine the art of music to its real object—that of aiding the effect of poetry by giving greater expression to the words and scenes; but without detriment to the action of the plot, and without weakening the impression by useless ornamentation; and I was of opinion that this ought to be effected in the same manner as brilliancy of colour and judicious contrast of light and shade heighten the effect of correct and well-designed drawing, and give life and expression to the figures without effacing the outline. Therefore, I do not stop the performer in the middle of a dialogue while he waits the termination of a tedious *ritornello*, nor do I allow him to pause on a word or a vowel in order to give him an opportunity of showing off the flexibility of his voice in a long *roulade*, or to wait till the orchestra gives him time to take breath for a long *cadenza*. It seems to me, that the *seconda parte* of an air, be it ever so emotional and important, ought not to be hurried over in order that the words of the first part be repeated four times regularly —the air occasionally concluding when the sense of the words is not completed, so as to enable the singer to show that he can vary the passage as much and as often as he pleases;—in short, I wished to do away with those abuses which common sense and good taste had inveighed against for some time past. My idea is, that the overture should prepare the audience for what is to follow, and, as it were, herald the substance of the piece; that the instrumental portion should vary according to the amount of passion or effect required, without making an abrupt transition from air to dialogue, neither should it form an untimely interruption to the recitative, nor interfere with, and weaken, the action. I thought, further, that my utmost endeavours should tend to acquire a noble simplicity of style; I have sought to avoid difficult passages where brilliancy would be obtained at the cost of distinctness; I only valued novel effects when resulting from the scene and expression, and I have never scrupled to sacrifice a *principle* for the sake of an effect. This is my theory. Fortunately for me (in this respect Gluck was always fortunate), the *libretto* suited my purpose exactly; the celebrated poet (Calzabigi) ventured on a new method with regard to dramatic and scenic arrangements; in consequence of which, flowery descriptions, superfluous comparisons, and instructive, but formal maxims (herein differing from Metastasio) are set aside for language expressing the feelings, powerful emotions, effective climaxes, and varied drama. The result has justified my theories, and the unanimous (?) applause of so enlightened a city has clearly proved that simplicity, truth, and naturalness are the true principles of beauty in every work of art."

The above views of Gluck concerning the nature of the Opera have recently made so much ado (we allude to R. Wagner's book, 'Oper und Drama'), that we think it incumbent on us (to avoid being identified with the cause) to correct this opinion by quoting two eminent art-critics—Kiesewetter and O. Jahn—for the especial benefit of those who will listen to no opinion unless endorsed by a great name.

"So much for Gluck's views. His high æsthetic feeling and refined taste have saved him from the stumbling-block of those—otherwise excellent—maxims which set forth that every consideration for the *music itself, which, nevertheless,* **must** *exist as a separate art, even in the Opera,* must be sacrificed to the poetry and the 'situation.' His genius, while giving every care to the integrity of the poem, has established the independence, as well as the beauty, of his music; she is *not* the servant of poetry; she is rather a loving sister, apparently only intent on setting her charms in the fullest light, yet too charming herself not to be acknowledged her superior. The melodies of Gluck delight us in connection with the words by the correctness of their musical expression; but, were they dissevered from the words, they would be considered excellent and beautiful on their own account. And if, indeed, his songs are *only fully effective when heard in connection with the scenes to which they belong, and, therefore, when disconnected are unsuitable for concert performances,* yet they are by no means without form, and their graceful *motifs* are so clearly recognisable, that after hearing his operas, the memory retains them as easily (?) as if one had come out of an Italian Opera house."*

"Musical performance touches the feelings and emotions so directly, and with so much greater intensity and force than poetry (which appeals principally to the mind and imagination), that it

---

* KIESEWETTER. *Geschichte der Musik,* p. 93. First edition.

may easily happen that the declamatory recitation **gives rise to an unnatural disproportion of effect, if music,** with **its more powerful means of expression, follows the words of the** poem too servilely. **It** is a mistake to say that music shall be subordinate to poetry—a mistake which **Gluck's simile** only the more clearly displays'; **for the** true artist does **not colour or** illuminate **his** picture, but conceives the whole **design as it shall appear in** the full glow of colour; he cannot imagine it other than complete, and represents it accordingly; the contrast between drawing and colour only applies to the mechanical part—not to the conception and production of a work of art. The final explanation to this phenomenon, viz., that he would restrict **music as** an independent art in its own peculiar province to a mere characteristic illustration of poetry, is evidently to be found in the inferiority of his musical organisation, for which this error of judgment served as a cloak."* This, we would observe, as contrasted with the learned pedantry **and** affectation of modern **Gluck-worshippers,** is indeed an honest, straightforward opinion.

We will conclude with a favourable verdict from **Heinse** :† " **Gluck** has indubitably ceded the highest place **to poetry ; and by reverently** serving **her, has incurred the** displeasure **of all musicians** and *dilettanti.* **But he refutes himself the best ; for in his** *best operas* the music **predominates more than in the others**—only it does not trifle and flutter about, but represents the emotions with powerful distinctness. It is *thus,* on the contrary, **that** in many of the Italian **masters the poem** predominates, for, frequently, if we did not know the words, the music would tell us nothing."

The subject of 'Alceste' (from Euripides) bears throughout such a strong resemblance to 'Orpheus,' that we are inclined to suspect Gluck has, in this opera, made use of much that he had not been able to treat in the former one, or, perhaps, had not as yet fully matured in his own mind—a proceeding which (though in different ways characteristic both of Gluck and Handel) is

* OTTO JAHN. *Mozart,* vol. ii., p. 226—229.
† *Hildegard von Hohenthal,* vol. ii., p. 308.

clearly evident in both the 'Iphigenias' and in 'Armide.' In short, the design of the new opera was to represent a perfect and complete whole, regardless of the egotistical proclivities of the singer. One important circumstance is the bold co-operation of the orchestra evident for the first time in Alceste, and appearing at once in the overture, and particularly in the recitative accompaniments, in a new and peculiar manner. Wind instruments (formerly employed only in the *tutti* and concerted passages) are used by Gluck in a highly characteristic style. By their aid, his somewhat cold, unimpassioned music receives the needful assistance to give animation and variety to the unadorned rendering of the words; while to the whole, as compensation for the absence of brilliant vocalization, they impart a rich instrumental colouring.

The first performance of 'Alceste' [in the 'Burgtheater' at Vienna, December 16th, 1767] is thus described by Sonnenfels:* "I am in the land of miracles. A serious melodrama with natural voices, music without *solfège*, or rather, without *chirrupping*, Italian poetry without affectation and bombast. The *Burgtheater* has been opened with this three-fold wonder." The success of 'Alceste' was, however, not so universal as the worthy reporter had anticipated. "Notwith-

* In the '*Wiener Diarium*.'

standing the splendid form in which it was given on the Viennese stage, as well as all manner of extravagant puffs and advertisements, its success was, after all, not a lasting one; for it did not appeal to the popular taste, and there was no middle class of sufficiently elevated taste to give encouragement and abiding interest to works of this calibre."* Gluck himself confessed, in the preface to '*Paride ed Elena*' [1769], that his expectations had been disappointed, and his endeavour " to restore dramatic music to its proper aim and object" had not succeeded in Germany. " Pedants and half-educated men, as well as fastidious *dilettanti*, whose judgment did not extend beyond their ears, inveighed against principles which, if correct, would have put an end to their conceit."

Gluck looked for a better reception in Paris. He rightly judged that the time had come when, after the operetta interlude, the *Grand Opéra*, with his amendments, would find favour. BAILLY DU ROLLET, attaché to the French Legation at Vienna, adapted Racine's '*Iphigénie en Aulide*' for music, and, at the instance of the Dauphiness, Marie Antoinette (whose singing master Gluck had formerly been), the opera was performed in Paris, February 11th, 1774. It was, however, not till the second performance, on the 19th of April,

* GERVINUS. *Geschichte der deutschen Dichtung*, vol. iv., p. 354.

that it obtained complete success. On that occasion, so enraptured were the audience, that when Achilles' air in the third act (" *Calcas d'un trait mortel percé* ") was sung, the military brandished their swords amid the general applause. During the subsequent eighteen years, this opera was performed no less than one hundred and fifty times.

What the French required of an opera was: truthfulness of expression; distinct, pleasing, simple melody; music suited to the action, and action to the music;—all which they found combined in Gluck's work. In addition to this, the national vanity was not a little flattered and soothed; for the assertion that the French language was not adapted for singing was thus substantially disproved, and even Rousseau admitted that Gluck had wrought a change in his views on that score.

In August of the same year, Gluck brought out (in a French and very unfavourable adaptation) 'Orpheus,' and, two years afterwards, 'Alceste,' on the stage. In the meantime [August 1755], he produced a gala opera (*Opéra ballet*) of inferior merit, called ' *Cythère assiegée.*' He was aroused to fresh and increased efforts by the arrival of the celebrated Italian maestro PICCINI — favoured by the Dubarry faction — towards the close of 1776. The old party spirit broke out afresh, and "Gluckists" and "Piccinists" carried on a literary feud with each other.* While his enemies were busily spreading reports that he had nothing new to give France, Gluck produced 'Armide' [September 23rd, 1777], of which the book was by Quinault and had already been set by Lully,—an opera differing entirely from any of his former ones. In accordance with Gluck's severe principles of art, this opera is no advance on the previous ones; it is rather a grand operatic display in the ancient style, with rich choruses and dances and great scenic effects, but little action. Handel's opera 'Rinaldo' [1711], adapted from the same story (the well-known episode in Tasso's *Gerusalemme Liberata*), depended for effect more on the portrayal of emotion in the airs—the "interior dramatic expression," as Chrysander calls it. To correspond with the subject matter, Gluck's music, especially in the splendid instrumental portions, is of brighter and more delicate hue; so that, on the stage, it would probably make a deeper impression on the less critical connoisseur. The choruses and ballets (compare these latter with the trivial dance music of the present day!) are indeed remarkably fine; but they are also by far the finest pieces in the opera. Therefore, we agree with Heinse, that though it has been the one most frequently performed in Paris, it is—even from a stage point of

---

* *Mémoires, pour servir à l'histoire de la révolution opérée dans la musique, par* J. Chr. Gluck. Paris, 1781.

view—far inferior to his 'Iphigénie en Tauride.' "Altogether, it is deficient in naturalness; the Devil and *Hate* personified are too artificial; and the choruses, generally speaking, are not well adapted to the scene. Nevertheless, some of the scenes are effective, as for instance, one where Armida goes to kill Rinaldo asleep; and another — the last — where she is alone — forsaken by Rinaldo."

Piccini followed suit with the opera of '*Roland*' [January 1778], from the composition of which Gluck desisted when he heard Piccini had been commissioned to write it. The latter (greatly esteemed even by his adversary Gluck) always diffident, anticipated failure, but, on the contrary, achieved a brilliant success! It was now for Gluck to conquer a rival who was becoming formidable, by producing a new composition. In this he succeeded when '*Iphigénie en Tauride*' was performed [May 18th, 1779]. It is by far his best work—one in which he combines both the French and Italian peculiarities of powerful dramatic expression and beautiful melody, in this respect surpassing all who had previously treated the subject—Jomelli, Traetta, Ciccio di Majo, Piccini. Gluck's 'Iphigenia in Tauris' is the grandest lyrical tragedy that could possibly be created in the antique spirit, but with modern appliances of art,—in music, what Goethe's tragedy is in poetry —the revival of Greek art in the German mind.

How noble and expressive are the female choruses, as also Iphigenia's and Pylades' airs! how faithfully is the old Greek feeling, from the first burst of the introduction to the last faint echo of the chorus, "To Greece, to Greece!" rendered! But what we admire most of all, is the sublime unity of the whole, the avoidance of anything that would be horrible or revolting, the correct taste which never failed the composer even when portraying mysterious and fearful occurrences—such as Iphigenia bewailing the murder of her father by her own mother, and Orestes pursued by the Eumenides. (What would Wagner, whose pretensions can only be understood by supposing him to be treading in Gluck's footsteps, have made of scenes like these?)*

After bringing out the opera of 'Echo et Narcisse,' [September 1778], and giving over the setting of the Danaïdes to Salieri, Gluck, worn out with strife and overwork, returned to Vienna, where he died [November 17th, 1787, a few days only after the first performance of Mozart's 'Don Giovanni']—leaving a considerable fortune. His bust was placed in the opera-house at Paris beside those of Lully, Quinault, and Rameau, and below it the following inscription : "*Musas praeposuit Sirenis*" (Il préféra les Muses aux Sirènes).

* This opera was performed for the first time in German at Vienna, October 23rd, 1781, and at Berlin (where Gluck's operas were more frequently, as well as better, performed than elsewhere), February 24th, 1795.

Gluck had raised the French Opera to a pinnacle on which it could not maintain itself without him; he had, to a great extent, weakened, though not counteracted, the influence of the Italian style introduced by Piccini, which still found numerous adherents, especially at Court. The multitude were, however, ardent seekers of novelty; and, not altogether unreasonably, preferred the pleasing, cheerful melodies of the national operetta, to the grave character of the *Grand Opéra* and "*musique tudesque*." Without predecessor, Gluck had, even in France, no successors or even imitators (with the exception of Méhul's exquisite opera 'Joseph') till Spontini appeared; yet was his influence sufficiently powerful to have "determined the salient characteristics of the French Opera even to the present day; though at different periods and in various ways, Italian influences have undoubtedly made themselves felt."*

Gluck's reforms were of no account whatever in Germany; though German poets (Klopstock, Herder, Wieland, &c.), as a matter of course, lauded him as "the only musician who was a poet,"—i.e., content to be subservient to the poet, and modestly sink his own individuality.†

---

* JAHN. *Mozart*, vol. ii., p. 257.

† Herder's opinion deserves to be recorded: "The progress of the century reveals one who, rejecting all this musical rubbish, sees the necessity for close relationship between the tale itself with his music. He descended from the lofty pedestal on which the vulgar musician was wont to glorify himself that poetry was subservient to

On the other hand, musicians — with Bach's learned panegyrist Forkel at their head, who declared Gluck's music only fit for rustics — attacked him without mercy. Even Leopold Mozart talks of Gluck's "dismal opera 'Alceste;'" and the Princess Amalia of Prussia (Frederick the Great's sister) did not hesitate to pronounce the following opinion with regard to the 'Iphigénie en Tauride:' "Monsieur Gluck," writes she to Kirnberger, "can never, in my opinion, be reckoned a clever composer. In the first place, he is not original; secondly, his melodies are tame and poor; and thirdly, he has no expression—no emphasis. There is a sameness throughout (in this last particular the worthy princess was not so far wrong); and, taking it altogether, this opera is a weak production."

The learned and accomplished Joh. Friedrich REICHARDT* [1752—1814] is one of the few who sided with Gluck; but his compositions of nearly all the poems of Goethe that can reasonably be set to music afford the most striking proof of the

his art; and, as far as was consistent with the taste of the nation for whom he wrote, made his music subservient to language, emotion, and action. He has imitators, and may be *some one will before long advance on him*, by scattering to the four winds the whole wretched, patched and pieced Opera system, and erecting a veritable Odeum—a compendious lyrical structure, in which poetry, music, action, and decoration form one complete whole." Has the deeply-read R. Wagner perchance stumbled on this passage?

* *Joh. Friedrich Reichardt. Sein Leben und seine musikalische Thätigkeit.* Dargestellt von H. M. SCHLETTERER. Augsburg, 1864.

inapplicability of Gluck's theories as a general principle, and apart from the stage. In the profound odes: 'Prometheus,' 'Ganymede,' 'Borders of humanity, &c.,'* his finely-imagined recitation —partly owing to its leaving untouched the rich polymetric form of poetry — is, on the whole, more successful than in the ballads; but his "*talking melody*" ("*Sprechmelodie*")—as it is now called—is wholly inadequate for the rendering of the songs (*Lieder*), in which, indeed, his music is far inferior to the poem in intensity of feeling and expression. The observation of Rochlitz † (generally so indulgent), in allusion to one of his compositions of the *Lieder*: that, with much art, he has done a great deal for the words, but far less for the expression, is a fair description of his whole style. Goethe, who in the lines ('To Lina'):

"No, not talking, only singing," &c.,‡

has said clearly enough what he required of a composer, denied in the 'Xenien'§ all knowledge of his conceited and officious friend. Reichardt's compositions of Goethe's melodramas: 'Claudine von Villabella,' 'Jery und Bätely,' &c., are of as little account as Anton SCHWEITZER's setting of

* '*Grenzen der Menschheit*, &c.'
† Compare *Reichardt's music to Goethe's songs*. See *Fur Freunde der Tonkunst*, vol. iii. p. 376—434.
‡ "*Nur nicht reden, immer singen.*"
§ The 'Xenien' was a collection of satirical poems, edited conjointly by Schiller and Goethe, and consisted of satirical lines and epigrams.

Wieland's great operas: 'Rosamunde' and 'Alceste'—pieces which at Mannheim (at that time enjoying a first-class musical reputation) were supposed to be the foundation of a "German national Opera." No highly-gifted musician attached himself to the great poets (Gluck had only set seven of Klopstock's odes—according to this latter " in real tones of truth "—; others, as for example the 'Hermannschlacht' and Gellert's songs, he only retained by heart and never wrote down, while Herder's sacred Cantatas remained almost unnoticed)—whereas inferior poets like Weisse, Gotter, Brandes, Kotzebue, &c., have attained to unmerited honour through their composers: Hiller, Benda, Himmel, and even Beethoven.

As in Italy and France the comic opera and the operetta displaced the more serious style, so in Germany, where a national Opera had as yet no existence, the *Liederspiel*, founded by Joh. Adam HILLER [born December 25th, 1728, died at Leipzig, June 16th, 1804] became highly popular. Hiller's idyllic *Liederspiele*, or operettas ('*Lottchen am Hofe*,' '*Die Liebe auf dem Lande*,' '*Die Jagd*,' &c.), written in partnership with Weisse, though now antiquated and forgotten, always drew a full house; and some of the songs which occur in these pieces (as for example " *Ohne Lieb und ohne Wein* ") still survive in popular recollection. It is, indeed, "father" Hiller's peculiar merit, that he, though a really learned musician, should have been content with such a humble sphere, and restricted himself to songs, and refrained from all operatic devices and embellishments; which is the more to be admired when we consider his partiality for Hasse and Graun. His deserts, as far as Handel's music is concerned, are beyond all praise, as also as regards the art of singing in Germany; indeed, in the opinion of Rochlitz and others, his pupils Gertrude Elizabeth MARA and CORONA SCHRÖTER (immortalized by Goethe) are equal to the best Italian singers.

After Hiller, the only composer of operettas whose name survives, is Friedrich Heinrich HIMMEL [born 1765, died at Berlin, June 8th, 1814] admired in his day as the "polite" musician, and whom Beethoven admitted to possess a "charming talent." His melodrama of '*Fanchon*,' which enjoyed a long run of popularity, but is too sentimental for the taste of our day, shows the altered direction which the German *Singspiel* had taken by adopting the French operetta and the Italian *aria* style. The forms were more finished and polished, but they lacked the genuine feeling and spirit of the German song. The German *Singspiel* only attained a vigorous, thoroughly popular, character, when Dittersdorf and the Viennese "*Volksoper*"* took it in hand, as, indeed, musical vitality and development may

* Literally, "the *people's Opera*."

be said now to have quitted Protestant North Germany, and taken up its abode in Catholic South Germany. The Northern, or Berlin school (represented by Zelter, Berger, Bernh. Klein, Friedr. Schneider and others,) is certainly inferior to the South Germany, or Viennese, school.

The numerous operettas of George BENDA [1722-95] are inferior to his melodramas: '*Ariadne auf Naxos*' and '*Medea*,' which quickly found their way into other countries. "The magnificent musical delineation of the passions—fear, joy, and horror—made a powerful impression on all who heard it." Mozart wrote to his father from Mannheim [Nov. 12th, 1778] as follows:—" I have twice seen such a splendid piece performed here, with the greatest pleasure! Indeed, nothing has ever astonished me so much! for I had always imagined that kind of thing would never be effective. You know, of course, that it is not sung, but declaimed, and the music is like a recitative *obligato*; sometimes there is talking amid the music, which has a splendid effect. The piece I saw was 'Medea,' by Benda. He has composed another, 'Ariadne auf Naxos,' and both are indeed excellent. You know that Benda was always my favourite among Lutheran composers. I am so fond of these two pieces that I have them always by me."

Benda's melodramatic music (taking into consideration the period in which it appeared) is in so far remarkable, that, absolutely reversing Gluck's principle of subordinating music to poetry, it allows the instrumental element, although bound to the words and the dramatic movement, a far freer characteristic development. 'Ariadne' appeared at the same time [1774] as Gluck's 'Iphigénie en Aulide,' whose still much admired overture* discloses, in a far grander manner and consistent form, the newly discovered power of instrumental music. "There is not so much as one phrase that resembles vocal song—not one that seems to require the aid of the book or the programme. Even were the overture detached from the opera, and the audience ignorant of the relation of each to the other, its musical significance would still be complete. In design, it is music as applied to a given purpose; but in result, it is music pure and unalloyed."† It was about this time also that Haydn originated the *symphony*, in which instrumental music became invested with a poetry of its own, and the magic power of depicting all the manifold phases of phantasy and feeling.

* As the overture leads directly into the first scene of the opera, Mozart has added a conclusion for concert performances. It is a truly sublime and brilliant addition, and far more in keeping with the tragic grandeur of the piece than Wagner's, which, however, has of late frequently received the preference (in Germany). Wagner's conclusion, which employs the first *motif* of the *allegro*, is cleverly imagined, but the colouring is too feeble and too modern. However interesting, it is not in Gluck's style.

† OULIBICHEFF. *Mozart*, vol. ii., p. 242.

CHAPTER XI.

FOUNDATION AND IMPROVEMENT OF INSTRUMENTAL MUSIC IN GERMANY BY HAYDN.

WE are now entering on the period when instrumental music attained to glorious distinction. Like painting, it is entirely of modern origin, and that branch of musical art in which Germany first bid fair to out-rival Italy, and was even destined to take the lead in all future progress. If the supremacy of the Italians in violin playing and technical skill on bowed instruments cannot be denied, to the Germans is due the credit of perfecting wind instruments, and being the first to employ them characteristically. Not until these were added to the resources of the orchestra could instrumental music attain complete and independent existence, warmth, animation, and expression. The clarionet was the most recently invented [at Nüremberg 1720] wind instrument, and Gluck—altogether the greatest instrumental composer previous to Haydn—had been the first to employ it in dramatic music (in the "*airs de ballet*" of his operas). With what application and zeal the technical features of instrumental music were studied and practised in Germany since the middle of the last century, is evident from the numerous *"Méthodes"* for various instruments which appeared in quick succession and constantly new editions. QUANZ wrote an 'Essay on Hints in playing the *Traversière* Flute'* (Berlin 1752); LEOPOLD MOZART an 'Essay on a thorough method of Violin playing'† (Augsburg 1756); and Phil. Eman. Bach an 'Essay on a true method of harpsichord playing'‡ (first part Berlin 1753)—a work still held in esteem, and lately re-edited by G. Schilling; its technical practice, being grounded on an uniform system of fingering, laid the foundation to modern pianoforte playing.

Haydn, the veritable originator of German instrumental music, in the first instance and in general, adopted the pianoforte sonatas of Phil. Eman. Bach (whom he was accustomed to designate as his master) for his studies and model. Eman. Bach had, in accordance with the paternal wish, applied himself to music "for his pleasure rather than as a profession"—a circumstance which imparted to his whole after-career a singularly free and distinct individuality, which remained unfettered by scholastic restrictions. "Entirely free from all that can be called man-

---

* '*Versuch einer Anweisung die Flöte traversière zu spielen.*'
† '*Versuch einer gründlichen Violinschule.*'
‡ '*Versuch über die wahre Art das Klavier zu spielen.*'

nerism in the music of those days, he allowed his own proclivities and, what we call, artistic individuality full scope—first of all in manual execution, and afterwards in his compositions."* Of these, the most remarkable are his pianoforte compositions, especially the 'Sonatas and Fantasias for connoisseurs and amateurs'†—compositions held in high esteem by young Haydn. "I could not get away from my harpsichord till I had played them through, and those who know me well must be aware how much I am indebted to Emanuel Bach, and that I have studied him thoroughly. Bach once paid me a compliment about it." Characteristic also are Mozart's words when he heard Bach extemporize on the harpsichord at Hamburg. "He is the father, we are the boys. If any of us can do a thing well, he has learnt it of him; and if he doesn't say so, he is a fool. *What* he does would no longer suffice us; but no one can come up to him in the *manner* of doing it." Some of Eman. Bach's 'Orchestral Symphonies,' which appeared about the same time as Haydn's earlier ones, have been revived of late, and, as is frequently the case with works of an early period, considerably overrated. For us they have a peculiar interest, inasmuch as they exhibit a wonderful advance on the orchestral "*suites*" of his father, and do not appear to have any visible

* ROCHLITZ. *Für Freunde der Tonkunst*, vol. iv., p. 299.
† '*Sonaten und Fantasien für Kenner und Liebhaber.*'

connection whatever with the *suite* form, which Riehl regards as the foundation of the modern symphony. The purely abstract succession of pieces in the dance form differs *in toto* from the inward development of Eman. Bach's symphonies. "To me it is evident that the '*suite*' is not the parent of our modern symphony and sonata; but this would not preclude the adoption of the former to a certain extent."* However inferior in point of genuine orchestral character, as well as general style and expression, Eman. Bach's symphonies may be to those of Haydn and Mozart, he it is, most certainly, who first prepared the way for the brilliant epoch of instrumental music which began with Haydn.

JOSEPH HAYDN—the eldest of fourteen children—was born of poor parents at Rohrau (a village on the frontiers of Austria and Hungary), March 31st, 1732.† He was put to school in the neighbouring village of Hainburg, where, under the severe tuition of a relative, he became familiar

* JAHN.

† GRIESINGER (the friend and companion of his later years): *Biographische Notizen über J. Haydn.* Leipzig, 1810.

ARNOLD'S (so-called) biography: *J. Haydn. Kurze Biographie und ästhetische Darstellung seiner Werke.* Erfurt, 1810.

CARPANI: *Le Haydine ovvero lettere su la vita e le opere del celebre maestro G. Haydn.* Milano, 1812.

A. ADAM: *La jeunesse d'Haydn* in the *Derniers Souvenirs d'un Musicien*, p. 1—39.

Haydn in London 1791 *und* 1792, von Prof. Th. von KARAJAN. Wien, 1862.

DIES: *Biographische Nachrichten von Jos. Haydn.* Wien, 1810.

with almost every kind of stringed and wind instrument till his ninth year, when he was sent to Vienna as a chorister. There, in the choir of St. Stephen's, he received a good practical education in music; his early attempts at composition were aided by Fux's '*Gradus ad Parnassum*' (at that time the standard work on composition) and Mattheson's 'Complete Chapel-master.'* After eight years, when his voice broke, he was dismissed, and for the ten succeeding ones, poverty and privation were his lot. His earnings, made first by joining small bands of music (*street-music* as he afterwards called it), and, subsequently, by teaching, were barely sufficient to eke out a scanty subsistence; but his innate cheerfulness of disposition, and, yet more, his genuine love of art sustained him through all the troubles and trials that befel him. "Sitting at my old worm-eaten harpsichord, I envied no king upon his throne." He had even to reckon it a privilege that he was allowed to accompany the renowned Porpora when he gave singing lessons. The latter, indeed, treated him no better than a servant; "but I put up with everything, for I learnt a great deal of Porpora, in singing, composition, and Italian."

In the meantime, some pianoforte Sonatas and Trios, published without his knowledge, caused his name to become known, which led to his being appointed [1760] chapel-master to Prince

* '*Vollkommener Kapellmeister.*'

Esterhazy—an appointment he held for thirty years. The prince resided during the greater portion of the year at his seat in Hungary, only visiting Vienna for a few months in winter, and maintained a band and choir of his own for opera —Italian of course—, concert, and church music. Haydn had not only to rehearse and conduct the performers, but, as was always expected of a chapel-master in those days, to write nearly all the music himself. This was the origin of most of his Symphonies and Quartets (together with those written at a later date, 118 and 83 in number); his *Concertos* and *Trios* (each 24 in number); 44 Sonatas; 19 Operas (14 Italian and 5 German *Marionnette* Operas); 15 Masses; the Oratorio '*Il ritorno di Tobia*;' and about 400 dances. Besides the above works, he wrote 163 pieces for the *baryton*—a species of *viola di gamba*, similar to our *violincello*, and the prince's favourite instrument. A good many of the Symphonies were *pièces d'occasion*—among them the '*Children's*' (for pianoforte and seven toy instruments) and '*Depart*' symphonies, which latter owes its effect more to the ingenious idea of letting one instrument after another cease, than to any great musical originality. Occasionally, some of the pieces in the symphonies written at that period, were headed with appropriate titles as: '*La Bella Circassa*,' '*La Roxelana*,' '*Elena Greca*,' '*Il Solitario*,' '*Il Maestro di scuola inna-*

morato,' '*La Persiana,*' '*Il Poltrone,*' etc., and (a circumstance deserving of notice) others he is said to have provided with a kind of programme, for instance: "God conversing with a hardened sinner," "Departure of an indigent family for America; grief of those left behind; the voyage and return;" "*Le matin, le midi, le soir.*" Thus, Haydn found, in his constant and varied duties, the best opportunity for improving his talents and forming his style. "My prince was pleased with my productions; I received commendation; as leader of an orchestra I was enabled to make experiments, to observe, and learn what constitutes, as well as mars, effect; to improve, add, withdraw, to make experiments. I lived apart from the great world, with no one near to confuse or annoy me; and, thus, I could not fail to become original."

After Prince Esterhazy's death [1790], Haydn, now verging on his sixtieth year, entered on a new career, whereby his future musical productions were materially influenced. Like Handel and Gluck, he, too, was to meet with the full measure of regard and appreciation in foreign lands—not indeed, as they did, by his own efforts, but by the valuable aid of a countryman and enthusiastic admirer. John Peter SALOMON from Cologne, manager of the famous *Professional Concerts* in London, and himself an excellent artist, had already made repeated but ineffectual attempts to induce Haydn to quit the service of Prince Esterhazy and come to London, if only for one winter. His terms were: that, for liberal remuneration, Haydn should write a new piece—if possible, a symphony—of which he was to conduct the performance himself, for each of Salomon's "Grand Concerts." Haydn, being now at liberty, Salomon hastened to Vienna in order to put his project into execution. That same year, Haydn accompanied him to London, where he remained a year and a half; and, after two years [January 1794], returned thither for the same length of time. During the three years of his residence in London, Haydn wrote—besides a number of smaller pieces—six of his finest Quartets, and those incomparable twelve (entitled) *London Symphonies*, which we all admire so much: one in C minor, with the lovely *minuet* trio (for violincello *concertante*); the truly sublime one in B with the grand *finale*; the so-called 'Military Symphony;' one in G (with the "clock movement"*), and others.

That Haydn was well received and remunerated

---

* The two last symphonies were surnamed from their beautiful *andante* movements, wherein, in one, the beat of a kettledrum falls unexpectedly on the softest possible piano; in the other, is a splendid "Turkish music." In other respects, the 'Military Symphony' has not a particularly military character; and, consequently, the comparison which Ambros (in his '*Grenzen der Musik und Poesie*,' p. 132) draws, to Haydn's disadvantage, with Beethoven's '*Eroica*,' is quite out of place. Of the "military" element in the '*Eroica*' we shall have occasion to speak hereafter.

in England, is evident from an entry in his diary referring to his farewell benefit concert at the Haymarket Theatre [May 4th, 1795]: "This evening I made four thousand florins. That is only to be done in England." He returned to Vienna, and purchased a house and garden in one of the suburbs, where he lived quietly and comfortably till his death (May 31st, 1809]. It was during this latter period that his great German Oratorios—'The Creation' and 'The Seasons'—were composed.

Haydn's works, more, perhaps, than those of any other master, form an epoch in the history of art; "Father Haydn," as he is called, is the ancestor of succeeding musical generations. He has opened out the widest field for free, artistic, individual expression by means of instrumental music, of which he fixed, and, in many ways, developed the forms. Unfettered by rules and traditions of art —grown up as it were in a school of his own— he carried music out of school and church into the freshness and reality of life—home to the feelings of the multitude " even as it weeps and laughs." As German poetry was improved by Goethe's and Herder's return to the poetry of early times — especially Homer, and the old German national song—, so was music benefited in a yet greater degree by Haydn, in whose compositions reminiscences of popular tunes, whether of song or dance, are clearly discernible.

In order to illustrate the newly-found subject-matter, the *form*, or manner of composition, had to be changed; in lieu of the contrapuntal harmonic style of composition, arose, since **Haydn**, the melodic-thematic, consisting of a leading idea or *theme* from which are derived a succession of *secondary subjects*. This is called thematic composition; and by it, unity of design is combined with constant variety. In this art—that of pursuing one thought or theme through all the shades and intricacies of which it is susceptible, and, without detriment to the original character, cause it to represent every possible alternation of feeling—Haydn, by the very clearness and simplicity of his style, remains to this day a model. "No artist has, with such innocence and simplicity, accepted every, the smallest thought which God has given him, and cherished it so heartily and fervently, that it grew to a mighty stock of artistic inspiration; no one has bestowed such admirable, judicious, and loving care on the instruments committed to his charge. He would be everlastingly enviable, if he did not equally command our respect, gratitude, and love."* "If an idea presented itself," says Haydn, "all my endeavours were directed to entertain and carry it out in accordance with the rules of art. Thus I tried to improve myself; and that is where many of our

---

* Compare the article '*Haydn*' in Gassner's *Universallexicon der Tonkunst*.

modern composers fail; they string one little piece on to another, and break off **when they** have hardly begun; but none of it touches our feelings **when** we hear it." Those would-be original **geniuses,** whose **supercilious vanity** teaches them **to** look down upon the **writer** of the 'Children's' Symphony, and, comparing his symphonies with the grandest **that** have ever been written—Beethoven's —, pronounce them antiquated or oldfashioned, would do well to ponder these words. Haydn, **to** whom Mozart dedicated his six finest Quartets [composed 1783–1785], **and** Beethoven his first Trios; to whose memory Cherubini (**too** modest to dedicate **to** him his *chef d'œuvre,* ' *Les deux Journées* ') composed the ' *Chant* **sur la mort de Joseph Haydn,**' is still (especially now-a-days, when **the feeling for simplicity and beauty in art-**productions **threatens to** become extinct) the master, from whom disciples of art may learn the most. **His** Symphonies and Quartets are, owing to their purity of idea and clearness of development, models of their kind; and even their short-**ness—so** derided by **the** ignorant—might be advantageously imitated by our " Grand Symphony" **writers, who** spin out everything to unheard-of lengths, **and** with dwelling **upon a** number of subordinate subjects are scarcely able to get to the end.*

* A **talented and** judicious art-critic of our own day expresses himself thus **decidedly** against the conceited assertion that Haydn's

We must not indeed expect to find profound ideality in Haydn's works; on the other hand, we cannot allow that his Symphonies (as **Riehl** even says of Mozart's) are nothing better than a combination of symphonic movements. **Haydn** imbibed his ideas directly from real life, just **as it** presented itself to his childlike, sunny temperament—keenly alive to impressions from without. The movements of his symphonies **and** quartets, notwithstanding their **close and complete** connexion with each other, **are not bound** together by abstruse or poetical ideas; but, as **Haydn** himself admits with regard to some **of them, rest on** the simple foundation of a particular circumstance **or** emotion. To seek effect by means of contrast, was utterly foreign to his purely harmonious disposition; with him all is right and joyous as a fine spring morning when our spirits are buoyant with cheerfulness and hope. In the Minuets which (like Mozart's *andantes* and *adagios* and Beethoven's *finali*) peculiarly characterize **Haydn**, he seems to take especial delight—revelling in playful humour and arch surprises.

That Haydn could make so much of an appa-

---

symphonies are **not destined to endure.** "Whereas, about twenty years ago, Haydn was **almost unanimously** allowed **to be** the first among instrumental composers, and his quartets and symphonies extolled as the acmé of perfection, it is now the fashion to fall into the opposite extreme, and to speak of them with a contemptuous smile, **as** of unpretending *bagatelles,* beneath the notice of our enlightened generation."

rently restricted field of sentiment, is the clearest proof of his wonderful musical gifts, as well as true artistic self-knowledge, which, rejecting the mysterious and ethereal, contented itself with a slight tinge of ideality. "The variety and delicacy of perception with which he illustrated so many different phases of a cheerful mood in the elaboration of a symphony, and, without the aid of forced contrasts, preserves its character apparently intact while describing infinitesimal shades of feeling, is, and ever will be, worthy of admiration. Take, for instance, the symphony in D. The first *allegro* movement portrays quiet felicity, mingled with tender loving kindness—unclouded even by a perceptible tinge of sadness; the *andante* following on it illustrates happiness and content; in the minuet, a delicious sense of enjoyment breaks forth into wilful sportiveness; while, in conclusion, the *rondo* describes the wild merriment of a joyous troop, and that with such marked and distinctive traits, that when listening to it, we almost fancy we see before us a picture of Teniers. Thus, we find happiness and joy represented in a variety of gradations, yet without inducing the least sense of monotony or weariness."* It was but seldom that Haydn attempted the delineation of the passions,—not, however, that he lacked either receptivity for grand emo-

---

* Fr. Hand. *Aesthetik der Tonkunst.* Vol. ii., p. 421.

tional sensations, or the faculty of rendering them in music. Of this his Oratorios furnish proofs to the contrary; for, besides tenderness and sweetness, sublimity and solemnity are therein strikingly expressed.

When in his sixty-fifth year [1797], Haydn composed the '*Creation*,' for which the book (it was said) had been written for Handel by Lidley. This Oratorio has a far more solemn and sacred character than his Masses (in which serenity and enjoyment break forth so charmingly and innocently), and the noble chorus: "The heavens are telling," and others, may be accounted equal to the sublimest achievements of sacred choral music. "I was," narrates Haydn, "never so pious as when engaged on the 'Creation;' I fell on my knees daily, and prayed God would vouchsafe me strength to carry out the work." To the orchestra, which forms a rich accompaniment to the recitatives and airs, is assigned the descriptive portion; while, towards the close, emotional transports find vent in the lovely duet: "Graceful consort." It is in this extensive range—embracing the Deity, Nature, and Humanity — that the 'Creation' stands alone, unrivalled. Were we to characterize the different parts more nearly, we should say: the first is the grandest, the second the most picturesque, and the third the most melodious.*

* Memorable is the performance of the 'Creation' in the Hall of the University at Vienna, March 27th, 1808, at which Haydn (then

The third part of the 'Creation' describes the life of our first parents before the Fall. It is a charming idyll, following on a grand epos. Altogether idyllic in subject is the pastoral Oratorio: ' *The Seasons*' [1801], after Thomson's poem. Unlike the everlasting "Odes to Spring" of modern poetry, and their accompanying music, Haydn presents us in the 'Seasons' with a

in his seventy-sixth year) was present. When at the famous passage "Let there be light" the audience broke out in loud plaudits, the old man raised his trembling hands deprecatingly, saying: "It is not mine, it comes from above." Dreading further excitement, he desired to be conveyed home before the end of the first part. And this was not the merely momentary weakness of old age; it was his firm persuasion that all blessing on his work came from above. His scores were headed " *In nomine Domini,*" or " *Soli Deo gloria,*" and ended with " *Laus Deo.*"

We cannot refrain from quoting an interesting passage, bearing on Haydn's Oratorios, in the letter to Mendelssohn from his father (see Lady Wallace's translation of Mendelssohn's letters, vol. ii., p. 78). "It seems to me that both the Oratorios of Haydn were, in their sphere, also very remarkable phenomena. The poems of both are weak, regarded as poetry; but they have replaced the old positive and almost metaphysical religious impulses by those which nature, as a visible emanation from the Godhead, in her universality, and her thousandfold individualities, instils into every susceptible heart. Hence the profound depth, but also the cheerful efficiency, and certainly genuine religious influence, of these two works, which hitherto stand alone; hence the combined effect of the playful and detached passages, with the most noble and sincere feelings of gratitude produced by the whole; hence is it also that I individually could as little endure to lose in the 'Creation' and in the 'Seasons' the crowing of the cock, the singing of the lark, the lowing of the cattle, and the rustic glee of the peasants, as I could in nature herself; in other words, the 'Creation' and the 'Seasons' are founded on nature and the visible service of God,—and are no new materials for music to be found there?"

M

complete picture of rural life, the conception of which is unequalled for naturalness and simplicity, and for which the tenderly executed musical colouring is as essential, as the portrayal of sentiments awakened by the contemplation of nature, were to Beethoven's ideal mind (in the 'Pastoral Symphony'). It cannot, however, be denied that these numerous and, as far as they go, attractive, instrumental details are prejudicial to the freedom of song in the airs. Even if we do not, with Zelter, regard the 'Seasons' as a symphony with singing, yet we do not hesitate to designate the greater portion of it as a recitative with unusually rich accompaniment. With the exception of the air: "Oh how pleasing to the senses," and the two songs in the last division, the tuneful, purely musical, charm of the solo songs is inconsiderable, or, at all events, not to be compared to the lovely duets and the *pièces d'ensemble*. But the *choruses*, besides the famous hunting and vintner's choruses, the pious—really inspired—choruses of prayer and praise, unite the whole in one complete composition. Without them, indeed, this work would consist merely of a series of fatiguing, only partially interesting, pieces; but they impart to it a oneness of form, as also to the Oratorio the required lofty and ethical significance—the religious element. Similar to the sublimer 'Creation,' the joyous idyll of the 'Seasons' closes with the double choruses in praise of everlasting spring: "'Tis come the great and glorious morn," in solemn devotional strains.

As to the intrinsic merit of these two works, when compared with each other, Haydn has expressed himself as follows: "My 'Creation' will endure, and probably the 'Seasons' also." On being congratulated, on every side, after the first performance of the 'Seasons,' he replied: "It is not the 'Creation;' there, angels sing, here, rustics." That is, in the jargon of the schools, there the *ideal,* here the *real* prevails; and "thoughtful" musicians, to whose palled taste the 'Seasons' fails to give satisfaction, would probably express themselves at yet greater length. Though the 'Creation' is indisputably the grander and more universal work of the two, yet in the 'Seasons,' Haydn's individuality shines forth so brightly and distinctly, that it takes a strong measure of modern conceit and affectation to find it tedious.

'*Il ritorno di Tobia,*' an Italian oratorio written during the Esterhazy period, and of late revived, is inferior in interest to those above mentioned; but the composition of the *Seven words: 'Musica instrumentale sopra le sette ultime parole del nostro Redentore al Croce'*—an *intermezzo* for Good Friday's Liturgy for orchestra alone—is a work of note and importance. Haydn, himself, set so great store by it, that not only did he afterwards publish it as a solo-quartet, but even adapted it for an oratorio, in which the 'Words' were simply recited in a choral tone, and the expression of the sentiments contained in the instrumental description, is allotted to the chorus.

In Church composition, properly speaking, Haydn gave the preference to the works of his younger brother MICHAEL, as being more consonant with genuine Church style. Michael's are the so-called 'Spanish Mass,' the 'Requiem,' 'Pax vobis,' 'Salve Regina,' 'Lauda Sion,' and other sacred compositions.

In dramatic music, Haydn was a copyist. His Italian Operas, of which his unfinished 'Orfeo,'— written for the London stage—is reckoned the best, reveal ignorance of scenic effect, as well as of correct dramatic expression. These high qualities were the portion of one, whom Haydn himself designated as "alone and incomparable," viz.—Mozart.

CHAPTER XII.

Mozart (The Opera).

WOLFGANG AMADEUS MOZART* was born [Jan. 27th, 1756] at Salzburg, where his father, Leopold Mozart (referred to above as the author of a violin *méthode*), was vice-chapel-master to the Archbishop. So extraordinary was the child's progress in everything appertaining to music, but especially in pianoforte playing, that so early even as 1762-1766, his father made professional tours with little "Woferl" and his sister (five years older than himself) to Munich, Vienna,

---

* OULIBICHEFF: '*Nouvelle Biographie de Mozart, suivie d'un aperçu sur l'histoire générale de la musique et de l'analyse des principales œuvres de Mozart.*' Moscou, 1843.

OTTO JAHN: *W. A. Mozart.* Vier Bände. Leipzig, 1856-1859. *Chronologisch - thematisches Verzeichniss sämmtlicher Tonwerke W. A. Mozart's*, von L. RITTER VON KÖCHEL. Leipzig, 1863. (Supplement to JAHN's Biography).

Mozart. Eine populäre Biographie des Meisters, von L. NOHL. München, 1863.

Mozart's Briefe, nach den Originalen herausgegeben von L. NOHL. Salzburg, 1865.

Paris, and London. Wherever they went, the "infant prodigies" were praised to the skies in German, Italian, and Latin, and in Holland were even permitted to give concerts during Lent, because it "redounded to God's glory." Mozart afterwards spent three years at Salzburg and Vienna in composing and studying the art of composition, during which time he attracted but little notice—perhaps, even, was purposely neglected, through the jealousy of rival artists. The juvenile composer (thirteen years old) met with a warmer reception in Italy [1770]. Whatever could most gratify the ambition of a gray-haired professor was freely bestowed on the ingenuous lad—the Papal Order, diplomas from the philharmonic academies of Bologna and Verona, the esteem of connoisseurs, and the adoration of the multitude. Mozart's operas: '*Mitridate Rè di Ponto*,' and '*Lucio Silla*,' both of which he wrote for the Milan stage (where the former was performed under the youthful *maestro's* leadership to the cries of "*Evviva il Maestrino*"), were performed no less than twenty times. It is scarcely necessary to add, that these operas (quite of the traditional type), together with the later gala pieces: '*Ascanio in Alba*,' '*Il Sogno di Scipione*,' '*Il Rè pastore*,' and the German operettas '*Bastien und Bastienne*,' '*Zaide*,' and even the *buffa* opera: '*La finta Giardiniera*' [1775]—a more matured piece in regard to instrumentation and dramatic expression—have **no value and importance now-a-days; but** (as Jahn justly observes), the boy's exquisite discernment of characteristic and national peculiarities in different branches of dramatic composition is evident in these pieces.

Mozart's classical period may be said to begin with '*Idomeneo*' [1781], the success of which (together with the consciousness of genius and respect for his calling) inspired him with the resolution of quitting the service of **the coarse,** uneducated Archbishop of Salzburg. He had, it is true, before this [1778 and 1779] endeavoured, though unsuccessfully, to obtain an appointment either at Munich, Mannheim (where he met his bride Constance), or Paris. Mozart now settled in Vienna, "in a private capacity," **gaining a** livelihood by giving concerts, lessons, by professional tours, and such trifling sums as his compositions brought him in.* It was not till the year 1787 that, with the title of Imperial Chamber Composer, an annuity of 800 florins was awarded him; **and**—on his death-bed—the ap-

* A few weeks after the first performance of the '*Entführung*' (for which, however, he got one hundred ducats), Mozart wrote, December 21st, 1782, as follows: "Altogether I am so hardly worked that I often don't know what I am about. The entire forenoon till two o'clock is occupied in giving lessons, afterwards we dine. After dinner I must allow my poor stomach a little time to digest; **there remains only** the evening when **I can attempt to write,** and that **not** always, for I am frequently **obliged to attend the academies** (public concerts).

pointment of chapel-master at St. Stephen's cathedral.

Idomeneo ('Idomeneo Rè di Creta ossia Ilia e Idamante') [performed for the first time at Munich, Jan. 26th, 1781], is, on the whole, constructed on the plan of the old Italian *Opera seria*; the large proportion of airs, and the circumstance that the part of Idamante is written for a now obsolete kind of voice, being of itself characteristic. But, notwithstanding these concessions to mere redundant vocalization in the airs, and setting aside the evident imitation of Gluck (particularly 'Alceste') in the treatment of the recitatives, Mozart's genius shines forth in all its might in the grand choruses, and, still more, in the wonderfully bold, yet delicate, colouring of the instrumentation with which this opera abounds. "Oulibicheff remarks with truth, that in 'Idomeneo' it is easy to distinguish how far Mozart still clings to the formal *Opera seria*, how far he follows in the steps of Gluck and the French Opera, and how far he does justice to his own original powers."* It is much to be regretted that the radically undramatic plan of the book, and a want of variety and movement, as also of effective *ensembles*, has hindered this opera, with its manifold beauties, from keeping the stage. It is not a musical drama—least of all one in

* JAHN. Vol. ii., p. 449.

Gluck's sense of the term—, but there is abundance of dramatic music in it. It is, therefore, all the more to be desired that this work—highly prized by Mozart himself—should be duly represented in the concert room by extracts of its best pieces.

If in 'Idomeneo,' Mozart appears (as is also the case in his two last Italian operas 'Così fan tutte' and 'Titus') still fettered by Italian influences, we find him in his other works attempting hitherto untried styles, and leaving in all of them works that may be called models of their kind. The opera that followed next: '*Die Entführung aus dem Serail, oder Belmonte und Constanze*' [performed July 12th, 1782] was written by command of the Emperor Joseph II. ("who even included the lyric theatre among his reform projects"). The plan of this work is, for the most part, in the manner, and according to the standard, of the *Singspiel* of that period; but it is far richer in the execution of the details, and, likewise, remarkable for its admirable keeping and warmth of expression—qualities which temper the exultation of the happy bridegroom by the tenderness of its lyrical strains. But Mozart did not content himself with the expression of contemplative sentiment alone; the delineation of constancy and affection is relieved by the wildest sallies of humour and a breadth of comic effect never again attained, even by himself. The "stupid, loutish, and wicked Osmin" (Mozart's own words) is, of a truth, the most original character that ever was imagined, and a downright root and branch *comic* personage, whose droll pathos and rough jokes temper the sentimentality of the piece in the happiest possible manner. And this best of bass *buffos* Mozart created, not only without the assistance of, but actually unbeknown to, his *libretto* poet—indeed he altered the whole plan of the piece to suit his views. "This Osmin," writes Mozart to his father, "has in the *libretto* only one small song and nothing besides, except in the trio and *finale*. So he is to have another air in the first part, and one in the second. I have indicated to Mr. Stephani (Bretzner was the *libretto* poet and Stephani the substitute engaged by Mozart) the plan of these airs, and the principal part of the music was finished before Stephani knew anything about it." In the same letter Mozart expresses himself on the means and object of art with so much penetration, that it seems astonishing people should say (as some do) that Mozart, through life artless and inexperienced, exercised his art instinctively and unreflectingly, without profound "self-consciousness"— in short, that he recked not how bad the *libretto* for which he wrote his music might be. His correspondence with his father regarding 'Idomeneo' and the 'Entführung' furnish proofs to the contrary; afterwards, since the death of his father

[May 28th, 1787], he had no further occasion to express himself concerning his works. "At that time, musicians were not in the habit of analyzing art and works of art, and especially the peculiar relations of the individual himself to art; such a proceeding was utterly foreign to Mozart's nature."* It is also worthy of observation, that Mozart has not made use of any former similar work (not even 'Zaide') when composing the 'Entführung,' and that he left unfinished and unemployed an already completely designed comic opera, 'L'Oca del Cairo' [1783], because he found the *libretto* poor, and the subject too nearly approaching the 'Seraglio' (yet the music of the first act, particularly the lively *finale*, is magnificent, "resplendent with genius, playfulness, and originality"). The case is the same with the following year's [1784] opera ' Lo Sposo deluso,' concerning which he writes at the time: " I have, I should think, looked through a hundred or more books." Not until the year 1786 did he (with the exception of the one act operetta ' *Der Schauspieldirector,* a comedy with music for Schönbrunn ')† produce a new *chef-d'œuvre* replete with originality and vigour.

* JAHN. Vol. ii., p. 299.

† "The pieces contained in this operetta (besides the overture there were only two airs and one trio which also forms the *finale*) have been embodied in Cimarosa's ' L'impresario in angustie,' which Goethe caused to be performed in Weimar, in 1791, with the title of ' Theatralische Abenteuer' (Stage Adventures). Several of Mozart's

In '*Le Nozze di Figaro*' [performed May 1st, 1786], which was composed in the space of six weeks to a subject of his own selection, Mozart's genius shines forth in full splendour. He has, almost in sport as it were, achieved the difficult task of infusing genuine sentiment into the "polite society" tone of Beaumarchais' lively comedy,* and embodying its broad merriment in musical forms. Mozart alone knew (what no Italian or French composer could have done) how to redeem the cutting satire and frivolous tone of the play. He sought out, as far as he was able, the poetry of which the subject was capable, and, taking love—genuine disinterested affection—for the motive of its perpetual intrigues, described it with wondrous depth and truth in every conceivable relation, and caused it finally to triumph over all obstacles and impediments. Frigid and narrow-minded critics, however, who are incapable of distinguishing between Mozart's glorious music and the subject on which it rests, can only be answered with the somewhat trite maxim, that the proprieties of art are the sole standard of beauty, and by them alone a work of art must be judged.

songs have of late been interpolated, and the piece performed with the title of 'Der Schauspieldirector, oder Mozart und Schikaneder.' (The Stage Manager, or Mozart and Schikaneder). Mozart himself is the hero who is represented as composing the 'Zauberflöte' at Schikaneder's suggestion." (Jahn.)

* '*Le Mariage de Figaro, ou la Folle Journée.*'

'Figaro,' from a dramatic, as 'Don Giovanni' from a musical, point of view, is unquestionably Mozart's *chef-d'œuvre*. The sprightliness of actual life bursts forth in this incomparable "musical comedy," more especially in the grand *ensembles* and *finali*, where each character is admirably in keeping. While Gluck invariably aims at the solemn, measured repose that is the exclusive attribute of Greek tragedy, and avoids whatever might interfere with the even tenour of the subject, Mozart attains his best dramatic effects in the *ensembles* and *finali*, in the vigorous treatment of which he is, perhaps, unequalled, and in the airs he reveals the profound emotions which stir the human heart, and the inborn power of melody. He understood and appreciated better than any other the aim and scope of dramatic music, and carried both music and drama a step higher. Even R. Wagner is compelled to admit this much, when (speaking of Gluck) he says: "Gluck took pains to express himself correctly and intelligibly in music, whereas Mozart, following his own natural instinct, could not help doing so."[*] "Mozart," he continues, "has, in the opera, brought to light the capabilities of music to respond generously to every wish of the poet; and the glorious musician has, in his own natural, uncalculating method, by *truthfulness of dramatic expression*, and the endless

---

[*] *Oper und Drama.* Vol. i., p. 132.

variety of his airs and tunes, discovered this faculty in music in a far greater degree than Gluck and his disciples."

Owing to party spirit and the intrigues of Italian singers and composers, Mozart's "favourite song" met with an indifferent reception at Vienna,* but, on the contrary, was enthusiastically welcomed at Prague. For Prague, accordingly, the great *maestro* wrote his next and best work: '*Il Dissoluto punito ossia il Don Giovanni,*' [performed Oct. 29th, 1787]. 'Don Giovanni' is, as Spohr justly remarks, the most energetic in character of all Mozart's operas. Here we have no mere outpouring of sentiment and emotion, but human nature, swayed alternately by love and hate; life, in all its aspects of keen enjoyment and passionate desire, forms the subject of this opera, while, combined with the utmost variety of character and "situation," the development of the plot is natural and simple. Differing from all other operas (but in this respect resembling the Shake-

---

* Strictly speaking, only at the first performance—intentionally marred by the Italian performers. L. Mozart wrote to his daughter that at the second performance five, and at the third seven, pieces were *encored*, "among which a small duet had to be repeated three times." From this statement we learn that the anecdote (so frequently retailed by way of consolation to unrewarded talent) that Figaro was a complete failure at Vienna, is a gratuitous invention. Even Mozart's opponents—envious rivals—knew how to appreciate this opera; for at subsequent performances *encores* were prohibited (ostensibly for the sake of the singers) by imperial decree, and before long, the opera was withdrawn from the stage.

spearean drama), the prevailing character of 'Don Giovanni' is a mixture of tragedy and comedy. To use Jahn's words, "Mozart's conception of this subject is drawn from his own deep sympathy with, and profound knowledge of, human nature."

Undeniable as is the force and richness of its musical structure, and irresistible the power of even a tolerable performance (which never fails to draw a full house), the poetical significance of this profound and carefully matured work is even yet far from being fully appreciated. "The grandeur, beauty and sublimity of the music of 'Don Giovanni' (writes a reporter in the year 1790) will ever be discerned only by a select few," and so it is up to the present time. Else how could Don Giovanni's frivolous carriage, Leporello's weak jokes, Zerlina's equivocal conduct, and above all, the shameful mutilation of the second *finale* (whereby the piece is made to conclude with the ridiculous caperings of infernal *masques* and a "brilliant display of fireworks") ever be tolerated? To satisfy the requirements of good taste, the closing scene should express the nobler emotions (*vide* the *finale* sestet with the fugued conclusion: "Questo è il fin di chi fa mal"). When the "devil takes the hero" there is, of course, an end of everything, so far as the musical rabble is concerned. But this concession to the "gods of the gallery" not only mars the ideal impression of a work of art, it utterly destroys the scenic illusion as well as the tragic effect; whereas Mozart has introduced the demonic element with such consummate skill and impressiveness that no one can help believing in the awful reality. For the rest, the common herd, accustomed to regard Mozart himself as a "Don Giovanni" incarnate, views this opera as nothing more or less than a revel in honour of dissipation and vice. Still more narrow is the view taken by some propriety folks, who really deplore that Mozart should have thrown away his "exquisite" music on such a coarse subject. By such discriminating people as these, a representation of the catastrophe alone—an enlarged second *finale*—would probably be the most admired. "This opera is not for the Viennese, rather for the Praguers, but chiefly for myself and my friends," said Mozart; and in the magnificent overture has he not, as it were in characters of fire, proclaimed the lofty pathos of the work—ay, so that the blindest might see, were it not that there are those who cannot realize "poetical justice" unless final retribution is awarded amid thunder and lightning, and Death himself appears to end the voluptuary's career!

Mozart's 'Don Giovanni' is, by its marvellous delineation of both the lights and shadows of life, its combined seriousness and playfulness, tragedy and comedy, an *universal*, unique, and deeply significant work; one to which, in the sister art of drama, Goethe's 'Faust' can alone be worthily compared. Both these productions are drawn from the mysterious depths of popular tradition; both are, from their very nature, inimitable; both are frequently taken as models, as well as illustrated by the sister art;* both are entirely commensurate to the grandeur of their scheme and the limits of their respective provinces, that, as Carriere † aptly remarks, 'Don Giovanni' in poetry and 'Faust' in music can never equal the originals, " because poetry can neither render individual character and feeling with such truth and impressiveness as music, nor can music reveal deep thoughts and self-conscious power with the precision and clearness of poetry." Goethe's 'Faust' and Mozart's 'Don Giovanni' may be regarded as the two greatest master-pieces of modern drama and modern music, notwithstanding that in both (especially in 'Faust') there is, to a certain extent, a want of completeness and dramatic coherence.

So admirable is Da Ponte's (Mozart's poetical coadjutor) musical appreciation in regard to the

---

* Viz., in poetry: 'Don Juan,' by BYRON, and also by LENAU. In music: 'Faust' (without reckoning SPOHR's opera) by SCHUMANN ('*Scenen aus Faust*'); BERLIOZ—after Liszt the musical translator *par excellence*—('*Damnation de Faust*'; several scenes in airs and choruses); LINDPAINTNER ('*Overture to Faust*'); R. WAGNER ('*An Overture*' [save the mark!] *to Faust*); and GOUNOD ('*Marguerite*,' an Opera).

† *Aesthetik.* Vol. ii., p. 581.

books for 'Figaro' and 'Don Giovanni' (the latter written, as he himself relates, with a bottle of Tokay before him and his landlord's pretty daughter at his side), that his failure—as competent judges consider it—in this, his third, *libretto* for Mozart is all the more glaring. The *libretto* of the opera: '*Così fan tutte, ossia La scuola degli amanti*' [performed Jan. 26th, 1790] is, in fact, so wondrously stupid, that no subsequent stage writer—desirous of rescuing Mozart's exquisite music from oblivion—has ever succeeded in arranging it satisfactorily for the stage. It were better far—at least we think so—to set aside "modern adaptations,"* newspaper strictures, and analyses; these ridiculous love affairs and childish surprises may indeed well be tolerated for the sake of Mozart's music. "It has indeed," writes L. Rellstab (on the occasion of the performance of this piece at Berlin), "always appeared incomprehensible to ourselves, that a foolish Carnival joke, which forms the plot of this opera, should be taken so seriously, and expectations entertained with regard to it which it is not in the least calculated to fulfil. Two lovers agree to put the fidelity of their mistresses to the proof by assuming an *incognito*, and tempting them to infidelity. The *ruse* succeeds; the ladies abashed seek forgiveness; they are pardoned as a matter of course,

* In 1863, an attempt was made at Paris to adapt Shakespeare's 'Love's Labour Lost' as a text-book for 'Così fan tutte.'

vows, &c., are renewed, and all goes merrily as before. That is no more than the way of the world in general and this piece in particular. The poet has treated the whole thing as a harmless frolic — a mere "*Vaudeville folie*" — whereby, indeed, he has neither had regard to probabilities nor to the moral of his tale. Mozart has composed the music to this trivial subject in a correspondingly light, free, and jovial strain." 'Cos fan tutte,' being of the downright *buffo* species, in which music is everything and the words are o no account, is averse to careful dramatic development of the plot; the vivacity of its musical expression makes up for poverty of invention and probability in the poetical department; merriment and joviality reign supreme, and whoever enjoys conviviality and fun is sure to enter heart and soul into it.

In 'Così fan tutte,' Mozart has, in general, retained the traditional Italian forms, but in the *pièces d'ensemble* (mark the farewell scene!) and the two *finali*, we detect the dramatic composer's earlier manner. The same may be said, perhaps in a still greater degree, of his last secular work —an heroic opera, written, in the short space of eighteen days, for the coronation of the Emperor Leopold II., and entitled: '*La clemenza di Tito*' [performed at Prague, Sept. 6th, 1791]. According to the plan of the poem (Metastasio's, and already frequently set to music) which Mozart was commanded to write for, the whole piece was intended merely for a Court and festival opera with brilliant solos and *finale* choruses. But Mozart, not content with this, created the *finale* of the first act, which, by its overpowering dramatic truthfulness, has ever since remained a model of musical tragedy. Similar to Shakespeare's grand Roman tragedies, Mozart has here represented the public life of Roman days heaving and surging under the pressure of a great national calamity. It is a grand historical *tableau*, than which it is impossible to conceive anything in music more impressive and lifelike. How incomparable is the distribution of the double chorus at the words: " *Oh giorno di dolor*," how profoundly imagined, how sublime! Among the airs we cannot fail to distinguish the one with *corno di bassetto* (a now almost obsolete instrument of the clarionet genus) *obligato:* " *Non più di fiori*," whose noble proportions and profound expression give it a foremost place among the (hitherto little known) *Concert* airs of Mozart.

On the whole, Oulibicheff (who also deals hard measure to 'Così fan tutte') considers 'Titus' as, undoubtedly, the least perfect of Mozart's severe classical operas. "Mozart wrote five or six pieces *con amore*; these are, indeed, masterpieces (besides the overture, the *finale* to the first act, the trio in the second act, and the above-mentioned air of Vitellia; to which may be dded the last air of Sextus, the last chorus but one and the concluding chorus); the other scenes, which he only sketched, are redolent of the varnish of the period, and, owing to the pressure of an incredibly short space of time for completion, he commissioned SÜSSMAIER to write those recitatives that were not *obligato*—merely reserving to himself the supervision. Tradition even ascribes to Süssmaier Vitellia's air: '*Deh si piacer mi vuoi*,' and Sextus' duet with Annius: '*Deh prendi un dolce amplesso*.' "

Scarcely had Mozart completed this highly honourable task, than he set himself to finish one of far greater importance, viz.: '*Die Zauberflöte*,' which was performed at Vienna so early as the end of the same month [Sept. 30th, 1791]. To those never-ending critics whom we already hear exclaiming against the foolish *libretto*, we would fain reply in Hegel's consoling words (taken from his *Aesthetik*). "How often do we hear this cant: that the subject of the 'Zauberflöte' is utterly contemptible; yet this patchwork subject forms one of the best opera books extant. Schikaneder has, after a number of strange, fantastic, and common-place productions, at last hit the right medium. The realm of Night, the Queen, the realm of the Sun, mysteries, wisdom, love, ordeals, and, withal, a kind of moral admirable in its universality; added to which, the depth, the enchanting loveliness and repose of the music, fills and enlarges the imagination while it touches the inmost heart." When Mozart wrote operas, he was indeed a poet; more so than ever when he composed the 'Zauberflöte,' whose solemn and mysterious music could alone invest the apparently childish drama with dignity and grandeur. Even the overture, with its exquisite varied melodic and contrapuntal beauties, the trombone triads, the glowing, irresistibly impetuous conclusion, seems to tell us that above and beyond the checkered fairy tale, a higher ideal world is about to be revealed. It is no ordinary trials and sorrows which here appeal to our sympathies, but an image of sorely-tried yet victorious humanity is presented to our view in deeply significant symbolism.* At the same time—apart from Mozart's masonic relations—, we can never sufficiently admire how naturally and truthfully he makes his characters think and feel, and (especially in the *naïve* and comic episodes of Papageno and Papagena, on which he has bestowed equal pains with the rest) what a charming

---

* That this was clearly discerned by Beethoven—himself prone to the ideal—is evident by his giving the preference to the 'Zauberflöte' among all Mozart's operas. Goethe, whose mystical tendencies during his latter years are well known, undertook to write a second part to the 'Zauberflöte' for an opera book. "If," says he of the 'Helena' (*Faust*, part ii., act 3), "only it find favour with the masses, its deeper meaning will, at the same time, not escape the initiated, as is the case with the 'Zauberflöte' and other works."

balance he maintains between the fairy creations of his own brain, and those scenes which are taken from life. He has here displayed that wonderful versatility which enabled him to conceive and describe every imaginable phase of life, that charming vivacity and happy temperament which literally revelled in beauty and variety, and (what exceeded the expectations of the more specula*ting* than specula*tive* Schikaneder) has succeeded in endearing this ideal and beautiful work alike to the multitude and the cultivated minority. The 'Zauberflöte' was performed at Vienna one hundred times during the first year; it was this piece which spread the fame of the (meanwhile deceased) musician far and wide through Germany.

'Die Zauberflöte,' though of far grander proportions, is *de facto* a *Singspiel*—as, indeed, it is entitled in the earlier editions. Mozart wrote it for a Viennese *Volkstheater*, in the unassuming garb of the fairy plays so popular at that time; yet there is no opera so difficult of production on the stage, none, unfortunately, of which the execution (especially in the subordinate parts) is frequently so imperfect. The Queen of Night has a notoriously difficult part, in which, indeed (in the grand *bravura* air), Mozart, out of compliment to the vocal powers of his *prima donna* (Mde. Lange, his sister-in-law), has introduced passages of, to say the least, questionable taste.

We trust the intelligent reader will require no apology for the foregoing detailed account of Mozart's operas. Mozart has obtained a foremost—nay *the* foremost—place in the annals of dramatic art. His operas, in truth, comprise (as Oulibicheff enthusiastically exclaimed) all the known species of musical drama. 'Idomeneo,' 'Titus,' and 'Così fan tutte,' represent the eighteenth century—the *Opera seria* and *buffa* (the first, indeed, viz., 'Idomeneo,' with reminiscences of the Gluck period); the 'Entführung' and 'Die Zauberflöte' are the foundation of an independent German school; while 'Figaro' and 'Don Giovanni' are works of *universal* interest, which have alike exercised influence on the Italian, French, and German Opera.

Mozart, the gifted heir of all hitherto available resources in musical art and science, was almost as great in sacred and instrumental, as in dramatic, compositions; though, *historically*, his importance in these branches of art — especially the former—is, comparatively speaking, inferior. His *Masses* date from the Salzburg period [1773—1780]—consequently, prior to 'Idomeneo.' The (4) earliest, called *breves*, are written in the severe contrapuntal style with organ and two violins only; one of them, in F [1774], reminds Jahn of the finest specimens of the earlier Neapolitan school. The later ones, called *solennes*, have full instrumental accompaniment; they contain some beautiful traits replete with religious feeling; but the generality of the Masses betray inequality of style and want of keeping throughout. Mozart himself did not esteem them highly; they were written under the depressing influence, and to please the superficial Italian taste, of the Archbishop of Salzburg, to whose service he belonged as "Court and Cathedral organist."* Among his other Church

* Of Mozart's Masses *solennes*, the two in C [1777 and 1779] (particularly the latter with the touching *Agnus* for treble solo) are worthy the attention of musicians, and—with the omission perhaps of the *Dona* movement—of more frequent performance. But alas! now-a-days even the 'Requiem,' as well as modern Church music altogether, is despised; in Germany, the cathedral choirs are disbanded, and in lieu of Bach, Beethoven, Mozart, &c., the prevailing taste for mediæval productions admits of nothing but artificial imitations of Palestrina, or the utterly art*less* Gregorian chant. We hold that the former beneficial alliance between the Church and contemporary art cannot be dissolved without signal danger to both. "The decline of sacred art," says even the learned WINTERFELD (Gabrieli, vol. ii., p. 124), "dates from the time when it contracted that fatal taint by which it was degraded to the service of the senses; but is due, likewise, to that frigid exclusiveness which demands the sacrifice of all genuine feeling and inspiration." Still more forcible is S. BAGGE's remark, that the Roman Catholic form of worship has pursued the same tendency to splendour and florid decoration as music: "Therefore, musicians cannot be blamed for having shared this tendency; more especially, as the *back stream* of civilisation, which saw danger as well as deviation from established lawfulness and propriety in redundance of ornament and influences brought to bear more immediately on the senses, had not yet set in." This reaction extended itself also to painting and statuary; the *Madonnas* of Raphael and other great painters are looked upon as profane—indeed, by some the element of actual beauty is altogether denied to religious art; whereas architecture—a merely *sublime* art—enjoys the utmost consideration, and architectural ornamenta-

compositions: the *Vespers* and *Litanies* [also between 1773—1780]; the elaborate contrapuntal Motet: '*Misericordias Domini*' [1781]; and the angelic prayer for chorus: '*Ave verum corpus*,' "that should only be listened to on bended **knee**" [composed June 18th, 1791], are specially deserving of notice.

tion—the shell of a shell—is allowed free play. It is the same crude materialism of the age that rears its head in other branches of musical art, which here appeals to the uninitiated in the sanctimonious garb of saintliness and Church discipline. With regard to Mozart, he has bequeathed his own confession of faith, than which nothing can be more sincerely attached to his church; and that Mozart's powers (even allowing for the external disadvantages under which he laboured) fell far short of his intentions, no one, we imagine, will be seriously inclined to maintain. Upon one occasion, when his Leipsic friends were lamenting that many great musicians had thrown away their talents on trivial church texts, Mozart became serious, and exclaimed in words to this effect: "What absurd nonsense they talk about art! As to you, if you carry your religion in your head, may be there is something in it—I can't say. But with us, it is different. You cannot feel what that means: "*Agnus Dei! qui tollis peccata mundi! Dona nobis pacem!*" But when one has been, like myself, brought up from early childhood in the mystical holiness of our religion, when one has—before one even knew what meant the secret feelings that welled-up within one, and, scarcely conscious of one's own desires—attended Divine service with the deepest devotion, and returned home with a heart relieved of its load and lifted up, and when those were esteemed blessed indeed, who to the melting strains of the *Agnus Dei!* knelt down and received the Sacrament, and from whose hearts, while receiving, the music spoke in serenity and joy—"*Benedictus, qui venit in nomine Domini*"—then it is quite another thing. Well yes, it is true, that gets lost by living in the world. But—at least, so it is with me—when I take the well-known words in hand with a view of setting them to music, it all comes back most forcibly and impressively, and stirs my very soul within me."

Mozart's genius was of that profound and comprehensive order that could achieve marvels even in those branches of art which seemed most remote from his decidedly dramatic temperament; but, during the period of his greatest activity, he had no leisure to devote himself in earnest to Church composition.

This circumstance would account for the rather slovenly composition of the so-called Oratorio: 'Davidde penitente' (*Cantata a due soprani e tenore con cori*, 1785), consisting merely of pieces selected from his earlier Masses and a few additional solos. It was not till death was rife within him that he concentrated his whole attention on sacred composition, and drew the plan of that stupendous work, that sublimest production of modern art—the *Requiem*. The very ideal of modern Church music, viz., inward devotional feeling and the measured solemnity befitting public worship—both uniting to form a work of admirable proportions, exquisite musical expression, and noble Church feeling—is, we think, most completely attained in Mozart's 'Requiem.' Its character is that of grand choral polyphony, which in the glorious solo-quartet pieces: *Tuba mirum*, *Recordare*, and *Benedictus* has a most striking and thrilling effect. Every one knows that while Mozart was engaged on the 'Zauberflöte,' he received an anonymous order for the 'Requiem,' and, with death staring him in the face, had to hasten its completion, so that—similar to Raphael's last work the Transfiguration*—it is not equally finished throughout. His pupil Süssmaier (the same who aided him in 'Titus') filled up, in accordance with Mozart's instructions and posthumous sketches, the gaps that were left in the instrumentation and the three last numbers (*Sanctus, Benedictus, Agnus*). Süssmaier, indeed, professed to have entirely composed these pieces; but, "with the exception of the *Sanctus*, we certainly have the Requiem—in all essential particulars—exactly as Mozart partly completed it, and partly intended it to be."† Doubtless, had life been spared him, he would, after the 'Requiem' (which "he wrote for himself"), have produced many a splendid work in Church music; perhaps indeed,—having already attained perfection in every other style—have devoted himself to sacred art with peculiar zeal, for which his recent appoint-

* The parallel between Mozart and Raphael has been frequently drawn, and insisted on even to the minutest details—latterly by Alberti in his '*Raphael und Mozart. Eine Parallele.*' *Vortrag, etc.* (Stettin, 1856). Equally striking is the resemblance between Beethoven and Michel Angelo, for which see H. Grimm's description of the great Italian artist. "Existing entirely in ideal realms of thought, absorbed in himself and sublime art, he is an enigma to his contemporaries, and frequently incomprehensible (Beethoven was so only in his latter years); conscious of his powers, self-sufficing, a man of few wants, he lived secluded; benevolent, though of a retiring disposition and habitually silent, his rare observations were frequently ironical and sarcastic; in never-ceasing activity pursuing his own way, he was an inventor in whatever he undertook."

† Rochlitz.

ment of chapel-master to St. Stephen's would have furnished ample opportunity. Indeed, the works written during the last six months of his life — 'Titus,' 'Die Zauberflöte,' and the 'Requiem' — warrant this supposition, as also his own pathetic farewell: "Even now I must go, when I might live peaceably; I must leave my art, when, no longer the slave of fashion and shackled by speculators (Schikaneder!), I could follow my own inspiration, and be free to write as my heart dictated!"

Mozart died — his last thoughts dwelling on the 'Requiem' — December 5th, 1791, in the thirty-seventh year of his age, — having been actively devoted to the pursuit of his art from early infancy. On the 4th of September, 1842 — more than fifty years after his death —, a bronze statue (by Schwanthaler) was erected to his memory at Salzburg; and, only a short time since, an allegorical monument (a weeping muse placing the score of the 'Requiem' on his other works) marks his — supposed — resting place.

Of Mozart's numerous instrumental compositions, a large number, being merely juvenile works or *pièces d'occasion*, are altogether of minor value; while others are important only as regards certain portions (generally the *andantes* and *adagios*). We allude, of course (besides the numerous Symphonies written before 1784), chiefly to the *pianoforte Sonatas,* which — in spite of Mozart's emphatic declaration: "He who judges me by such *bagatelles* as those is a fool!" as well as his father's: "You would not surely judge of him by his pianoforte Sonatas, which he wrote when a mere child?"—have frequently been taken as a standard of comparison between Mozart and Beethoven. Almost all of them, like the Masses, are of inferior merit, especially in their concluding pieces. The only pianoforte composition that may be reckoned equal to his other productions is the rich and carefully-finished '*Fantasia and Sonata*' [1785 and 1784], to which five or six of the Sonatas (viz., two in D, two in F, one in B, and the one in A with variations) may be reckoned as but little inferior. Of the remainder, the greater portion is "music of the past." In the estimation of severe critics, they contain "a peculiar intermixture of original ideas and musical commonplaces, deep sentiment and shallow trifling, unrivalled art and careless workmanship."

In Mozart's chamber music we discern the matured musician, viz., in the (6) *Quartets* dedicated to Haydn; the more brilliant and pathetic *Quintets*; the splendid (for its resources almost too powerful) *pianoforte Quartet* in G minor, which—contrary to his usual habit—Mozart himself arranged as a violin quintet, and others. The most remarkable of the smaller compositions for orchestra are the graceful, exquisitely finished *Serenades* for wind instruments; likewise, a number of miscellaneous works, among which **the greater part of the violin Sonatas were the offspring of casual suggestion, and were frequently** written, amid the pressure of more important business, to oblige his friends **and pupils.** With the exception of **Fr.** Schubert, no other great musician has manifested such extraordinary facility and fertility of **production** as Mozart, whose autograph **catalogue,** during the last few years of his life, exhibits an average of three compositions per month.*

Of the *Symphonies,* the finest **are** those in **E** flat major, G minor, and **C** major (with the fugue), which were written **in the above order in** the space of one month and a half during the summer of 1788. The *E flat Symphony* has been entitled, ' *Chant du cygne* '—an appellation which (apart from its peculiar signification) may be taken as answering to the contemplative repose, the elegiac feeling of the *andante* movement. On the other hand, the two *allegro*

* "It would be past comprehension how works differing essentially from each other—works, too, of unusual magnitude, depth, and beauty—could have been produced in so short **a** time, were it not a fact that, amid the multitudinous impressions of daily life, the artist's mind is ever at work, secretly and unceasingly preparing the **threads from which a work** of art shall ultimately be woven." This graceful simile, taken by Jahn (*Mozart*, vol. iv., p 128) from Mozart's own words, but applied in a wider sense, is perhaps more applicable to Mozart than to any other composer; for the facility with which he wrote (for example, the overture to ' Don Giovanni ' was composed during the night previous to its performance) might by many **be mistaken for** carelessness or haste.

movements have a youthful, joyous, muscular character; and how bright and cheerful is the Minuet with its gentle Trio! The character of the entire work is not so much that of an autumnal elegy, as of a quiet summer's evening mood, when calmly and contentedly the impressions of the day are gathered up and poured out in melody. Emotion and passion, glimpses of which we already discern in the impetuous *finale* where (contrary to Mozart's usual practice) the musical flow is interrupted and the conclusion suddenly broken off, are allowed full sway in the grander *G minor Symphony*. "The whispered murmur of sorrow continues with increasing vehemence, till it becomes a raging passion striving to drown its own devouring grief."* The most emotional of Mozart's symphonies is, of course, far removed from Beethoven's deep pathos,—perhaps, gifted connoisseurs deem it weak and tame; yet it sets forth Mozart's peculiar greatness, his wondrously correct and refined taste, his admirably tempered portrayal of deep emotion. Of its *andante* movement (which bears some resemblance to the " portrait air" in the 'Zauberflöte'), the young F. Schubert declared " he could hear the angels sing therein."

The *C major Symphony* with the fugued *finale* ('*Jupiter Symphony*') celebrates the victor's triumph. Earthly anguish is overcome; all is

* JAHN.

peace, prosperity, and grandeur. It is the apotheosis of the master himself, whose triumphant brow beams with immortality. With true artistic discernment, Mozart selected for the *finale* of his majestic work (as in the overture of 'Die Zauberflöte') the most intellectual and ideal of forms— the fugue—for the embodiment of his ideal subject; and, in both instances, achieved "a real triumph of art, in which observance of legitimate principles of art and freedom of creative power conduce to the utmost perfection, order, and beauty."*

It is evident that these three magnificent works —produced consecutively and at short intervals— are the embodiment of *one* train of thought pursued with increasing ardour; so that, taken as a whole, they form a grand *trilogy*, which it would be intense enjoyment to listen to in the order in which they were originated. These three grandest of Mozart's symphonies (the first lyrical, the second tragic-pathetic, and the third of ethical import) correspond to his three greatest operas: 'Figaro,' 'Don Giovanni,' 'Die Zauberflöte,'— or if we select their instrumental counterparts, the overtures of those operas.

Far more complete, and of greater intrinsic merit than many of the movements in his other (30) symphonies (among which, however, we would distinguish the D major, in three move-

* Jahn.

ments, teeming with freshness and melody), are Mozart's *Pianoforte Concertos*, composed for his own performance, and, consequently, with unusual care and partiality. He gave to the *Concerto* (to use his own definition, the acmé of refinement, in contra-distinction to the Symphony, which is the acmé of grandeur) its grand symphonic character (carried to perfection by Beethoven); in accordance with which, the pianoforte performance combines with the orchestra in an animated and delightful whole, by means of mutual interchange of effect. Hoffmann, who owned to "a downright dislike of all pianoforte *concertos* whatsoever," described those of Mozart and Beethoven as "not so much *concertos*, as symphonies with pianoforte *obligato*."

CHAPTER XIII.

ZENITH OF INSTRUMENTAL AND BALLAD COMPOSITION. BEETHOVEN AND SCHUBERT.

LUDWIG VAN BEETHOVEN, the last great master of the so-called " classical " period (so fertile in men of genius) in Germany, was born at Bonn on the Rhine [December 17th, 1770], where his father was tenor in the Elector of Cologne's private chapel.* Devoting his vast powers principally to the composition of instrumental music, he achieved in this branch of musical art results hitherto unattained. So early as his eleventh

* *Biographische Notizen über L. v. Beethoven*, von DR. F. G. WEGELER und FERD. RIES. Coblenz, 1838.

A. SCHINDLER (Beethoven's intimate friend during the years 1814-1827), *Biographie von L. v. Beethoven*, &c. Münster, 1840. Third edition in 2 vols., 1860. W. v. LENZ. *Beethoven et ses trois Styles.* 2 vols. St. Petersbourg, 1852.

OULIBICHEFF. *Beethoven, ses Critiques et ses Glossateurs.* Leipzig, 1857.

MARX. *Ludwig v. Beethoven's Leben und Schaffen.* Berlin, 1859. 2nd edition, 1863.

Beethoven's Leben von L. NOHL. Erster Band Wien, 1864.

Chronologisches Verzeichniss der Werke L. v. Beethoven's von ALEXANDER W. THAYER. Berlin, 1865.

year, he published variations on a march, three pianoforte sonatas, and several songs. But the peculiarity of his genius was even then, and subsequently in a still greater degree, more especially apparent when he extemporized on the pianoforte. At Vienna, during the winter of 1786, when playing on a theme given him by Mozart, the latter remarked to the bystanders: "Mark this young man, he will make a name for himself some day." Being sent, when twenty-one years of age [1792], by the Elector, to complete his musical education at Vienna, he studied composition firstly under Haydn—whose course of instruction, however, was too precise and gradual for an ardent spirit like Beethoven's—and, afterwards, under the learned contrapuntist and thorough-bass master, ALBRECHTSBERGER. His exercises in harmony and composition (interspersed with delightful marginal notes against "bookworms" and "pedants") were published in 1832, and entitled: '*Beethoven's Studies in Thoroughbass, &c.*,' by SEYFRIED—likewise a pupil of Albrechtsberger, and Beethoven's intimate friend. The biographical notes which accompany this work are of considerable interest; but recent researches have pronounced the book, so far as the greater part is concerned, a fraud. In 1795, Beethoven's first compositions, which are entitled "works," made their appearance, viz., three Trios (op. 1) dedicated to Prince Lichnowsky, and three pianoforte Sonatas dedicated to J. Haydn. These works at once proclaimed the young musician the first of the age. The compositions of the following years (Sonatas, Trios, the two first pianoforte *Concertos*, the Septet, the first Symphony) established his reputation as a composer, so that he could write with complete satisfaction to Wegeler [June 1800] as follows: "My compositions bring me in a good deal, and I may say, that I have more commissions than I can well get through. Indeed, for all my pieces there are six or seven publishers, and more even if I wished: I am no longer bargained with, I ask what I choose, and I get it."

Highly beneficial, in regard to his artistic career, was the society of aristocratic and intellectual Viennese families who freely and cordially welcomed Beethoven—already too prone to live "only in his music"—among them on terms of equality and intimacy. Prince Lichnowsky even received him [1794] as an inmate of his establishment, and, when he desired to live independently, granted him [1799] a pension of 600 florins* per annum, and the Princess "would have put him under a glass case to shield him from rough contact." Refined and cultivated women have ever been the first to acknowledge true genius, and Beethoven was, in truth, so adored by ladies of high rank, that, oblivious of the accidents of birth

* £60.

and fortune, he, for several years, actually contemplated marriage with the young Countess Julia Guicciardi. According to the prejudices (even more in force at that time than they are now) of her station, such an alliance was, of course, out of the question; and Beethoven faithfully kept his promise never to love another—for, like Handel, he never married. The *souvenir* of this pure and ideal affection is preserved in the so-called 'Moonlight Sonata' in C sharp minor [op. 27, No. 2] dedicated to "*Madamigella Giulietta di Guicciardi.*" "Life apart from thee"* is the stern decree; patient resignation to which is pathetically described in the tender melancholy *adagio*, but against which the whole soul of the strong man rebels and pours itself out in the *presto agitato* of the same sonata.

Thus blighted in his affections, and—so soon even as his thirtieth year—afflicted with deafness, he withdrew more and more from human intercourse.† In 1809, King Jérome offered him the

---

* Beethoven's own words in a letter to "Julia."

† So early as 1800, he writes to Wegeler as follows: "But that envious demon, my health, has played me a plaguy trick; my hearing has got worse in the last three years. Indeed, I may say life is a burden to me. For the last two years I have avoided society because I cannot bear telling people I am deaf. If my calling were other than it is, it wouldn't so much matter, but in my calling it is a fearful thing; besides which, my enemies, of whom there are plenty, what would they say? To give you an idea of this extraordinary deafness, I must tell you that when I go to the play, I am obliged to lean close to the orchestra in order to hear the

lucrative appointment of Chapel-master at Cassel, but which his noble patrons at Vienna dissuaded him from accepting, and secured him an annuity of 4000 florins* in order to retain him at Vienna. This sum (owing to the disordered state of Austrian finance) was, so soon even as 1811, reduced to one-fifth of its original value; but it had the effect of debarring Beethoven from undertaking duties which, with his increasing infirmity, he would have been scarcely competent to fulfil, and

---

actors. At a little distance I am unable to distinguish the high notes of the instruments; it is astonishing that some people have never noticed it when speaking to me; as I used frequently to be absent and abstracted, it went for that. . . . I have often cursed my existence; Plutarch taught me resignation." And in the same letter (1801) in which he speaks of the sweet girl whose station was, unhappily, superior to his own, he thus laments: "You can hardly imagine how forlorn and desolate my life has been for the last two years; wherever I went, my deafness seemed like a spectre, and I shrank from society, and appeared as though I were a misanthrope, which indeed I am far from being. Oh, I would embrace the whole world were I freed from this calamity. . . . . Were it not for my deafness, I should have travelled half round the globe before now, and indeed I must. *I will struggle with my fate;* it shall not break me down." In the will which he drew up at Heiligenstadt, near Vienna, in 1802, he alludes almost exclusively to his deafness, which isolated him, " naturally of an ardent temperament and highly susceptible of social enjoyment," so early as his 28th year, and forced him, against his will, to turn philosopher. (" It is no easy matter for any one, least of all for an artist," said Beethoven in the aforementioned will.) It was his art alone that prevented him from putting an end to his existence. " Oh! it seemed impossible to me to leave the world before I had completed all I felt myself inspired to do."

* About £400.

thus he was left free to follow his own bent. Though ever since 1816 almost stone deaf, he went on originating and composing, in increasingly deeper strains, till, at length, on the 26th of March, 1827, death released him from his lonely position and the hardships which his solicitude for ungrateful relatives had brought on his latter years. "*Plaudite, amici, comœdia finita est*" were his last words.

Beethoven's appearance is thus described by Fr. Rochlitz in his second letter " on music and musicians at Vienna,"* dated July 9th, 1822. "The sight of him would have shocked me, had I not been previously prepared; though it was not so much his neglected, almost wild exterior, his thick and matted hair hanging dishevelled about his head, as his whole aspect, that impressed me. Imagine a man about fifty years of age, rather small in stature, but thick set and powerfully built, large-boned—somewhat similar to Fichte,† only stouter, and the face fuller and rounder; colour ruddy and healthy, eyes restless, flashing, and, when fixed, absolutely piercing. His movements are few, but quick and sudden; the countenance, especially the quick intellectual eye, is a mixture of, or rather an oscillation between, extreme kindliness and shyness; his whole manner betokens that restlessness and anxious attention

---

* *Für Freunde der Tonkunst.* Vol. iv., p. 350.
† The renowned German philosopher.

which we frequently observe in persons of quick feeling who are similarly afflicted; occasionally, a cheerful expression escapes him; then he relapses into gloomy silence. With all this, whoever sees him cannot help saying to himself: 'This is the man who has provided enjoyment for thousands —genuine intellectual enjoyment.'"

The bronze statue (by Hähnel) erected at Bonn, in 1845, to Beethoven's memory, with its multitudinous folds of drapery, is scarcely a fair representation of the great master; and the expression of the face—similar to the generality of those gloomy portraits of Beethoven—is too old and serious. The *bas-reliefs* representing the Fantasia, the Symphony, Sacred music, and Drama, are by far the best part of it. It is much to be regretted that, owing to insufficiency of funds, Schwanthaler's splendid cast (representing Beethoven as Apollo with the lyre) could not be realized in bronze. The impetuous Fr. Liszt, disgusted with the tardiness of contributors, has undertaken to defray the still remaining expenses connected with the monument.

It has been usual, when treating of Beethoven's life and works, to assume three separate periods or styles, viz., the first [1795—1804], called the Haydn and Mozart style; the second [1804—1814], the matured period, as being stamped with his own distinctive individuality; and the third or latter period 1814—1827], that of his decline.

It is, however, impossible to assign definite limits to these supposed periods by the aid of dates or compositions; still less can it be a question of three distinct and separate "styles." We should be disposed to admit this classification for general purposes, and to select the first, third, and ninth Symphonies as types of the three periods, were it not that a large number of works taken indiscriminately from any one of these periods bear a marked resemblance to each other; but to assume a *first* period at all, appears to us both arbitrary and superfluous. As might be expected, Beethoven began by adopting the forms established by Haydn and Mozart; but the spirit and expression he infused into them are his own, and these stamp him at once as an original genius. This was freely acknowledged by Haydn himself, when he seriously endeavoured to dissuade the young composer from publishing the last of the three trios which had been dedicated to him by the former. We have only to glance at Beethoven's pianoforte Sonatas (among which the *Pathétique,* the one in A flat with variations, the *Grande Sonata* in B [op. 22], those in C sharp minor [op. 27] and D minor [op. 31] would be allotted to the "first period"), and compare them with the most finished Sonatas of Mozart, to see the fallacy of this arrangement; and who would perceive in the pianoforte *Concertos* [op. 15, 19, 37], in the celebrated *Septet* [op. 20], in the second Symphony, and those compositions which were written prior to 1804, a "decided imitation of Mozart?" We must admit, that in Beethoven's works a richer and warmer colouring prevails; the ideas are cast in a grander mould, are profoundly intellectual, and fraught with a noble and deep pathos. The manner in which Beethoven treats the Variation —the most formal of musical forms—is of itself characteristic. Variations, such as those of the A flat and Kreutzer Sonatas and others are widely removed from the merely formal cast of Haydn's and even Mozart's *thèmes variés*, for they keep in view the idea contained in the theme; each time presenting it, as it were, in a different light, they repeat and envelope the theme, which thus takes the character of a musical phrase of deep import, and produces a corresponding impression on the listener's mind. In no instance do we find the form influencing his musical inspirations; but, on the contrary, the poetical idea which he seeks to embody in music itself determines the form— the work developes itself, as it were, from the nucleus outwards.

Thus, to take one instance among many, instead of the minuet (which on some occasions he retained), he made use of the richer and more elaborate *Scherzo*, a form peculiar to himself, and suggestive of playful wit disporting itself in a variety of ever-changing moods. "To sum up, this great master," says Griepenkerl,* "possesses one marked characteristic which is the foundation of all the others, and which distinguishes him from every other 'tone-poet,' viz. :— keen sense of humour, such as only a Shakespeare and a Jean Paul have displayed in literature. This subtle and powerful gift, which had never before found expression in musical forms, was a mine of wealth to a genius like Beethoven's." Of a truth, wit and humour are essential characteristics of Beethoven's grand originality, and must be regarded as all the more significant of his noble disdain for mere sentimental outpourings as the musical form which this intellectual attribute requires for its expression is frequently repulsive to amateurs, and by them decried as faulty; for, the embodiment in musical art of this species of wit necessitates the employment of striking changes and contrasts which interfere with the flow of the melody or leading idea, while foreign, or seemingly incongruous, elements are employed, as well as quaint abrupt turns and other peculiarities which have been denounced as eccentric and unintelligible in Beethoven's works. Beethoven's "tone-poetry" is contemplative, emotional; and though in its impetuous flight it soars— apparently heedless of form—far above ordinary thought and comprehension, it invariably retains

* *Das Musikfest oder die Beethovener*, p. 77.

that true proportion which is apparent, not so much in isolated phrases, as in the profound connexion with which each and every thought combines to produce a complete and harmonious whole. And although we are fain to admit that Beethoven has not always attained to the purity and perfection which characterize Mozart's writings, yet he possesses, as no other does, the secret of stirring our hearts. After listening to a work of Beethoven's, we seem lifted into a higher sphere of thought and sentiment; we experience, as it were, a feeling of repose—grateful, according as our emotions have been previously more or less roused by this wonderful music. Thus, the enthusiastic BETTINA VON ARNIM represents Beethoven as writing to Goethe as follows: "When I look around, I cannot help sighing; for what I behold is contrary to my religion, and makes me despise the world, which does not dream that music is a higher kind of inspiration than even wisdom and philosophy; it is the wine which invigorates men to fresh efforts; and I am the Bacchus who mixes this glorious wine, and so intoxicate men's minds, that when they are sober, they find they have gained lasting treasures.—I have no fears for my music, no harm can happen to it; whoever understands it will be freed from all the misery that others drag about them."

This lofty ethical significance Beethoven's music has in common with Schiller's poetry;

while, at the same time, its naturalness and grace in some measure correspond to that of Goethe. We do not make this comparison because Beethoven's prime was precisely contemporaneous with the renowned classical period of **German** poetry (represented by Schiller and Goethe), but because Beethoven was, in fact, the first "tone-poet" to whom such a comparison is applicable; for he was the first musician who (apart from mere song composition) was thoroughly imbued with the spirit of contemporaneous poetry, and whose creations it manifestly influenced. O. Jahn[*] aptly remarks that "poetry must first bring to light the faculty of minutely describing the innermost depths of reflection and emotion before these could be adequately represented by means of music." Beethoven, accordingly, was the truly original master whose **creations** emanated from himself alone, and—far different from the musicians of our day, who simply transcribe **written** poetry into musical phrase—displayed his **grandest** powers where (as Schindler writes in his conversational notes of the great master) "words are of no avail, because they are **inadequate** to express the **divine word** which music alone can render." Thus, the ancient poets and Shakespeare, as well as Klopstock, Goethe, and Schiller, **were** not so much his poetical models and guides, as intellectual friends and companions when his

[*] *Mozart.* Vol. ii., p. 393.

sad fate debarred him from human intercourse and society.* This it was that kept his creative fancy healthy and vigorous, and preserved him from a too dreamy tendency—an error, however, into which Schumann, the most poetical of musicians, has occasionally fallen.

Let it then be clearly understood from the foregoing remarks, that a high intellectual standard, and the habit of attention which the perusal of the great poets demands, is absolutely necessary to a thorough comprehension and appreciation of Beethoven's works;—an average musical education will not suffice for this. Thus, his rich and carefully-finished *pianoforte Sonatas*, in especial, are replete with profound significance; they represent his entire artistic development. What wonderful musical conceptions are these! how ideal and spi-

---

* With what true appreciation Beethoven studied the great poets is evident from his conversation with Fr. Rochlitz, in 1822, when alluding to Klopstock: "Ever since that summer in Carlsbad (where he made Goethe's acquaintance in 1811), I read Goethe every day—that is, when I do read. He has quite destroyed Klopstock with me. You are astounded? Well, you smile? Ah, because I have read Klopstock! He has been my companion for years; when I went out walking, and wherever I went. Well, I don't say that I always understood him. He flies too much from one thing to another; he begins by soaring too high, always *maestoso!* D flat major! Is it not so? But he is grand, and he elevates the soul. When I could not understand him, I guessed what he meant—about. If he would only not be for ever dying! That's sure to come in its own good time. At all events, it sounds well. But Goethe; he lives, and we are to live too. That's why he can be set to music." But Shakespeare was, above all others, his "*poète de prédilection.*"

ritual their subject-matter! how admirably do they portray the loftier emotions and experiences, mental conflict and triumph, in distinct and well-defined forms, and present to the attentive listener's imagination, not only particular moods and phases of feeling, but an entire psychological development and progress! The question has over and over again been raised: what is the real meaning, the poetical theme or subject of these pieces? and frequent attempts have been made to render the sentiments they contain in language, or even to make them patent to common comprehension and reduce them to philosophical axioms. The querists, for whose benefit various exegetical commentaries have been framed,* belong chiefly to a matter-of-fact, and not very musical, class of people, who are incapable of appreciating a work of art, and therefore imagine that fine words, analogies, and so-called "ideas," can assist in fathoming its depth and meaning. This feeling prompted several of his friends to urge Beethoven, when a new edition of his Sonatas was in contemplation, to " add some explanatory notes as to the leading ideas of many of those works."† He declined the suggestion; and, as we know, has only enlightened us as to a few of them by a

* We allude only to ELTERLEINS' writings: *Beethoven's Clavier-Sonaten erläutert, &c.* Leipzig, 1856; and *Beethoven's Symphonien nach ihrem idealen Gehalt.* 2nd edition. Dresden, 1858.

† Compare Mendelssohn's answer to a similar query. Vol. ii., p. 298 of the '*Letters*' (translated by Lady Wallace).

short heading or an occasional word or two. In the days when he wrote his Sonatas, said he to Schindler, people's minds were more poetical; they had, therefore, no need of the like explanations. Now-a-days, people are too apt to endeavour, by interpreting even to the smallest detail and colouring of a musical movement, to obtain a confused and unsatisfactory intellectual reading of that which can only be accurately apprehended by the feelings. Such lengthy poetical descriptions as we are now alluding to may perhaps find favour with sentimental readers; as to their usefulness, the fact speaks for itself that, particularly as regards Beethoven, rarely do two expositors agree in their reading of the same work. It would rather assist the true understanding of his works if Beethoven's life and artistic progress were written with a view to the exact date of all his compositions, and their reference to the great musician's own circumstances considered and duly pointed out. " Beethoven is never uniform or restricted, nor is his conception limited to one particular view or phase of feeling.—Yet this wide intellect proclaims its own individuality so strikingly, that Beethoven's works are but a reflex of his own experiences. He did not, like most other composers, appropriate and proceed to work out ideas and feelings external to himself; on the contrary, his 'tone-pictures' faithfully represent himself, his inner life, his experiences; even when the ideal (as, for instance, Napoleon, his ideal of a republican hero in the 'Eroica') claims his ardent admiration, or, when harassed and afflicted, he manfully struggles with cruel destiny till light and cheerfulness illuminate the gloom (as in the C minor Symphony), or when (as in the 'Pastorale') he revels in the full enjoyment of nature and rural life. The ideas he imbibed became a part of himself before they took form in music; it follows, therefore, that a biography of his own life and experiences written by the **composer** himself could alone furnish a complete and satisfactory commentary on his works."*

The theory we maintain concerning the purely amateur origin and object of the numerous analyses and descriptions of Beethoven's Sonatas and Symphonies (similar to the *fata morgana* which *inverts* the image it reflects) is further strengthened by the **circumstance, that** those compositions which are less accessible **to the** general run of amateurs and concert audiences (as, for instance, the violin Sonatas, the **Trios, the** Quartets and *Concertos*)—have not **been treated of** in works of the above description. Are such compositions as the Kreutzer Sonata, Trios op. 70 and 97, Rasumowsky Quartets (op. 59), and others we **cannot here** enumerate—are these gems of chamber music, whose true appreciation will ever and everywhere be a standard of correct

* F. Hand. *Æsthetik der Tonkunst*. Vol. ii., p. 425.

taste, less poetical in conception, less profound, less intelligible? As to the smaller works for wind instruments, viz. the Quintet op. 16, Sestet op. 71, and the Serenades (op. 25 and 41), an interpretation of their subject-matter is scarcely needed, so absorbing are the charming instrumental combinations and the sweet, graceful expression of these pieces. Ambros would probably designate them as "Music of the moment" as distinguished from "Intellectual music;"* the former, as he asserts, being the music of Haydn and Mozart, the latter—they did not attain to.

The *Concertos,* five for pianoforte (of which those in C minor and E flat major are the most remarkable) and one for violin (op. 61), are reckoned among the best and most matured of Beethoven's works. These compositions hold a middle place between the Sonata and the Symphony; and, like a species of instrumental *Cantata,* combine splendour of effect and dramatic vigour. When Hoffmann (in allusion to their symphonic character) designated the pianoforte *Concertos* "Symphonies with pianoforte *obligato,*" it is evident he thereby intended only to describe their grandeur and richness when compared with pianoforte *Concertos* in general, (which are merely calculated for the display of manual execution), not that they were beyond the province of legitimate pianoforte composition; on the contrary,

* *Grenzen der Musik und Poesie.* P. 123.

the pianoforte **part comes** out so prominently and effectively, that it is much **to be** regretted these *Concertos* are not more frequently performed—now-a-days, especially, when mere execution is still held in high repute—and that, too, without the introduction of those wretched *cadenzas* with which performers are in the habit of disfiguring these splendid works.

The '*Kreutzer Sonata*,' so called because dedicated to the celebrated violinist Rudolf Kreutzer (op. 47, "*scritta in uno stilo molto concertante, quasi come d'un Concerto*"), may be regarded **as a** second smaller violin *Concerto*, though in plan and general development it more nearly resembles the sonata. The sixth pianoforte *Concerto* is the exquisite '*Fantasia*' for pianoforte, orchestra, and chorus (op. 80), with its grand *finale*—a truly sublime masterpiece, and withal so joyous, so thoroughly popular **and** fascinating; altogether, forming a charming prototype of, and contrast to, the ninth Symphony. The plan of this **work is** bold and vigorous. It opens with a pianoforte *fantasia*; to which succeed delicious **variations for** the several instruments which, as it were, dispute one another the possession of the lovely theme. Joining in the now general contest, the pianoforte once more takes up the theme, followed presently by solo voices, male and female, and afterwards by the whole chorus; till, at the close, chorus, orchestra, and pianoforte unite in glorious strains in honour of the divine art. The ' *Grand Concerto concertant* ' for pianoforte, violin, and violoncello (op. 56 C major, called also the ' *Triple Concert* '), is a most singular composition, and might with propriety be styled a concerted Trio with orchestral accompaniment, or *Symphonie Concertante*.

In order to the full and true appreciation of those grandest achievements of modern musical art — Beethoven's *SYMPHONIES* —, not only the great composer's life and genius, but also the *period* in which he lived and thought—those stirring times which ushered in the present century and gave birth to political freedom and philosophical research, when literature and music put forth new and splendid shoots—must be taken into consideration. A mind like Beethoven's could not fail to be imbued with the spirit of times like those, and his powerful imagination excited to great creative efforts. When Beethoven summoned all the resources of the orchestra, it was not merely to provide a vehicle for the effusion of sentimental strains, or the abstract delineation of events or circumstances; he seized and reproduced the prevailing tone of thought and feeling and the impression which remarkable events were calculated to produce, while dwelling on that view of a subject which more especially harmonized with his own sentiments. Just as Schiller's dramas take their character from great and decisive historical events, do Beethoven's

Symphonies (and that not the 'Eroica' alone) reflect that brilliant intellectual period which shed, as it were, a halo over his glorious "tone-pictures." At the same time, it is as absurd to talk of Beethoven's political—much less democratic—tendencies, as to force a symbolic interpretation upon works of art perfect and complete in themselves. Beethoven was no philosopher; he was, like Schiller, a poet endowed with the spirit of philosophy, who, appropriating the ideas of the age in which he lived, rendered them out of his own experiences—the offspring, as it were, of a particular phase of sentiment. He was, above all, an artist in the true sense of the word; one who never lost sight of the principle that a real work of art should not depend for success on any adventitious explanation or meaning. Thus, in those magnificent specimens of modern historical painting—Kaulbach's frescoes—the object and essence of all true art is so admirably understood and kept in view that, notwithstanding their deep significance, even the least educated spectator can enjoy and appreciate them. We should be inclined to define it as follows: what the philosopher seeks in a work of art is the *idea*, whereas the artist conceived an *ideal*; and the apprehension of a work of art in the spectator or auditor is in proportion to the degree of *ideality* with which he happens to be endowed—in short, *artistic perception*. It follows, therefore, that it is as ignorant to deny significance to a work of art as it is absurd to be for ever asking what the artist intended thereby to express. "Beethoven, in his Symphonies," says Lewis in his Life of Goethe,* "may have expressed grand psychological conceptions, which, for the mind that interprets them, may give an extra charm; but if the strains in themselves do not possess a magic, if they do not stir the soul with a keen delight, then let the meaning be never so profound, it will pass unheeded, because the *primary requisite* of music is not that it shall present grand thoughts, but that it shall agitate the audience with musical emotions."

Thus was Beethoven understood, and according to this standard was he judged by his generation; no one then thought of mysterious meanings, tendencies, and the like. Perhaps people were not so clever in those days; indeed, some newspaper critics gravely affirm that not even the *musical* merit of these great works was properly understood. In order to confute this assertion, we quote the opinion of a learned contemporary.†
"Beethoven has taken up musical art at that point where Haydn and Mozart left it; he adopted the *manner* of those great masters, but developed and improved it till it became absolutely transformed

---

* Vol. ii., p. 543.

† KRAUSE. *Darstellungen aus der Geschichte der Musik.* Göttingen, 1827. P. 221.

by his genius. In especial, did he carry orchestral music a step farther—as far indeed as is possible with our present means and methods of art. He has, likewise, the great merit of having developed the resources of pianoforte music, and enriched it with all the magnificence and power of which it was susceptible. But it is in grand orchestral music that his chief merit lies. Those splendid descriptive Symphonies, the 'Pastorale' and the 'Eroica,' exhibit an intellectual depth and force such as had never before been revealed in music. What the opera is to music in general, Beethoven's Symphonies are to the rest of instrumental music. In these matchless compositions, the several instruments seem possessed with one leading idea, which, conjointly with the rest, is taken up and worked out by each according to its own peculiar tone and character; no two of the parts are alike, yet all, as it were, intimately related, and inspired with the same sentiment, combine to produce the loveliest effects. All the ingredients of the orchestra, from the larger and more imposing masses to the smaller groups, as well as all the instruments severally, conduce to unity of effect in such a manner that their own individual significance is thereby enhanced. More especially are these masterpieces remarkable for the admirably maintained balance between string and wind instruments, and for the bold, vigorous treatment of the basses. Extreme richness in the instrumentation in no way precludes clearness and precision—that is, with a well proportioned orchestra of which the execution (especially as regards expression) is unimpeachable, and an audience composed of those, who, by a due course of study and attention to musical works of a high order, have qualified themselves for the comprehension and enjoyment of such noble and profound emanations as have never before found expression in musical art. But even the less cultivated lover of music is fascinated and enthralled by these majestic compositions, though he may not fathom their deeper meaning."

A noble spirit struggling with fate, surmounting all obstacles, and breaking forth from bondage to liberty, out of darkness into light, is the sublime—we had almost said tragic—theme which lies at the root of Beethoven's magnificent Symphonies—the 'Eroica,' the C minor, and A major; but is most powerfully developed in the Ninth Symphony, where it is carried through all the changing scenes of happiness and sorrow, even to the sublimest visions of glorified rapture. It is worthy of observation, that the above-named Symphonies (3, 5, 7, 9), throughout which this, the leading idea, is perpetually surging, are universally acknowledged to be the finest. Of the remainder (2, 4, 6, and 1), whose general tone is pleasing, tender, and joyous, the D major and 'Pastorale' Symphonies (more especially in female estimation and that of the majority of amateurs) are reckoned equal to the first-named.

The *FIRST* Symphony, in C major [1799, op. 21], which is dedicated to the noble patron of art, van Swieten, presents, both in design and general features, no marked difference from one of Haydn's best Symphonies, when—as for instance in the grand B flat major—his imagination takes a higher flight than usual. The powerful **pathos** and dramatic effect for which the *finali* of Beethoven's other Symphonies are remarkable are not, it is true, apparent in this one; yet we hold it to be mere affectation to esteem this, his first Symphony, which K. **M. v. Weber designates** " bright and fiery," a weak production.

The *SECOND*, in D major [1800, **op. 36**], **opens a series of** Symphonies worthy of each other. We **have listened to it over and over again**, and each time were **strengthened in our conviction that** it is the most *beautiful* of all—so even and flowing are the **parts, so** admirably complete and finished is the whole—a revival, as **it were,** of Mozart in the Beethoven spirit. In entire keeping with **the** joyous character of the prevailing key,* the work is an ideal reflex of that happiest period of the composer's life, when reliance on his own powers, the energy and enjoyment of life inherent to youth, and the sweet illusion of first love lent a charm to existence. True it is, there were sadder moments in which, shortly before the completion of this work, he complained to his friend Wegeler that the "envious demon" was threatening to obscure his horizon; but the world **as yet** was to ignore this, and, out of his hidden treasures, he has presented us with a work of art in which the *actual* **and the** *ideal* **unite** in perfect harmony.—We subjoin a specimen **of "in**terpretation" from Oulibicheff, who, however, finds **the lovely** *Larghetto* "somewhat too long." "*Elans guerriers* **et** *parade militaire splendide dans l'allegro; entretien prolongé avec une douce et charmante amie dans le larghetto; jeux folâtres commencés dans le scherzo* **et poursuivis** *avec un surcroît d'ardeur dans le finale.*"

The *THIRD* Symphony, in E flat major [1804, op. 55], entitled '*Eroica*,' by **Beethoven** himself, was (according to Ries) originally composed in **honour** of the "*Général bourgeois*" Buonaparte—the

---

* Equally characteristic is the employment of the sombre D minor key in the ninth and **last** (a striking contrast to this second) **Symphony.**

hero of the Revolution. He had actually placed Buonaparte's name on the title-page of the score, with the signature "Luigi van Beethoven" beneath; and, thus entitled, it was waiting to be forwarded to **Paris** when Ries brought the great news to Beethoven **that Buonaparte** had declared himself **Emperor.** "After all he is no better than the rest," exclaimed **Beethoven, at the same time tearing** up the title-page and throwing down the score with reiterated curses on the tyrant. Some time elapsed before the work made its appearance (in the original form, though Oulibicheff affirms with the addition of the funeral march!), entitled '*Sinfonia eroica composta per festeggiare il sovvenire di un grand uomo*,' and dedicated to Prince Lobkowitz. With this narrative before us, can any doubt be entertained as to what Beethoven intended **to** portray? Certainly, no other than the ideal of a hero—such as Buonaparte appeared to be—one who rids the world of oppressors and tyrants; or else, that inborn heroism **which** rejoices in the fray, mourns for the fallen brave, and, regardless of death or danger, earns for itself a name that survives **in the** hearts of a grateful posterity. We do **not perceive in the** *Andante* episode any incongruity with **the ideal scheme** of this composition; though, perhaps, **the** *Scherzo*—**which by some has been** taken to mean spectral apparitions, by others the pleasures of camp life, and again by others the phantom revels of unburied slain—might incur this imputation. We hold this to **be one** of those pieces which **must** be grasped by the feelings rather than the imagination, and that it is intended as a kind of interlude (mark those enchanting horns in the trio!) between the mournful funeral march and the burst of joy and triumph in the *Finale*.

The *FOURTH* Symphony, in B flat major [1806, op. 60], is one of those which precludes the idea of any particular subject; but, as Oulibicheff would say, it contains its own programme. The fundamental idea of Beethoven's Symphonies,—viz., conflict and victory—is likewise evident in this one; but the tone is exulting, as if assured of victory. As compared with the breadth and detail of the 'Eroica,' this (by Beethoven entitled) "grand" Symphony is, especially in the *allegro* movements, remarkably condensed and energetic. **Schindler,** who never enlarges in analytical disquisitions on **Beethoven's** works, calls it "the most *polished* of all the Symphonies." **One marked** characteristic of this one—as contrasted with the almost stereotyped introduction to Haydn's **symphonies and** those of his imitators—is the sublime *Adagio*, **so full** of subdued pathos; presently the gloom disperses—for not **yet will** the great master give vent to his anguish in a musical composition—and makes way for the bright, joyous *Allegro*, which, rushing onwards in delightful rhythmical cadence, enthralls and captivates the listener's senses. "Emotion is only fit for women; music should strike fire from a masculine mind" are the sentiments which Bettina von Arnim attributes to Beethoven, and which might here be quoted against Oulibicheff, who is of opinion that love—its joys and sorrows—are not alluded to in the *Adagio* alone. We agree, however, with his view that this Symphony is a pendant to the second, and, like it, a faithful picture of happier times gone by; but the colouring throughout is of deeper hue, and already dark shadows hover round the fair prospect —monitors, as it were, of how transitory a thing is earthly happiness.

The *FIFTH* Symphony, in C minor [1807, op. 67], whose central position with regard to the others is not without a significance of its own, is universally and rightly acknowledged to be the most perfect instrumental work of Beethoven, and, consequently, the most splendid Symphony that ever was written. It is a veritable tragedy in music; one in which the great problem of the composer's life, viz., struggle with destiny, is brought to a decisive issue. "Thus fate knocks at our door," says Beethoven of the *Allegro* theme, and: Be it so, is the reply of one who, through the drear night and the horrors of death, unflinchingly progresses towards immortality. We here subjoin *Hoffmann's* celebrated description,* which, though somewhat diffuse, is comparatively the best. Having compared Beethoven with Haydn and Mozart, and pointed out the profound unity and proportion he observed in his instrumental works, Hoffmann proceeds as follows: "Of all his works, perhaps none displays this in a higher degree than the glorious, profoundly significant Symphony in C minor. How this wondrous composition carries the imagination with ever-increasing mystery and grandeur into the unknown spirit-world! Nothing can be simpler than the leading idea of the *Allegro*, which consists merely of two bars, and begins with a unisonal phrase, while the key in which it is written remains at first a mystery. Oppressed and harassed with forebodings of some dire catastrophe, it would seem to denote one venting his anguish in sharp cries; but soon a bright image appears and illuminates the gloom (the exquisite theme in

---

* *Phantasiestücke in Callot's Manier.* Vol. i., p. 48.

G major, first indicated by the horn in E flat major). How simple, we repeat, is the theme which the master has selected for the corner-stone of this imposing structure; but how exquisitely does the rhythmical proportion of the secondary and intermediate subjects unite them with it in such wise that they assist in developing the character of the movement indicated by the theme itself! The phrases are one and all short, consisting for the most part of only two or three bars, and are, besides, constantly changing from the wind to the stringed instruments. One would have been inclined to suppose that such materials could produce nothing but a disjointed, unsatisfactory result; but, on the contrary, the proportion observed throughout the whole piece, as well as the continual repetition of the phrases and chords, suggests the idea of an indescribable yearning after a higher existence. Does not the lovely theme of the *Andante con moto* in A flat major (introduced by the violas and violins solo) sound like a sweet voice from spirit-land, filling the heart with consolation and hope? But even here the dread shadow which loomed so threateningly in the *Allegro* bursts from out the storm-clouds, and from before its terrible aspect vanish the sweet forms which hover around us. What shall I say of the *Minuet (Scherzo)*? Mark those singular modulations, those concluding choruses in the dominant major, which the bass repeats in the minor key and takes for the tonic of the succeeding theme, while the theme is for ever extending itself through additional bars.* But, like a bright sunbeam, the glorious theme breaks in amongst the jubilant concord of instruments in the concluding movement. What wondrous contrapuntal passages are these! To many, indeed, the whole may appear nothing more than a splendid rhapsody; but the more intelligent listener will realize the idea of unspeakable anxious yearning, and this thought will pursue him to the conclusion; and, not even when the magic sounds cease to fall on his ear, will he at once awaken to the consciousness that he is no longer in the unseen spirit region, where joy and grief surround him in musical form."

Mendelssohn, in one of his letters, gives an interesting narrative of a visit to Goethe at Weimar, on which occasion he played the first movement of the C minor Symphony on the pianoforte, "though the

---

* Spohr, who also finds fault with portions of the other movements, calls the bass passages in the Trio (frequently a failure in the execution) too quaint and noisy for his taste! The *Finale* is a continuation of the third movement.

old gentleman would have nothing to say to Beethoven. He was wonderfully impressed. He **said,** 'That does not stir the feelings; it astounds one; it is grandiose,' **and** so went on muttering to himself; after some time he resumed: 'It is very grand, quite awful—as if the house were tumbling about one's **ears;** and what must it be with all that number of performers?'"

The *SIXTH* Symphony, in F major [op. 68], was **entitled '*Pastorale*' by** Beethoven himself, and was performed for **the first time** December 22nd, 1808, on the self-same occasion with the **splendid** *Fantasia* [op. 80]. The composer has here subjoined a programme which renders further explanation superfluous. It runs as follows: "Cheerful sensations awakened by an arrival in the **country.** Scene by a rivulet. **Rustic** merry-making. **Storm. Songs of the** shepherds. Feelings **of joy** and gratitude after the **storm."** In the additional notice, **"The** expression **to be emotional rather than** pictorial," Beethoven **has** tersely **and concisely declared the** dissimilarity between himself and his predecessors, especially **Haydn** (in the 'Seasons,' of which a grand performance, warmly seconded **by** Beethoven, had taken place March 27th of the same year). Whilst Haydn delights in simply portraying a foreground without distance, Beethoven finds in the ever-varying aspect of nature a reflex of his own feelings; by continually mingling his own sentiments with his description of rural scenes, he throws around **the** landscape an ideal atmosphere; his **work expresses, as** it were, a longing for country life common **to persons of imaginative temperament.** Thus our musician—" the **strange** man escaping **from city life "*** in the genial spring time—pursues his rambles " o'er hill and dale," **to mingle with** the jovial, simple country folk :

"Both great and small send up a joyous cheer;
Yes! I am still a man—I feel it here."†

It is well known that Beethoven spent the greater **portion of summer time in** the country, and that he delighted in long rambles, frequently **returning only at nightfall.** We have no difficulty therefore in **tracing the origin of** the Pastoral Symphony. As to the objections so **continually** brought forward against the imitation of birds' notes (the **quail, cuckoo,** nightingale) **in** the second part, we will reply in the **words of Carriere :‡** "Imitation of natural sounds

---

* Hölty.   † Goethe's *Faust.*   ‡ *Aesthetik.* Vol. ii., p. 342.

for their own sake is not art; but Beethoven presents us, in the first instance, with a charming landscape view, and in the second, with a retired valley scene; the impressions which these call up in our minds are so unmistakeable, so distinct, and, consequently, the very essence of rural life is so fully realized, that the musical element it contains is clearly brought to light; accordingly, should the 'tone-poet' hesitate to complete the picture with reminiscences of the sweet sounds more especially typical of rural enjoyment, he would fall into the error of that mistaken idealism which despises natural forms, however beauteous, and endeavours to replace them with inventions of its own."

When Wagner expresses himself as follows: "The concert-going public of our day only plays the hypocrite when pretending to appreciate symphonic composition," he would probably account for the partiality of the public for the 'Pastorale' by the circumstance that this Symphony happens to be furnished with a programme. We have had occasion to observe that inferior amateurs have a strong preference for the 'Pastoral' Symphony—probably on this account. On the other hand, the verdict of severe judges runs thus: "The work, as regards form, is by no means free from defects, particularly the *andante* movement with its numerous repetitions."

The six first Symphonies succeeded each other at short intervals from 1800 to 1808; but from the sixth, a period of five years elapsed before the *SEVENTH* Symphony, in A major [1813, op. 92],—the most majestic and powerful of the whole series—was given to the world. It was performed for the first time, together with the 'Battle of Vittoria,' December 8th, 1813, and again December 12th, as well as in January and February 1814. The Symphony at once called forth "enthusiastic applause; and Beethoven, who conducted the orchestra, received quite an ovation. This latest achievement of Beethoven's genius must be heard in order to be truly appreciated."[*] A great deal has been written and said concerning this splendid composition; some think it is intended to represent Moorish chivalry;[†] others, marriage festivities;[‡] others again, a masquerade[‖]—all, in short, who have sought to interpret this music

---

[*] *Leipz. Allg. Mus. Zeitung.* Vol. xvi., No. 4. NOTE BY THE TRANSLATOR. We presume the reviewer hereby means that a perusal of the score alone will not suffice to disclose its beauties.

[†] MARX.   [‡] AMBROS.   [‖] OULIBICHEFF.

literally, agree in the **idea of a festive celebration.** We think L. Bischoff's reading of the A major Symphony, which views it as an autumn sequel to the 'Pastorale,' is the most ingenious. Perhaps one would at first be inclined to take the *Allegro* immediately following on the superb introduction for a scene of rustic festivity, or does the 6/8 time and the instrumentation remind one rather of a grand and brilliant hunting expedition? Even for that the movement is too rich, too bold and majestic. We repeat, that Beethoven **had no** intention of representing any particular external or picturesque scene; but simply himself, his life and circumstances viewed **in connexion with the world—at** that time the theatre of mighty **events—around** him. Nor should we lose sight of the circumstance that this Symphony was first performed in the year 1813 (so important in the annals of history), and on the same occasion as a commemorative piece ('*The Battle of Vittoria*' composed in honour of Wellington's victory, June 21st, 1813), as well as **for a patriotic** object. ("For the benefit of Austrian **and Bavarian warriors** invalided at the battle of Hanau.")* The celebrated *Allegretto* **in** A minor was, as Spohr relates, encored at the first performance. It opens with a long-drawn 6/4 chord by the wind instruments lasting from *forte* to *piano* through two entire bars; after which, the violoncellos execute a measured theme of ineffable sadness, whose every note stamps its melancholy on the mind. In ever-increasing numbers sob and sigh the mysterious voices till the utmost expression of **woe is attained ; when, amid the general lamentation, peals** the

---

* **Beethoven, in his circular** of thanks to those who assisted at the concert, expresses himself as follows : " It was a rare assemblage of first-rate musicians ; each of whom, animated solely **with the desire of** employing his talents for the advantage of his **country, without any** scruples of precedence or **merit took their places at the** orchestra indiscriminately, whether subordinate or otherwise. The **command of the orchestra** was entrusted to me, because the music was of **my composition ;** if any one else had written it, I would as cheerfully **have taken my place at the big drum,** as did Herr Hummel ; **for we had no other** object **than that of** serving our country gladly **and** joyfully—that country which had done so much for us. Herr **Schuppanzigh** led the first **violins;** Herr Spohr and Herr Mayseder played **among the second violins ;** the first chapelmaster, Herr Salieri, **marked time for the** cannonades and drums ; Herr Sivori and Herr **Giuliani likewise occupied subordinate places.**

gently-healing melody in A major, assuaging the bitter grief which alas! is too deep-seated to be at once removed. Again the voice of lamentation is heard, though this time not in passionate accents, but gently and gradually melting into calmness and resignation. The incomparable *Scherzo-presto* sparkles with life and enjoyment, to which the expressive *Assai meno presto* (Trio) presents a wondrously beautiful contrast. After the repetition of the *Presto*, the *Meno presto* again returns, when it is suddenly broken off by a most original and singular termination. The *Finale* carries the merriment of the *Scherzo* to the utmost limits of wild bacchanalian excitement. To Oulibicheff's taste, formed exclusively on Mozart's music, this **theme** appears commonplace and trivial. "*Les fanatiques, pour lesquels tout est génie dans Beethoven, appellent cela de l'humor.*" Yes, verily, genuine humour it is which sparkles throughout this colossal *finale*—delighting in contrast and opposition; and this sense of humour which, as we have already shown, was a powerful ingredient of Beethoven's character, is wanting to Oulibicheff and other "*hommes de goût.*" Accordingly, we are not surprised that he finds no merit in—least of all the *Finale* of—the eminently vivacious

EIGHTH Symphony, in F major [1817, op. 93]. He **calls it** "*La moins réussie et très probablement la moins goûtée de toutes les symphonies de Beethoven. Ecrité peu après **la** septième, elle **en a tous les** défauts, sans aucune des grandes beautés qui y font compensation.*" Whilst inveighing against the "eccentric, incoherent, contradictory" *Finale* which, besides, includes nearly half of the entire work, Oubilicheff is so obtuse to the merits of the rest that he can see nothing in the lovely *Allegretto Scherzando* but a satire on Rossini (!); while of the charming Minuet with the playful Trio he affirms that any other composer of the eighteenth century might have written it. On the other hand, O. Jahn remarks with great discrimination that the Minuet has the slowest *tempo* of the whole Symphony, and that its serious and dignified grace contrasts most humorously with the lively tone of the remaining movements. We certainly agree that the first movement is the least successful; but whoever despises the *Finale*—the theme of which is alone a wondrous conception—has not properly understood Beethoven—the great humorist, who in extraordinary contrasts and combinations of apparently irreconcilable **elements displays** a fund of originality and imagination **as wonderful as it is rare. One** reason, perhaps, why this composition **enjoys an inferior degree** of popularity to the others is (apart from **the very high** intellectual range requisite for its due appreciation) principally owing to the fact that it requires the utmost precision and delicacy, and in the *Allegro* movement great freedom and power, in the execution; the *Finale*, especially, is quite a *tour de force* for the orchestra.

Beethoven's *NINTH* Symphony, in D minor, "**with** a choral *finale* on Schiller's 'Ode to Joy,' for full orchestra, four **solo** and four choral **voices**" [1824, op. 125], is a truly colossal conception, typical **of a great** soul unsubdued by the weight of affliction. **For the last time,** when his days on earth are drawing to a close, the great composer depicts in vivid and powerful traits the indomitable **fortitude of** a noble mind under the pressure of unutterable woe, its **secret trials and conflicts,** and ultimate peace and resignation.

"Pain is short, but joy—eternal,"*

says **the poet** most akin to Beethoven; and this **sentiment is,** we opine, the thought which lies at the root of **this great work,** particularly the last movement. Most certainly **this** Symphony **is,** in regard to conception, the loftiest of them all; but, judged **by a** purely musical and artistic standard, it is, undoubtedly (apart **from** some eccentricities of modulation), inferior to the earlier ones. It outsteps the legitimate province of musical art; for in the principal movements, viz., the first and the last, it deals more in ideas than emotion;—Marx's definition, "that it exhausts the resources of instrumental music," **is,** therefore, singularly appropriate. The imposing grandeur **of this** Symphony in some measure justifies its creation; but it **would be a** mistake **to exalt it into a** precedent, or regard it **as** the model of a genus, **and we hold that view to be erroneous** which regards the eight preceding Symphonies **as mere preparatory** studies for "that marvel of composition, **the ninth.**" BERLIOZ, **who** endeavoured **to continue a** style inaugurated **by Beethoven, has** furnished the most striking proof **that** imitation **of exalted genius is liable to** degenerate into caricature. "**In connection with** music, **poetry**— the language of humanity — **heals** the deepest sorrow," **says Goethe.** This **is** the profound **thought on** which the great **composer has reared** his singular and incomparable edifice. And yet its **chief** peculiarity—the introduction **of the** chorus in the concluding movement—does not add to **the** effect; indeed, the measured, almost monotonous concourse of voices intoning,

"Joy, thou spark of heavenly fire!"

---

* SCHILLER's " Maid of Orleans."

would seem at first to produce an unpleasing impression. Beethoven intended, apparently, to express the awe which seizes those who contemplate the *sacredness* of joy, as Schiller describes in the 'Ode to Joy;' and, therefore, the expression is intensified after the words "thy hallowed fane."* The *Adagio*, breathing solemnity and repose in every chord, is highly suggestive of inward peace and content—a farewell, as it were, to the happy past. As to the *Scherzo* (which in this Symphony constitutes the second movement), the majority of connoisseurs have agreed in pronouncing it the most original and beautiful portion of the work. We have here given a short sketch of our own ideas concerning this magnificent—we had almost said *weird*—composition, which, like the second part of Goethe's 'Faust,' will ever remain a *poema reconditum* and æsthetic problem.

The ninth Symphony ("which not one in ten can understand" says Hans v. Bülow) is the greatest and most admired of Beethoven's *last compositions*; this work, the *Missa solemnis*, the four last pianoforte Sonatas (op. 106, 109—111), and the five last Quartets with the great fugue in B (op. 127, 130—133, 135) are the works which have, in our own day, given rise to much diversity of opinion. While some regard them as the *ne plus ultra* of Beethoven's productions, and extol them as the *only* correct standard worthy of future imitation, the great majority pronounce them unintelligible, eccentric, and unpleasing. As usual, the truth lies between these extreme opinions.

* "*Dein Heiligthum.*" NOTE BY THE TRANSLATOR. Sir E. B. Lytton's excellent rendering of the 'Ode to Joy' does not adapt itself to Beethoven's music, the metre being somewhat different from that of Schiller's poem. The English version usually employed in connection with the choral Symphony deviates so widely from the original, that the effect alluded to in the text is entirely lost.

As in the later works of other men of genius, but especially Goethe, a vein of serious contemplation verging on mysticism runs through these last compositions of Beethoven, supplanting, in great measure, the pathos and emotion which distinguish his earlier works, and replacing clear, well-defined melody by richly developed polyphonous and contrapuntal phrases. At the same time, we cannot fail to be struck with the number of passages still replete with the purity and grace of his earlier works; as, for instance, the second and third movements of the ninth Symphony, which are quite equal to anything he produced during his prime. It cannot, on the other hand, be denied that Beethoven has occasionally, and sometimes even throughout an entire movement or work, overstepped the limits of true beauty and proportion, and in his lofty soarings over-taxed the resources of musical art. But are not these very works the genuine expression of his own feelings, existence, and destiny—swayed alternately by despair, resignation, and hope? Regarded from this point of view, how differently do the gloomy, melancholy *adagios*—like unto sorrowful old age lamenting in touching strains the happy days of yore, and yearning, oh! how earnestly, for the "peace which passeth understanding"—appear; as also those impetuous *allegros* and *finali*, which resemble a mighty torrent rushing headlong over the rocks to the dark abyss beneath!

For those whose imagination cannot sympathize with that of the great master, these works will, as a matter of course, possess but few attractions; while, to the purely *musical* taste, their elaborate contrapuntal combinations will not compensate for the absence of beauty in form and conception.* We can quite understand that profound and educated musicians *grow* to these compositions; also, that the exclusive admiration of the disciples of the "development theory" as applied to music answer all objections advanced against their own confused productions by quoting the immortal name of Beethoven in support of their wild inventions.

Further, it appears to us especially worthy of notice that, during the latter period of his life, Beethoven exhibited a remarkable partiality for the quartet—that genus of musical art which Weber designates "intellectual music."† A deve-

---

* "Increasing deafness could not fail to act banefully on the imagination. His continued efforts at originality could not, as formerly, be guarded from errors of judgment. Is it, therefore, to be wondered at if his productions became more and more eccentric, incoherent, and unintelligible? True it is, there are people who profess to understand them, and are so overjoyed at this privilege, that they esteem them far above his earlier masterpieces. For my part, I confess that I have never been able to appreciate his later works. The ninth Symphony, as regards the first three movements, is, in spite of occasional traits of genius, inferior to any of his former ones; but the conception of Schiller's ode in the fourth movement is so utterly monstrous and absurd, that it is beyond my comprehension how Beethoven could write such a thing."—SPOHR's *Autobiography*.

† Of the *musical* subject-matter of the five last quartets, an

lopment of the tendency of Beethoven's last sonatas and quartets could only lead to a most undesirable *spiritualization* of music. The embodiment of spiritual in material forms (which **Bettina von Arnim** regards as the summit of **all true art**) is, **we think**, not satisfactorily attained in **modern music**; but in Beethoven—who, like Goethe, gave form and utterance **to his** own sensations—*that* was a simple and natural form of expression which in others becomes downright exaggeration. We should, therefore, lay particular stress on the fact that, previous to his decline, not only **were the great master's efforts expended in endeavouring** to render instrumental music capable of a contemplative tendency, but, likewise, in endowing the forms—enlarged owing to increased importance **of the** subject-matter—with a greater amount of variety and colouring.

---

excellent analysis has been written by SELMAR BAGGE, the talented editor of the '*Deutsche Musikzeitung*', (Nos. 36—40, 1862). He is of opinion that those in B major (op. 130) and C sharp major (op. 131) are the finest; and that, of the E flat (op. 127) and F (op. 135) quartets, the two central movements are superior to the principal ones. "It is worthy of observation that, as is well known, this disproportion in the relative parts of a quartet has gained ground ever since Beethoven's time; and that in modern quartets and other sonata forms the principal movements are, generally speaking, inferior to the central ones." The superscriptions of two movements in the last—somewhat abstruse—quartets should not be overlooked: "*Canzona di ringraziamento in modo lidico offerta alla divinità da un guarito*" (*Adagio* of the quartet in A minor op. 132), and: "Hesitation. Shall it be? It shall be!" (*Finale* of the Quartet in F major, op. 135).

The other great work of Beethoven's latter period is the *Missa solemnis* in D major, for four choral and solo voices, full orchestra, and organ (op. 123); the first performance of which took place April 1st, 1824—a few weeks previous to that of the ninth Symphony. It is one of the grandest and profoundest works of art ever created; one, however, in which the composer's peculiarities are all the more conspicuous, as Church music, especially, requires that artistic individuality should assert itself as little as possible. Taken as a whole, this Mass is rather a sublime than a religious conception;—not a *Mass*, properly speaking, with music adapted to the text, but a lofty expressive composition on words from the Church service—a composition whose astounding grandeur leaves no room for religious feeling and worship. Of this work, the *Kyrie* is the most devotional; the *Gloria*, with its scarcely practicable *Presto finale*, the most vigorous; the *Credo*, the richest and profoundest; and the *Benedictus* (where a violin solo soars, as if on angels' wings, over the whole orchestra), the sweetest and purest. In direct opposition to the *a capella* style, which Beethoven himself in a letter to Zelter (March 25th, 1823) calls "the only genuine Church style," the orchestra holds here a prominent place, and the singing is entirely subordinate, particularly in passages where the capabilities of the human voice are not duly considered. "To him men were as instruments, and instruments as men."*

The first *Mass* in C major, likewise for chorus and solo voices, orchestra and organ [1804, op. 86], is the exact opposite of this "grand and solemn" Mass—the expression being eminently sweet and melodious. For this music (with Beethoven's approbation) an additional German text was written; and thus it is known to many as the '*Three hymns.*' Beethoven's Oratorio, or rather Cantata, '*The Mount of Olives*' [1800, op. 85], is, "in fact, only the first part of a 'Passions' oratorio; but so much drawn out in detail that he never designed a fitting termination."† Beethoven's own admission, in after years, that his conception of Christ was too theatrical, is applicable to the whole work. Ambros is even of opinion that it is "scarcely equal to Rossini's *Stabat Mater,* and a Beethoven association—if ever such come into existence in Germany (which we hold to be neither essential nor desirable)—should therefore do its utmost to obliterate the memory of this work."‡ Taken by themselves, the march of the Roman soldiers and the final chorus are admirable pieces.

Beethoven was no Church composer—less so even than Haydn and Mozart; indeed, so much

* MARX. † ROCHLITZ. *Für Freunde der Tonkunst.*
‡ *Culturhistorische Bilder aus dem Musikleben der Gegenwart.* Leipzig, 1860. P. 26.

did he withdraw from communion with the Church that the orthodox and pious Haydn called him a downright atheist. Marx says: "Not only was Beethoven too much wanting in Church feeling and sympathy for the composition of Masses, but he was not thoroughly at home in choral writing, which, like every other branch of art, has its own peculiar conditions." Beethoven and the later musicians have carried musical art to its furthest limits; but in a very different branch to *sacred* music.

In his sole opera, '*Fidelio*,' Beethoven has adopted the Mozart form; but how different the essence and spirit of this opera from one of Mozart's—indeed, from every other opera! What an enormous distance between a so-called *opera seria* and the lofty pathos of this music!* But much as we admire this noble music (the prisoners' choruses, Leonore's grand *aria*, the jubilant duet which precedes the second *finale*, and other pieces), we cannot deny that, as such, it

* Let us not, however, be understood as praising Beethoven's opera at the cost of every other. Music is, in its very essence, a *cheerful art*. Therefore, even in sacred music, except on special occasions (such as, for instance, a requiem), the expression is never continued in one uninterruptedly solemn strain. In the opera which, more than any other genus of musical art, demands variety and piquancy (as well as great experience and knowledge of the world on the part of the composer), prolonged seriousness is scarcely tolerable. The lofty ideality of Beethoven's music could alone cause it to maintain a hold on the interest of an audience already favourably inclined; Cherubini's opera '*Les Deux Journées*' met with inferior success. Less gifted composers who have endeavoured to do

does not answer the highest demands of the genus. Neither the dramatic **action of** Mozart's operas nor the climax of effect in Gluck's *drame lyrique* **are** here discernible; the interest of the piece centres solely in Leonore, who appears as Fidelio in masculine attire. As to the **other personages**, little or no interest attaches to them; but Leonore, the heroine, is a part in which the most renowned singers, viz., Schroeder-Devrient, Schechner-Waagen, Milder-Hauptmann, **Malibran-Garcia, and, of** late, Louise Köster and Titiens have achieved their greatest triumphs. Leonore is Beethoven's ideal of a loving **woman,** whose affection, faithful unto death, inspires her with the strength and courage of a true heroine; the remaining characters are quite subordinate— the ideal, ethical, and expressive element alone being that in which he delighted. Florestan is a purely passive personage; besides whom, " Pizarro **and** the Prime Minister (without, however, **their motives** being distinctly accounted **for—the latter** appearing like a *deus ex machinâ* **at the conclusion**

---

the same, have invariably lapsed into hopeless monotony, as, for instance, BELLINI in '*Capuletti e Montecchi;*' though, musically speaking, there is a great deal of merit in this opera. The modern school of Italian composers, DONIZETTI and others, make not the slightest attempt (even in occasional scenes) to emulate the solemn tone of tragedy in music—their heroes encounter death to the tune of a lively waltz. In the Symphony—a far more serious branch of composition—the **necessity for a downright** lively—nay, mirthful— interlude (such as **the Minuet or** *Scherzo*) is recognized by **every composer.**

of the piece) represent the "antagonistic principles" (to quote Beethoven) "of good and evil. Midway between both stands Rocco, the obedient servant and abettor of evil, though good-natured, and ready to forward the prisoner's release. In order to give variety and action, but without exercising any influence on the plot, Marcellina and her jealous admirer Jacquino are introduced — episodically, as it were. The choruses of prisoners, soldiers, and populace are mere *garniture*, in order to assist the delineation of suffering, tyranny, and succour."* It is in the domestic scenes (Rocco, Marcellina, Jacquino) that Beethoven is least at home. When an opera book arranged from Schiller's '*Bürgschaft*' was proposed to him for composition, he actually requested WEIGL to compose the second act (the wedding feast) because "such cheerful gaiety did not suit him."† It is worthy of remark, that in this, his only opera, Beethoven celebrates an extraordinary instance of *female* heroism (Schiller's female creations have likewise, in general, more pathos than strict adherence to nature), whereas Mozart— who may in truth be styled the bard of love—, like Goethe and Shakespeare, portrays the female sex with all the reality of life.

* MARX. Vol. i., p. 331.

† In 1816, Franz Schubert wrote an opera (left unfinished at the third act) on another adaptation of Schiller's ballad; the score contains fifteen pieces of music. Lindpaintner's opera on the same subject has fallen into oblivion.

This opera was performed (with a somewhat inferior cast) for the first time November 20th, 1805, with the title of ' *Leonore, or Conjugal Affection;*' but met with a cold reception from an audience composed chiefly of French officers. After the third representation, Beethoven withdrew his work from the stage. The following year, it was again brought out with the suppression of a whole act. " I rearranged the whole book for him," writes Breuning to Wegeler, " so as to give action and variety to the plot ; he curtailed a good many of the pieces, and it was performed three times with the greatest applause. But it roused his enemies at the theatre, and, as he had given offence to a great many at the second representation, they have succeeded in preventing the performance of the opera in future." In 1814 Beethoven made several alterations in the opera, particularly in the two *finali,* and gave it the name of ' Fidelio.' " This business of the opera is the most tedious in the world," wrote he in a note to Treitschke, who had undertaken to alter the text. " I am dissatisfied with the greater part, and there is scarcely a piece that I have not been obliged to alter." In this its present form, the opera met with universal applause and approbation.

For the several performances of this opera [1805, 1806, 1814], Beethoven wrote four *Overtures,* the first of which he subsequently withdrew; it was not published till after his death. The *third* Overture, which is now very appropriately given between the first and second acts, is an arrangement and completion of the *second*. No other overture can be compared with this Leonore Overture. It is more than an overture,—it is a *fantasia*, a downright symphonic poem; while as a *musical* work—apart from its *ideal* excellence in connection with the rest of the opera—it is beyond all praise. The vigorous and impetuous *fourth* Overture (in E, written for the performance of 'Fidelio' in 1814) is the most perfect and beautiful of them all; it varies from the three other Leonore Overtures in this respect, that it makes use of no themes from the opera, but, on the contrary, forms an independent introduction to the opera.*

The second work of importance which Beethoven wrote for the stage is the music to Goethe's play *Egmont* [1811]; and which, along with Weber's 'Preciosa' and Mendelssohn's 'Midsummer Night's Dream,' is the best work of the kind ever written. Besides the Overture (which in point of dramatic significance and musical per

* Lyser narrates that, shortly before the performance of 'Don Giovanni,' Mozart played three splendid overtures for that Opera to a friend of his; the first was in E flat major; the second in C minor (a *fugued fantasia* like that to '*Die Zauberflöte*,' but totally different in character), and the third in D major, which he subsequently penned so quickly. But he could not be persuaded to write down the others.

fection can only be compared with the one he composed for Collins' tragedy *Coriolanus*), he wrote four unique and admirable *Entr'actes*, in which he has, with exquisite taste, united the last scene of each act with the commencement of the succeeding one—an interesting instance of how far Beethoven esteemed instrumental music capable of delineating particular situations and even words. "He has," says Ambros,* "with admirable tact, preserved the exact medium between allowing his music to degenerate into a meaningless mass of sound on the one hand (Meyerbeer's 'Struensee!'), and, on the other, maintaining a due subordination of the music to the words of the play" (unlike, for instance, Prince Radziwill's music to 'Faust'). The other pieces are: Clara's two songs, Egmont's monologue, the music which accompanies Clara's death, Egmont's vision of Clara as Liberty, and the triumphal symphony, which also forms the conclusion of the Overture. Beethoven wrote Egmont, as he himself told Rochlitz, with enthusiastic delight—having shortly before made the poet's acquaintance at Teplitz.

A subsequent homage to the great poet was that remarkable composition "*Meeresstille und glückliche Fahrt*, the poems by J. W. von Goethe, set to music and respectfully dedicated to the immortal poet by Ludwig van Beethoven, op. 112." The poems, especially the first, are not well suited

* *Grenzen der Musik und Poesie*. P. 94.

for songs; and the entire composition is, we think, so thoroughly *orchestral* in conception that we are inclined to surmise Beethoven originally intended to write a purely instrumental piece. There was certainly no idea of a programme-overture, of which the poem was the key, in those unsophisticated days. It is well known that Mendelssohn has given a detailed instrumental translation of the poem in his overture of the same name ('A Calm Sea').

Beethoven further wrote three small *pièces d'occasion* for the theatre : the ballet *Prometheus* ('Gli uomini di Prometeo,' 1801), of which the lively compact Overture is well known ; and, subsequently [1812], two Festival plays with chorus and songs by Kotzebue, entitled, ' *The Ruins of Athens*' and '*King Stephen*, Hungary's first benefactor.' Among the pieces contained in the first named of these plays, the choruses are remarkably fine, particularly the wild Dervish chorus and the Turkish march which precedes it. Of the second, the overture alone is known; it is—like the ' Ruins of Athens '—by itself (*i. e.* disconnected from the play), of no great importance as a concert overture. Likewise a festival overture (and what a one !), is that intended for the opening of the new theatre in the Josephstadt [1822]: *Zur Weihe des Hauses* (op. 124)—a splendid and highly imaginative work, yet complete and clear as anything of Mozart's.

Beethoven's best vocal compositions are the very beautiful '*Scotch Songs*' for one voice—(sometimes with one, two, or three others) with pianoforte, violin, and violoncello accompaniment [1815, op. 108]—taken from national melodies. Far more popular—perhaps because less difficult—are the songs and ballads with pianoforte accompaniment alone; especially, *Six Sacred Songs of Gellert* (op. 32, among them the famous 'The heavens declare the glory of God'), '*Adelaide*,' by Matthison (op. 46), *Six Songs of Goethe* (op. 75, 'Know'st thou the land,' 'Heart, my heart whence this emotion,' &c.,) and a collection of songs of Jeitteles, '*An die ferne Geliebte*' (op. 98). What a variety, both of style and character, do we find in these songs! how admirable are declamation, melody, and accompaniment in each one of them! Yet Beethoven—as he observed to Rochlitz in his later years—did not "like writing songs." His grave temperament was as little suited to the action and variety of the opera as his ardent fancy could brook the restraining influence of words in song composition. Thus, in his grand vocal works, as well as in the song proper ('Adelaide' for instance), the instrumental part rivals the vocal in importance and character. In conclusion, however highly we rate his genius as compared with others, we find that Klopstock's epitaph on Em. Bach may even more appropriately be applied to Beethoven:

"He was great in music derived from words, but greater still in that loftier music without words."

Vocal composition, so uncongenial to Beethoven's masculine temperament, was carried to unrivalled perfection by FRANZ SCHUBERT [born at Vienna, January 31st, 1797, died there, November 19th, 1828], who wrote quite in the Beethoven spirit.* His fame having been spread by the celebrated song 'Erlking' [1816], others ('The Wanderer,' 'Lob der Thränen,' 'Suleika,' &c.) appeared in quick succession. But the most remarkable of his vocal compositions are the two great collections of songs: *Die Schöne Müllerin* and *Winterreise*† (both containing as many as forty-four songs), which were probably suggested by Beethoven's collection of songs *An die ferne Geliebte*,' and which, together with others of his finest songs, form, as it were, a worthy supplement to that great master's works—so rich in harmony and profound expression are they, so full of charming variety—sorrow, joy, love, melancholy being in turn depicted in the most vivid and telling manner. The collection of songs entitled *Schwanengesang* contains Schubert's last and best-known songs ('Ständchen,' 'Aufenthalt,' 'Das Fischermädchen,' 'Am Meer,' &c.).

* *Franz Schubert*, von Dr. H. Kreissle von Hellborn. Wien, 1864.
† By W. Müller.

Whereas the old-fashioned *song*, derived principally from the operetta, aimed at a *popular* style (in accordance with the simple verses to which it was set), scarcely any of Schubert's songs or ballads contain the slightest reminiscence of national or popular tunes and rhythm;—of Schubert's six hundred songs, not one (so far as we are aware) has ever become a *popular melody*. The clear, concise form requisite for a popular melody, differs radically from the delicate characteristic delineation, the varied, almost dramatic action—in short, the *subjective* tendency, to which the pianoforte accompaniment lends effect by a local and emotional colouring in keeping with the words and melody. Schubert metamorphosed the poet's thoughts into melody; and, embodying them in sweet vocal strains, created a musical form answering to lyrical poetry (then recently revived in Germany by Goethe, Uhland, Rückert, and Heine), and raised ballad music to one of the highest branches of vocal composition. Schubert's songs — next to Beethoven's sonatas—represent the completion of modern musical art; they are the key-stone to the edifice commenced about a hundred years previously. Oratorio, opera, and symphony had reached their apogee in Handel, Mozart, Beethoven;—it remained for Schubert to complete the grand series of choric works by that branch of musical art which appeals more particularly to individual sentiment, and provides for him who, wearied and disgusted with the ignoble elements which, alas! too frequently degrade the musical profession, turns to the privacy of home and seeks refreshment and solace in what may, in truth, be called " fire-side" music. " Franz Schubert," says the poet Mayrhofer (Schubert's friend and companion), " was my good genius, who faithfully escorted me through life with melodies suited to every occasion, whether of trouble, peace, change, anxiety, sorrow, or joy." Beethoven himself, during his last days on earth, keenly relished Schubert's songs; and Jean Paul requested to hear the 'Erlking' once more before he died. As the bard himself says in the narrative of his vision ('My dream'), even the dying were " moved alternately by love and sorrow."—"And for the second time, with a heart full of unspeakable affection for those who had spurned me, I once more bent my steps to distant lands. For many a long year, I sang songs. If I would sing of love, it turned to pain; and if I would sing of pain, it turned to love. Thus was I swayed alternately by love and pain."

Schubert's *part songs* have only recently been brought into notice. We give the names of those best known and most frequently performed :* Quartets for male voices with pianoforte accompaniment, entitled: '*Das Dörfchen*,' '*Nachtgesang im Walde*,' '*Nachthelle*,' '*Schlacht-*

* NOTE BY THE TRANSLATOR. We believe only in Germany.

lied' (Klopstock) for eight part male choir; 'Ständchen' (Grillparzer) for mezzo-sopran and choir of female voices; 'Miriam's Siegesgesang' for *soli* and choir (the instrumentation by Fr. Lachner); 'Gesang der Geister über den Wassern' for eight part choir and bowed instruments.

Some of Schubert's *pianoforte pieces*, viz., two *Fantasias* in C (arranged for pianoforte and orchestra by Liszt*) and F minor respectively (the latter for two performers), the *Impromptus* and *Moments musicals*, are replete with originality and rhythmic vivacity; but exuberance of fancy too often interferes with just and true proportion in the form in his sonata writings. Schumann—an enthusiastic admirer of Schubert—says, with great truth, of the three last Sonatas (dedicated to himself by the publisher): "Brimming over with invention, never at a loss, always musical and tuneful, Schubert pours forth a rich stream of melody, only occasionally interrupted by emotional interludes, which, however, quickly subside.

---

* Liszt has therein rightly appreciated the symphonic character of this piece; and Schumann's surmise (principally in relation to the Sonata for two performers, op. 140) — that a good number of Schubert's compositions were originally intended for orchestra, but that he had only time for a pianoforte sketch—is, we think, worthy of attention. His active, ever-prolific mind sought an easier mode of expression, for which the pianoforte offered the readiest advantages. Hence, Schubert is the exact opposite of the later musicians, who *endeavoured* to write symphonies, but, in fact, only produced quartets.

This is the impression they made on me. He concludes in such a strain of sweet contentment and ease, as if he were ready to begin again next day." In another passage he writes about the Sonatas (op. 42 and 53) and the *Fantasia* op. 78 as follows: " Without much ado, we may pronounce these three Sonatas splendid; but his *Fantasia Sonata* is, we think, the most perfect in form and matter. After it, comes the one in A minor " (op. 42, but we prefer the second in A minor op. 143, and dedicated to Mendelssohn by the publisher).*

Of Schubert's remaining instrumental composi-

* Equally characteristic is Schumann's opinion of Schubert as a bard and composer in general. " If fecundity is a proof of genius, Schubert is one of the greatest. He would probably in time have set the whole of German literature to music. Whatever he tried, broke forth into music; Æschylus, Klopstock (so difficult to compose) yielded to his touch, yet he discovered unsuspected depths in W. Müller's simple verses." " Schubert will ever be a favourite with the young; he has that for which they most sympathize—ardent affections, bold imagination, vigorous action; he tells them that which they like best—tells them of strange adventures, maidens, love-affairs; he is by no means devoid of wit and humour, but never allows these qualities to destroy the tender impression of his music. At the same time, he excites the imagination as no other, except Beethoven, has ever done. We find reminiscences of Beethoven in his music; but had Beethoven never existed, Schubert would still have been the same, though his peculiar bent might perhaps have been longer in declaring itself (?). Compared to Beethoven, Schubert is a feminine character—more talkative, gentler, tenderer. True, he has powerful movements, nor is he wanting in breadth and vigour; but it is as a gentle entreating woman beside a commanding masculine character—though only in comparison to Beethoven. Compared to others, he is masculine enough; for he is the most vigorous and original of modern composers."

tions, the most remarkable are: the Quartet in D minor for stringed instruments; the Quintet in C major, the (so-called) *Forellen Klavierquatuor*; and, above all, the great *Symphony in C* [written March 1828]—which Mendelssohn and Schumann have pronounced to be the finest orchestral composition after Beethoven. The last (and only one in print) of Schubert's seven Symphonies is a work teeming with imagination; unfortunately, its extreme length deprives it of much of the effect which a due observance of proportion and form would have insured. "As to analysing the several movements, it would afford satisfaction neither to ourselves or others; we must be at the pains of copying the whole Symphony if we would have an idea of its romantic conception. Of the second movement, which appeals to us in such touching strains, we would, however, say a few words. It contains a passage in which a horn is heard, as if a long way off, and always seems to me to come from distant spheres. Hush! one listens and waits as though an angelic visitor were stealing through the orchestra."* That Schubert left a considerable number of works, especially instrumental compositions, unfinished is easily accounted for when we bear in mind his intense activity ever since his thirteenth year. It is a fact, that he never corrected his compositions—he had "no time" for that.

* R. Schumann.

Of nearly twenty—mostly unfinished—*Operas* (Kreissle aptly calls them "song" operas), *Vaudevilles*, and *Melodramas* of Schubert, the operetta, '*Der häusliche Krieg oder die Verschworenen*,' by Castelli, is the only one which has recently been brought on the stage (at Francfort, Vienna, &c.) The greater number have never appeared on the stage,—and are not very likely to do so at a time when plays and operas borrowed from French examples monopolize the boards of first-class theatres. Of the charming and graceful music to '*Rosamunde*' we wrote as follows on the occasion of its performance by the Academy of Music at Coblentz: "Since the 20th of December, 1823, when the following notice appeared in the Viennese papers—'Rosamunde, Princess of Cyprus, drama in four acts, with chorus, incidental music, and dances, by Helmina von Chézy, née Baroness Klenke, music by Herr Schubert'—this music has probably been seldom heard in a concert room. The overstrained sentimentality of Frau von Chézy's style (which caused even Weber's Euryanthe to become '*l'ennuyante*') would alone prevent this piece from keeping the stage. The tuneful *andante* and vigorous *allegro* of the Overture are so delightful, that we cordially echoed the loud 'encore' it called forth. Its loose structure—as compared with the great classical models—reminds one of Weber's style, particularly 'Preciosa,' to which

Schubert's music (inasmuch as it consists of a few songs and choruses) bears some resemblance. We prefer the choruses to the dreamy Moonlight Ballad; and, of them, more especially the chorus of spirits, whose solemn strains are worthy to be compared with the priests' choruses in the Zauberflöte." When a reviewer of far greater merit than ourselves declared of the aforesaid operetta that, notwithstanding its unpretending style, it contains more true beauty than all Wagner's operas put together, we presume we are not far wrong in supposing that Schubert's other dramatic compositions are of sufficient merit to warrant their performance at concerts.

Among Schubert's very numerous sacred compositions (Masses, Oratorios, Hymns, &c.) the *E flat Mass* is considered the finest; this, as well as the grand Symphony, was written in the year of his death.

Schubert was, in every respect, a wonderfully gifted man—admirably calculated to combine Beethoven's depth with Mozart's facility and grace. He was, unfortunately, prematurely snatched away whilst in the full enjoyment of his powers, so that a great many of his works never attained that maturity and finish which we admire in his songs and ballads.

So little is known of Schubert's life, that we borrow from *Kreissle* a few passages bearing on the subject—reserving to ourselves the privilege of some alterations and abbreviations. "His daily work was usually begun in the forenoon, and continued without intermission till dinner-time. When writing, his whole being was absorbed in music; his compositions had such an effect on him, that eyewitnesses affirm they could frequently observe in his flashing eye and altered speech that he was labouring under intense excitement. The rest of the day was almost invariably devoted to social pleasures; and, in summer, to country excursions with his friends. But the slightest encouragement sufficed to awake the slumbering muse; as we learn from the anecdote of his setting Shakespeare's exquisite sonnet ('Hark, hark! the lark at heaven's gate sings,') to music during one of these excursions; after being put on paper it was sung off at once at sight. Whoever gave Schubert lines to be set to music might be certain, if he took a liking for the subject, that the work would be completed in the shortest possible time. Thus the well-known song 'The Wanderer' was written in an incredibly short space of time; likewise the 'Erlking,' which, immediately after perusing Goethe's poem several times in the greatest excitement, he sat down and composed as fast as he could write the notes.

"When visiting at the houses of the great—which he only did when invited for the purpose of accompanying his own songs—Schubert was reserved and shy. No sooner had he finished his exquisite playing of the accompaniment to his songs than he put on a serious face, and withdrew to an adjoining room. Indifferent to applause, he avoided all compliments, and sought only the approbation of his intimate friends. Though he never danced, he was sometimes present at private parties given at friends' houses, when he would obligingly seat himself at the pianoforte and, for hours together, extemporise the most beautiful dance music. (What a contrast to some amateurs, who would not condescend to this, let alone *extemporising*!) Such passages as took his fancy he would repeat, so as to fix them in his memory, and afterwards write them down. When not invited out, he would spend the evening at the inn with his friends—the minority of whom were musicians. At those times he was always communicative, amusing, and witty withal; but downright mirth was foreign to his disposition. Maybe these meetings were prolonged into the small hours of the night, and the bounds of strict sobriety now and then over-passed. As to the stories current of Schubert's intemperate habits, they are, if not absolute inventions, at least gross exaggerations. It is true, Schubert was an epicure* in wine, and frequently indulged in a glass or two more than was good for him. On these occasions he was apt to be noisy, and his society became unpleasant.

"Of the Operas performed at that time, WEIGL's 'Schweizer-familie' interested him greatly; indeed, it was the first opera he had heard. He also admired CHERUBINI's 'Medea,' BOIELDIEU's 'Jean de Paris,' 'Cendrillon,' by ISOUARD, but principally GLUCK's 'Iphigénie en Tauride.' This opera always delighted him; and its noble, lofty simplicity caused him to prefer it to every other. It would appear that the melodious but shallow (?) tunes of the Italian Opera (then at its zenith) had fewer charms for him. For the rest, he admired LABLACHE, and ROSSINI's 'Barbiere di Seviglia'—which never yet displeased any one—was a favourite with him; he also liked some of the pieces in 'Otello.'"

CHAPTER XIV.

The Successors of Mozart. The Italian, French, and German Opera.

"Music has to bewail not only a great genius, but blighted expectations." Such is Grillparzer's* epitaph on Franz Schubert; and, in truth, never had the tuneful muse sustained a heavier loss. Haydn, Mozart, and Beethoven, like Bach and Handel, had gloriously fulfilled the promise of their youth; but to Schubert—the one of all others who might have taken his place beside the three great Viennese musicians—only a short sojourn was allotted here on earth; and the "spark divine," which Beethoven perceived in young Schubert, was destined never to expand into a warmth and light diffusing flame. Consequently, his genius left no impress on the period which immediately succeeded him. Song composition was, as yet, quite a new branch, and Schubert's instrumental—especially his pianoforte—compositions could not hold their ground beside the great

* Grillparzer was the author of several tragedies: *Sappho, Medea,* and others.

classical models. The lofty ideality and harmony of proportion which characterize these latter is wanting in the writings of Schubert, whose tendency is altogether a more *personal* and *realistic* one. His instrumental compositions represent his own feelings exactly as they were, and rarely with the refined, artistic grace which we admire in his songs. They are tinged with the *sensational* (if we may be allowed the term) element of modern literature, which was only fairly recognized and artistically treated by Mendelssohn and, more particularly, Schumann. The *Impromptus* and *Moments musicals* remind one strongly of the Mendelssohnian 'Song without words' and the Schumann *Phantasiestück*. Thus, Schubert denotes the transition between the "classical" period and the "romantic" school of modern days. But his own generation knew but little of Schubert, and Beethoven's lofty originality was unattainable. "Who can write anything after Beethoven?" was Schubert's own exclamation. Accordingly, Haydn and Mozart were the masters whom the next generation took for their models. History cannot take count of the enormous undergrowth of musicians who followed in the steps of these great masters; a few instances, however, may be selected from among the multitude—not so much for their originality, as for their judicious and masterly treatment of the *forms* in music.

In *symphonic* composition we find little that

recommends itself to our notice; for without poetical imagination and powerful resources in harmony—indeed, without a certain *heroic* character—this branch of art is scarcely conceivable. These high qualifications were, however, not vouchsafed to the " Viennese school," and their Symphonies (judging from their purely lyrical style and reduced dimensions) are nothing more than adaptations of the quartet. What Rochlitz misses in the operas of the charming violoncellist and song composer DANZI, viz., brilliancy, originality, distinctness, and character, is wanting also in the symphony writers of the period— Ferd. Ries, F. E. Fesca, Onslow, A. Romberg, &c.; though (as schoolmasters are wont to say of their pupils) they took great pains with their work. The symphonies of George ONSLOW [1784—1853]—still occasionally performed—are models of form, being free from eccentricity, but likewise from imagination, faultless in the detail, . . . in short, plain and straightforward like himself and whatever else is of true British origin. Riehl* is quite right in laying so much stress on the excellence of Onslow's quartet composition in regard to form, as, now-a-days, it is so much the fashion to exalt the " idea" in works of art at the expense of proportion and true beauty. " On the other hand, Onslow's Symphonies," continues Riehl, " are nothing more than quartets for

* *Musik. Characterköpfe.* Vol. i.

orchestra; and of his operas ('*Le Colporteur,*' &c.) the Overture is the best part. Onslow could not get beyond chamber music, as Platen could not get beyond lyrical poetry."

On the whole, the quartet was the best off; the quartets of F. E. FESCA [1789—1826] and ANDREAS ROMBERG [1767—1821] can, in K. M. v. Weber's and Rochlitz' judgment, bear listening to even after those of Haydn and Mozart. ROMBERG's *Cantatas* with orchestral accompaniment': 'The Song of the Bell,' '*Die Kindesmörderin*' (which latter he considered his best composition), 'The Power of Song' by Schiller, '*Die Harmonie der Sphären,*' '*Was bleibt und was schwindet*' are the only songs of the kind still performed and listened to with interest. A modern audience, as a matter of course, finds them old-fashioned and tedious—as it were, "homely fare" for commonplace folks. After all, it is more palatable than many of our modern concoctions. We cannot deny that the fire in the 'Song of the Bell,' for instance, is rendered much too tamely; but it was in accordance with the taste of the day, which preferred melody to the more vigorous movements and *ensembles*. (Our generation must have striking effects—mere beauty of expression is comparatively disregarded.) Of a similar calibre, but more in the modern taste, are the tuneful, melodious Symphonies of J. W. KALLIWODA [born at Prague 1801] which may be reckoned among the best works of their day, but they fail to satisfy the highest requirements of taste. His concert overtures, however, are distinguished by completeness of form and effective arrangement, while the brilliant pianoforte piece '*L'engagement de danse*' should be compared with Weber's far richer and more refined '*Aufforderung zum Tanz.*'

Mozart's influence on form and construction, which we discern in the above-mentioned works, found its most complete expression in *JOH. NEP. HUMMEL* [born at Presburg, November 14th, 1778, died chapel-master at Weimar, October 17th, 1837]. After the three great masters, Hummel is the best pianoforte (not sonata) composer; and, as such, is the founder of a school which has cast into the shade DUSSEK ('*La consolation,*' '*La chasse,*' &c.), STEIBELT, PLEYEL, WÖLFL, &c. His compositions (principally calculated for the display of finished execution) are models in point of form. The most remarkable are his Rondos, and the well-known Polonaise '*La bella Capricciosa.*' Equally admirable are his *concertos*, though the accompaniment is occasionally too florid—a fault from which we must, for very different reasons, exonerate modern *concerto* composers, (who, *en revanche*, make all the more noise in the interludes). Hummel's grand *Septet* for pianoforte, stringed and wind instruments, is generally, and with justice, considered his best work; it is a sterling, as well as **brilliant and flowing** composition, though **not** sufficiently profound to be compared with anything of Beethoven's. In pianoforte playing, especially extempore, Hummel **was** esteemed the first of his day. Even Spohr—so apt to find fault—concedes this much.* With all this, he did what many of Liszt's pupils hold to be incompatible with genius—*he played strictly in time.* "The *tempo rubato*—that insufferable fashion **of hurrying on in one place and** holding back in another, now in vogue, with which a great many pianists (**and almost all singers**) torture real lovers of music—was held in abhorrence by Hummel."† In order to appreciate his *Masses*, one has only to compare them with NEUKOMM's (of the **same** period), still occasionally performed. In after years, Hummel wrote excellent arrange-

---

* "For me, his extempore playing had the greatest charms; no pianoforte player has ever equalled him in this. Being once asked to play waltzes for some dancing that was going on in the adjoining room, he executed a series of *fantasias*, but always in waltz rhythm, so that the dancers were not disturbed. Afterwards, he took easy themes and passages from pieces which I and others had been playing that evening, introduced them into a waltz, and repeated them each time with brilliant and striking variations. He even introduced one of the themes into a fugue, and came out with all his contrapuntal resources; and that without in the least interfering with the enjoyment of the waltzers. Then he went back to the old-fashioned style, and finally went off into a *bravura* surpassing anything that had ever been heard of him. Throughout the *finale*, the airs were clearly discernible, so that the whole thing was a really artistic production." SPOHR's *Autobiography*. Vol. i., p. 206.

† *Musik. Briefe von einem Wohlbekanten.* P. 217 of the second edition. Leipzig, 1860.

ments of some of Haydn's and Mozart's Symphonies, and of the first seven Symphonies of Beethoven (for pianoforte, flute, violin, and violoncello).

The classic MOSCHELES (Professor at the Leipsic Conservatory since 1846) followed up Hummel's style (*concerto* for two pianofortes: '*Hommage à Haendel*,' &c.); but KALKBRENNER (his rival in Vienna in 1823), and yet more THALBERG [born 1812] (unequalled for graceful and brilliant pianoforte execution) restricted themselves solely to manual dexterity on their instrument. In a certain sense, K. M. von WEBER may be regarded as successor of Hummel in pianoforte composition, although he surpasses him in originality, vigour, and variety. His florid Variations, Rondos, Polonaises, and Concertos are well worthy the study of thoroughly efficient pianists, but his Sonatas betray (though not to the same extent as Hummel's) incoherence in the design;—their *Adagios* and *Minuets* are lovely; but in the *Allegro* movements, especially in the secondary subjects, we frequently meet with diffuse, meaningless phrases. The chamber sonata, says Riehl, gave way to the concert sonata.

Compared with Hummel's compositions, the scholastic and formal Sonatas of CLEMENTI [born at Rome 1752, died in London 1832] are of small account. Mozart said—what none but a Mozart could say—he was a mere mechanician. His best work is, in fact, that great collection of Etudes 'Gradus ad Parnassum,' which has, however, been in great measure superseded by those of his pupil, Joh. B. CRAMER. The *Etudes* of this latter are still held in high repute, but his other compositions are, happily for him, forgotten; and of Clementi's remaining pupils only two have distinguished themselves as composers: John FIELD, who wrote *Notturnos* in a sweet and tender strain, and Ludwig BERGER, whose Sonatas were, however, no longer suited to the taste of the day. The pianoforte became the instrument of fashion, and '*L'étude de la vélocité*' the stereotyped compendium of musical tuition. Karl CZERNY [1791—1857], the head of the Viennese pianoforte teachers, was really a good musician and excellent teacher (Liszt and Döhler are among his pupils), but an all too prolific writer (*composer* we may not call him), whose works, written *invitâ Minerva*, and amounting altogether to nine hundred, have, till quite recently, ruled the musical market. "Ever since I can remember, I have given lessons for twelve hours daily; I require four hours for composing, one for reading, one for eating, and six for sleeping." It is a fact, that he had three or four pieces of music lying on as many desks, all of which he worked at at once. With inferior resources and less exertion, this profitable trade was continued by the French firms: François Hünten, Henri Herz and Co., &c.; who, in their turn, are succeeded by Charles Voss, Th. Oesten, Henri Cramer, &c., in Germany.

In vocal composition we distinguish ZUMSTEEG [1760—1802], Schiller's intimate friend in youth. His settings of Bürger's ballads contain several points of interest, especially in the picturesque accompaniments; in other respects they are, because devoid of vigour and originality, now quite antiquated. Among the songs of that period, two of ROMBERG's: 'Know'st thou the Land' and '*Flüchtiger als Wind und Welle*' (Herder) are worthy of notice.

The Opera followed in the footsteps of Mozart's 'Entführung' and 'Zauberflöte;' and, along with it, the Viennese *Volksoper* founded by Dittersdorf, which, on account of its peculiarity, must not remain unnoticed. Karl von DITTERSDORF [properly K. Ditters, born at Vienna November 2nd, 1739, died a retired officer of the Prince Bishop of Breslau's household, October 31st, 1799] introduced, in lieu of the *Vaudeville* and *Liederspiel*,* the genuine *Opéra Comique* with *ensembles* and *finali* into German dramatic music. His best work is '*Doktor und Apotheker*.' "After that, I patched a number of operas to-

* Sort of operetta.

gether," says the poor destitute fellow in his highly interesting autobiography, "of which a good number have been played in various German theatres." Dittersdorf is especially happy in ridiculous and comic scenes, and is, perhaps, the only genuine caricaturist Germany ever produced; he is also an excellent musician, but, unfortunately, too careless of his talents—talents which called forth Gluck's admiration, and are evident in his more serious compositions, such as Oratorios, Symphonies, &c. Although more musically gifted than most of his successors, he was fully conscious of the true aims of art, as is proved by his essay in the *Leipziger Allgem. Musikzeitung* entitled: 'On the limits of the Heroic and Comic in Music.'[*] His comic operas may be called perfect in vivid characteristic and true observance of form in the several pieces of music; Spohr esteems them in regard to "innate musical value" far above Grétry's operettas.

A. KAUER, SCHENK, and the wonderfully prolific WENZEL MÜLLER [1767—1835]—whose clever farces were relished even by the refined Hoffmann—wrote operettas in a light, popular style. The music of these popular composers (who would have been quite equal to a higher walk of art) is, in its way, thoroughly original, and its tone healthy and vigorous, though by no means devoid of the tender element ("So leb denn

[*] *Ueber die Gränzen des Heroischen und Komischen in der Musik.*

wohl, du stilles Haus" and other **songs by Müller** are favourite tunes in Germany). The dry humour of these pieces is immeasurably superior to the allusive verses of the modern burlesque, whose wit consists solely in vulgar puns and alliterations. But they also require a better musical and vocal cast than the small summer theatres of Germany are able to command.

As to the Opera itself, few signs of life were visible in Germany. The greater number of composers (when they did not write Italian Operas) wisely estimated their own powers by restricting themselves to the *Singspiel* modified into Opera form; as, for instance, Joseph WEIGL [born at Eisenstadt, in Hungary, 1766, died at Vienna, February 3rd, 1846], whose '*Schweizerfamilie*' is remarkable for masterly treatment of form. While admiring its delicate, vivid instrumentation and exquisite vocalism, we cannot but protest against the excessive sentimentality which pervades the whole piece. Peter von WINTER [born at Mannheim 1754, died at Munich 1825] aimed at a loftier style of pathos in his opera compositions, but fell short of Mozart in rhythmical structure of the *aria* and dramatic movement. Only one of his operas, '*Das unterbrochene Opferfest,*' **is** still held in repute. It is characterized by the sweetness and clearness of its melodies, by powerful choruses and rich *ensembles*.

Mozart's influence is far more discernible in some of the masters of *Italian* Opera. Increased richness of harmony, fuller instrumentation, and dramatic vigour, imparted a higher style to the Italian branch of operatic art. RIGHINI [1756—1812] almost equalled Mozart in the construction of his vocal pieces, but cannot compare with him for dramatic action. His operas are, in fact,—what Abbé Armand called Italian Operas in Gluck's day— *des concerts dont le drame est le prétexte*. SACCHINI [1735—1786] wrote more in the Gluck style ('*Oedipe à Colone*'). Antonio SALIERI [born at Legnano in the Venetian territory 1750, died at Vienna 1825, after having, during fifty-nine years, served under four Austrian sovereigns] is almost a German in the style and character of his music. He resembled Mozart by adopting a medium between the lyrical tenderness of the Italian school and Gluck's severely chaste style. His French opera '*Les Danaïdes*,' the composition of which was entrusted to him by Gluck (at that time desirous of leaving Paris and returning to Vienna), was, in the first instance, attributed to the latter; and that the Viennese actually preferred his '*Axur, Rè d'Ormus*' to 'Don Giovanni' (as also, by the way, MARTIN's opera '*Una cosa rara*' to 'Figaro') is a fact which speaks for itself. Mosel considers it the finest Italian opera

---

* *Ueber das Leben und die Werke des Anton Salieri.* Wien, 1827.

extant, not excepting Mozart's 'Titus.' His comic operas ('*La Grotta di Trifonio,*' &c.) are, likewise, said to contain many pieces of merit. At the present day, **Salieri's** operas (especially as compared with the vapid music of some of the modern Italian composers) meet with unmerited neglect. Like Winter and Righini, whose vocal exercises are still in repute, Salieri was an excellent and influential master, especially in composition (Weigl, Hummel, Moscheles, Schubert, Liszt, and others, are of the number of his pupils).

Foremost in comic opera stands PAESIELLO [1741—1816], Cimarosa's rival, and, like him, remarkable for dramatic action in the *finali*. In Germany, his favourite operas were '*La bella Molinara*' and '*Il Rè Teodoro in Venezia.*' FIORAVANTI [born 1764, died 1837] displayed considerable talent for comedy; his opera '*Le Cantatrici villane*' was for a long time the stock piece of German theatres. Almost as superior to Fioravanti as Mozart to Dittersdorf, is CIMAROSA [born at Naples 1755, died at Venice, January 11th, 1801] a genuine master of musical comedy. Like Mozart, he excels in those parts of an opera which decide its merit as a work of art, viz., the *ensembles* and *finali*. His admirable, and by no means antiquated, opera '*Il Matrimonio segreto*' (the charming offspring of his " secret marriage " with the Mozart opera) is a model of exquisite and graceful comedy. The Overture bears a striking resemblance to that of 'Figaro,' and the instrumentation of the whole opera is highly characteristic, though not so prominent as in Mozart. Especially delightful are the secret love scenes—written evidently *con amore*, the composer having practised them many a time in his youth. On the occasion of its first performance at Vienna [1791] the opera was repeated by imperial command; and at Naples it was performed fifty-seven times consecutively.

Between Cimarosa and Rossini we find a stationary period, represented chiefly by F. Paër and Simon Mayer. The operas ('*Sargino*,' '*Camilla*,' '*Agnese*,' '*I Fuorusciti*,' &c.) which PAER [1771—1839] furnished to order for various royal personages (of whom Napoleon was the last) are, in accordance with the style of the day, brilliant and flowing but vapid and meaningless. His imitation of Mozart's forms is exclusively external, consisting principally in enriched instrumentation. Even less remarkable was Simon MAYER [1763—1845], who endeavoured to germanize the Italian Opera. It sounds curious to hear G. Weber, the thorough bass master, assert that "Germany gave to England a Handel, to France a Gluck, and to Italy a Simon Mayer!"

To these mediocre composers succeeded a great and original genius — GIOACCHINO *ROSSINI* [born at Pesaro in the Romagna, February 29th, 1792].* Rossini set at nought the efforts of his immediate predecessors to improve the **national music** by foreign adaptations, and even ventured to caricature the **renowned** Paesiello (who had composed the 'Barbiere' before him) in the *rococco* songs of the two old people (Bartolo's *arietta* and Marcellina's *aria*). The "saucy favourite of the **graces**" **threw** precepts to the four winds (" *Che cosa? parole? Effetto! Effetto!*") and acknowledged no other schoolmaster than his **own genius** and experience. Learned Germans might shake their heads and talk about his superficial work, unlawful modulations and orchestral effects, **his** *crescendo* and *stretto* passages, **and even the tameness** and uniformity of his melodies—about want of artistic finish in short; all these objections **were** "dispelled by Rossini's opera airs as if they were mere delusions of the fancy."† Everybody was enchanted, even Oulibicheff (more candid than most people) admitted, that when listening **for** the first time to an opera of Rossini's he forgot, for the time being, all he had ever known, admired, played, or **sung**—it seemed as though he had never heard music before. And no wonder: **the main** charm of Rossini's operas was melody—

* *Rossini's Leben und Treiben vornehmlich* **nach den Nachrichten des Herrn.** v. *Stendhal* (Vie de Rossini, 2 vols. Paris, **1824**), with opinions of contemporary writers on his music, by **Amadeus Wendt.** Leipzig, 1824.

† R. Wagner.

pleasing, grateful melody, rendered by the singer's art in such a manner as to dazzle and utterly preclude sober judgment. Towards this object, viz., fluent melody and vocalisation, Rossini managed to render, not only the orchestra, but even the chorus (almost entirely disregarded by his predecessors) serviceable, by frequently replacing the full-voiced *finale* with a *bravura* air and chorus ("*aria col pertichini*"). Finally, to insure effect in any and every case, he wrote out the vocal embellishments (*fioriture*) in detail (whereas formerly these were left to the taste and judgment of the vocalist); in doing which, however, he took into consideration the individual capabilities of those he wrote for. Thus, he avoided *cantabile* pieces, because Mad. Colbran, his *prima donna* (and wife into the bargain) was no longer in her *première jeunesse*, and, consequently, plain long drawn notes were unsuited to her. With such faultless *mise-en-scène*, Rossini's operas went the round of all the theatres in Europe. His monopoly of the opera stage—unprecedented in the annals of art—occurred, moreover, during the Restoration [1813—1830], when, after the troublous times which preceded it, people were only too susceptible to the charm of superficial, pleasing impressions. Tancredi's air "*Di tanti palpiti*" was the favourite song of the period—a period of political exhaustion and musical poverty; and, certes, it is no mere coincidence that, contemporary with Rossini's operas, dance music enjoyed a pre-eminence of its own in STRAUSS and LANNER at Vienna, though their successors, GUNG'L, LUMBYE, LABITZKY, MUSARD, &c., have worthily represented this light branch of musical art.

Having first tried his hand at farces and one-act operas, Rossini produced [1812] an opera *buffa* ('*La Pietra di Paragone*') at Milan, '*Tancredi*' and a *buffa* opera, '*L'Italiana in Algieri*,' at Venice. From 1815—1822 he wrote for the stage manager Barbaja at Naples his far-famed opera '*Il Barbiere di Seviglia*' (the Overture of which was taken from his opera *seria*, '*Elisabetta*,' as he had only fourteen days wherein to complete the whole opera); afterwards: *Otello, Cenerentola, La Gazza Ladra, La Donna del Lago, Moisè in Egitto*, &c.; for Vienna: *Zelmira* [1822], *Semiramide* [1823], and, finally, for the *Grand Opéra* at Paris, *Le Siége de Corinthe* and *Guillaume Tell* [1829].

Rossini is universally allowed to be unequalled in genuine *buffa* Opera; but he is quite as great in Opera *seria*, into which he infused the energy of the *buffa* ('Semiramide,' 'Moisè,' 'Otello'). Rossini is altogether the most comprehensive, and at the same time national, composer the modern Italian Opera has ever had—he is the Mozart of Italy. Conceited German reviewers, however, were never weary of denying to this highly gifted man invention, depth, and character;

but they had to retract everything when 'Guillaume Tell' was brought out. "Of all that peculiarly characterizes Rossini's earlier operas, nothing is discoverable in 'Tell;' there is none of his usual mannerism; but, on the contrary, unusual richness of form, and careful finish of detail combined with grandeur of outline. Meretricious embellishments, shakes, runs, and cadences are carefully avoided in this work, which is natural and characteristic throughout; even the melodies have not the stamp and style of Rossini's earlier tunes, but only their graceful charm and lively colouring. In short, Rossini seems metamorphosed, as it were by a magician's wand, from the Rossini of 'Tancredi' and 'Otello' into an entirely different artistic personage. If Rossini's extraordinary talents could ever be doubted, this work would furnish undeniable proofs to the contrary."* In his Italian operas, and, we think, yet more in the *Stabat Mater* ("*le joli Stabat*") Rossini remained, of course, what he always was— essentially Italian; and, why indeed should he, like Simon Mayer, deny his country? "Profound study and workmanship are rarely to be met with in his work; not because he was unequal to it, but because he would not take the trouble. As it was, his audience was always pleased, and applauded him."

* AMBROS. *Culturhistorische Bilder aus dem Musikleben der Gegenwart*, p. 41.

'Guillaume Tell' was the last song of Pesaro's minstrel. Resigning the field of his labours to others, the great *maestro* lives in retired ease at his villa at Passy near Paris. All we ever hear of him is now and then a small *pièce d'occasion*, or some humorous observation regarding modern musical art.

BELLINI [born at Catania in Sicily 1802, died at Puteaux near Paris 1835] restricted the opera mainly to brilliant vocalisation in the solo parts. He endeavoured to adopt the grave character of the *Opera seria*, but possessed little or no dramatic talent; his operas are essentially lyrical. Herein he mistook the nature of the genus; and, accordingly, deviated more and more from the true aim of the Opera. The doleful, almost sickly sentimentality which prevails in '*Capuletti e Montecchi*,' '*La Sonnambula*,' and his other operas ('*Il Pirata*,' '*La Straniera*,' '*Beatrice di Tenda*,' &c.) has, in spite of the sweetness of the airs, a monotonous and tedious effect. His elegiac pathos rises to powerful and genuine emotion in *Norma*—his *chef-d'œuvre*—which is, notwithstanding the weakness of its choruses, the last of the veritable *Opera seria*. His immediate successor, DONIZETTI [born at Bergamo 1797, died there 1848], was, even for an Italian, far too careless of his very superior talents. From 1822 to 1844 he wrote upwards of sixty operas;—when required, he could even write a whole act in one day. We consider 'ced *Lucrezia Borgia*' his best *Opera seria*; in '*Lucia di Lammermoor*,' '*Belisario*,' '*Anna Bolena*,' '*Marino Faliero*,' &c., the march and dance tunes of the music too often afford a strange contrast to the action of the piece; but of both the first named works the *ensembles* are good. Of '*La Favorite*' (written for the Parisian stage) Riehl says: " it is superbly tedious." Donizetti did violence to his Italian nature in writing this opera; Bellini, likewise, in his last opera, '*I Puritani*' (written for Paris), approached the French style; but it remained for Verdi (whom we shall consider hereafter in connection with Meyerbeer) to give musical expression to the modern school of French romance. Although inferior to Rossini in vivacity and colouring, Donizetti displays vigour and originality in comic opera ('*L'Elisire d'Amore*,' '*Don Pasquale*,' '*La Fille du Régiment*,' &c.)

MERCADANTE ('Il Giuramento'), CARAFA ('Masaniello'), and others, were but weak imitators of Rossini, who endeavoured to conceal poverty of invention by richness of instrumentation. In general, modern Italian composers are the reverse of Rossini in this respect:—that their lively pieces, as compared with the *cantabile* pieces of the same opera, are, for the most part, inferior and frequently trivial; they cannot do anything except in dance rhythm; accordingly, the manufacturers of *Grandes Fantaisies sur des motifs de l'opéra* .... have easy work of it.

The Mozart influence is not discernible in Rossini's successors, though he himself esteemed Mozart the first of musicians (his own 'Barbiere' he called a musical farce, but 'Le Nozze di Figaro' a *dramma giocoso*). On the other hand, the representatives of the *French* school prior to Auber—Spontini, Cherubini, and Boieldieu—turned their whole attention to the development of Gluck's and Mozart's principles.* As a worthy successor of Gluck we would cite, in the first instance, MEHUL [born 1763, died at Paris 1817], whose sterling opera '*Joseph*' K. M. von Weber admires for its thoroughly biblical expression and discreet management in the instrumental parts. Deserving of mention is his programme-Overture '*Une chasse du jeune Henri*.'

GASPARO *SPONTINI* [born at Jesi in the Papal States, Nov. 14th, 1784, died there January 29th, 1851] is the foremost and most gifted of Gluck's successors. He has not, as is frequently asserted, merely polished and adorned Gluck's style, but,

---

* *De l'Opéra en France*, par M. CASTIL-BLAZE. 2 vols. Paris, 1820. This work is not so much a history as a cleverly executed conception of the French Opera as it ought to be. This well-written book failed however in its principal object—that of improving the style of the so-called *Grand Opéra*.

on the contrary, has endowed it with vigour and action, and altered and modernized it to suit his views, the people for whom he wrote, and the requirements of modern stage practice, in a manner at once original and pleasing. To the majestic repose and lofty ideality of the Gluck drama—so thoroughly commensurate to antique tragedy — Spontini added that indispensable feature of modern opera, viz.—dramatic action. Remarkable alike for grandeur of conception and delicacy of detail, powerful delineation and graceful melody, his music, when the context requires it, is replete with brilliancy and military splendour. "He is more successful in the delineation of masses and groups," says Riehl,* " than in the portrayal of emotional scenes (?); his rendering of the national struggle between the Spaniards and Mexicans in *Cortez* is, for instance, admirable. He is, likewise, most (?) successful in the management of large masses in the instrumentation. In this respect he was, like Napoleon, a great tactician."

On the other hand, ' *La Vestale* '—in which the French ideal of "*gloire*" has found its highest expression—his *chef-d'œuvre*, displays Spontini's talents in a new light. His portrayal of character, and truthful delineation of passionate emotion in this opera are masterly indeed. The

* *Musik Characterköpfe.* Vol. i.

subject of 'La Vestale' (which resembles that of 'Norma,' but how differently treated!) is tragic and sublime, as well as intensely emotional. Julia, the heroine, a prey to guilty passion; the severe, but kindly high priestess; Licinius, the adventurous lover, and his faithful friend Cinna; pious vestals, cruel priests, bold warriors, and haughty Romans are represented with statuesque finish and relief. Both these works, 'La Vestale' [1807] and 'Cortez' [1809], are among the finest that have ever been written for the stage; they are remarkable for naturalness and sublimeness—qualities lost sight of in the noisy instrumentation of his later works (but noisy only as compared with those of contemporary stage writers). Unfortunately, they can only be performed in the largest theatres, and great tragic singers are rarely to be met with now-a-days.

The opera '*Olympia*' [1819] (principally based on splendour of effect) not obtaining the success which he had anticipated, Spontini quitted Paris, and was appointed General Music Director at Berlin. But the grand heroic spirit which animated his earlier noble creations appears to have deserted him in the German Athens; for there, he could produce nothing better than showy Court and gala operas ('Nurmahal,' 'Alcidor,' 'Agnes von Hohenstaufen'). One work only of intrinsic merit did he bequeath—

when compelled by continued annoyances from the Berlin press to resign his appointment—one in honour of the Prussian name :—'Borussia,' a song for male voices with orchestra.

MARIA LUIGI *CHERUBINI* [born at Florence, September 8th, 1760, died at Paris, March 16th, 1842) who, if not equal to the greatest masters (for in every style he fell short of perfection), was at least a kindred genius and worthy representative of the Haydn and Mozart school. Having heard his *chef-d'œuvre*, '*Les Deux Journées*' [performed for the first time June 1800], we are quite able to understand why his operas are no longer performed in France, and rarely in England and Germany. This opera is, as Riehl expresses it, "emotion dramatized," and that in accordance with nature and truth; but for stage effect, especially now-a-days, we think it is too finely chiselled, and the characters are not drawn with sufficient clearness. The music itself is perfect, being equally distinguished for tenderness and expressiveness as for noble simplicity and purity of form. How would a modern composer, had it fallen to his lot to compose "the days of danger," have filled the house, from gallery to pit, with fear and trembling!

Of Cherubini's remaining works (among which *Medea* and *Faniska* are the most remarkable), only the *Overtures* are known. The vigorous and tuneful one to *Lodoiska*, those of **Medea** (in which emotional expression is so admirably treated), of the 'Abencerages,' of 'Anacreon,' &c. All these Overtures are replete with vigour and character; their admirably drawn outline, exquisite finish, and instrumentation cause them to be reckoned models of their kind.

What was wanting to Cherubini's operas was only too prevalent in his sacred music; his Masses, especially, wherever the text afforded the slightest opening, are too dramatic; some of the pieces are quite operatic—nay theatrical—in style. Thus it came to pass, as a matter of course, that modern church music found its way from the church to the concert room. Accordingly, it was written with a view to this, and—as a reviewer observed of a modern requiem—presented to the listener's imagination a rich and picturesque array of tones in lieu of the former close connection of the music with the liturgy. If (in opposition to the one-sided views of some critics) we admit the lawfulness of this tendency of modern Church music in consideration of the circumstances of the age, we must allow that Cherubini's expressive as well as brilliant *Mass in D minor*, and especially his *Requiem in C minor* [1810], are noble and sublime conceptions. Notwithstanding the most lavish employment of orchestral and choral resources, these works are characterized by lofty simplicity, exquisite proportion, distinctness of form, and powerful imagination. When the

'Requiem' was about to be performed [1835, in honour of Boieldieu's memory], the clergy objected to the employment of female voices: Cherubini, accordingly, wrote a second requiem, similar to the first, for a choir of male voices. Of the ' *Hymnes Sacrés*' (of which the composition was probably suggested by Marcello's Psalms which Cherubini undertook to edit) we distinguish two of the best known : the *Ave Maria* for treble voice with hautboy *obligato* is, in truth, a piece of vanity and affectation—a mere theatrical display; but the four part *Pater noster* (with the exception of the secular tone of its conclusion) is not devoid of Church-like expression and genuine devotion.

Taken altogether, Cherubini's music is characterized by masculine vigour and earnestness. It is of a noble calibre, and savours more of German depth than Italian sweetness, and that in a greater degree even than Mozart's music; for which reason, Beethoven reckoned him "the most estimable of living composers." But the French said—what Napoleon said of the funeral Cantata for General Hoche—that Cherubini was too learned, especially in his operas—in other words, too German.

Cherubini's pupil BOIELDIEU [born at Rouen, December 16th, 1775, died at his country seat Jarcy near Paris, October 9th, 1834] inclined to the light French style. His operas, '*Jean de*

Paris' [1812] and '*La Dame blanche*' [1825]—the result of long years' practice in the national operetta ('Le Calife de Bagdad,' 'Ma tante Aurore,' &c.) and the study of Mozart—are the best French operas extant; they are admirable and thoroughly popular works. While the musician's taste is gratified by the carefully executed *ensembles* (of which the second *finale* to 'La Dame blanche' is absolute perfection), by the neatness and gracefulness of the instrumentation, and correctness of the composition throughout ("which alone can insure perpetuity to a musical work"),* the popular taste is delighted by the charming ballads and songs, which have, as it were, become its inheritance; even the airs are more popular in Germany than those of almost any other opera. Not long since, 'La Dame blanche" was performed in Paris for the thousandth time.

Another pupil of Cherubini's was Boieldieu's successor, AUBER [born at Caen in Normandy, January 29th, 1784, since 1842 Director of the *Conservatoire* at Paris]. He created that opera style which corresponds to (while frequently taking for its subject) the tales and comedies of Eugène Scribe, as also to Parisian life and taste, and in which the simple unadorned expression of feeling makes way for the artificial tone of polite society. Auber is the offspring of modern French

* K. M. VON WEBER.

civilisation, to which the conventionalities of life are, as it were, second nature; and although far less original, he is in his best works (*Le Maçon, Fra Diavolo, La Part du Diable, Lestocq, Le Domino noir,* &c.) quite as *real* as the easy going jovial Rossini is in his. Auber's opera music is, we admit, by no means profound; on the contrary, it is too frequently superficial—dancing, as it were, " on the light fantastic toe ;" but, generally speaking, pleasing, full of lively coquetry, piquant, and withal gracefully frivolous (take, for instance, the undressing scene in 'Fra Diavolo')—in short, the genuine expression of modern Parisian life. It addresses itself, therefore, principally to the French *esprit*, and the clever stage performance of the French *acteurs chantants* is as requisite to this light style as florid Italian vocalisation is to the Rossini opera.

Encouraged by success, Auber, unfortunately, exhausted his powers by all too prolific exercise, and repeated himself in a series of works each one inferior to the last, till, at length, the graceful opera composer degenerated into "*un habile faiseur d'opéras.*" But true genius is never exhausted; it either goes on producing like Mozart, or leaves off at the right time like Rossini.

Immeasurably superior to the rest of his compositions is the bold revolutionary opera, '*La Muette de Portici*' (*Masaniello*) [1827]—a truly grand conception in which the composer has quitted the gay field of Parisian society for the more stirring scenes of political excitement. The music which accompanies the dumb girl's pantomime, the national dances, and the insurrectionary crowd is perhaps unequalled for powerful and passionate expression. 'Masaniello' is the most effective of show operas; its performance at Brussels in 1830 was the signal for revolt.

Of Auber's successors, HÉROLD [born of German parents at Paris 1791, died 1833], by returning to a simpler form of opera and developing his own genial inspirations (advantages apparent in his pretty opera '*Marie*') might have been the man to restore the opera—now degenerated to a mere *spectacle*. Unfortunately, he understood the times better than he understood himself. His endeavour to improve upon Auber's talent and manner is only too evident in his shallow and noisy opera, '*Zampa*' [1830]. His last opera, '*Le Pré aux Clercs*,' is remarkable for the brilliant air for treble and violin *obligato*. ADOLPHE ADAM [born at Paris 1803, died there 1855], who possessed technical abilities, but "*sans la moindre prétention au style et au sentiment*," repeats Auber's opera style in the weakest of imitations ('*Le Postillon de Lonjumeau*,' '*Le Brasseur de Preston*,' &c.). The same may be said of the English composer BALFE, whose vapid, flimsy operas ('The Bohemian Girl,' 'The Castle of Aymon,' &c.) are nothing but effete imitations of French and Italian opera writers. He is inferior to WALLACE ('Maritana,' 'The Amber Witch,' 'Lurline,' &c.), in the instrumentation of his pieces as well as in *ensembles*. JUL. BENEDICT [born at Stuttgardt 1804], in his operas ('The Gipsy's Warning,' 'The Rose of Erin,' and 'The Bride of Song'), as well as in the popular cantata, 'Undine,' confines himself to the lighter style; while, in our opinion, MACFARREN's attempt to revive the old English music in modern opera is scarcely a successful one.

Somewhat better than the foregoing is the German FRIEDRICH VON FLOTOW [born at Teutendorf in Mecklenburg 1811], whose operas, *Stradella, Martha,* and *Indra* (written for the French stage), are cleverly and judiciously adapted to the taste of his audience. According to the severe standard of high-art critics, his talent is esteemed of the weakest; but we think he is entitled to a milder verdict, for the distinguishing peculiarities of French life are so genially rendered in his works (shall we call it the German element frenchified, or the French element germanized?) that the result is decidedly pleasing, and unquestionably—popular. To the external brilliancy of Auber's opera style he has added the two most effective ingredients of Iffland's plays, viz., homely and familiar, as well as touching scenes.

The play-going public likes to see every-day life, its familiar in and out-door scenes ("*nam his plebecula gaudet*") represented on the stage with all the embellishment of music and scenic effect. But, along with the absurdest trivialities, we discover many traits of genuine feeling, and the connoisseur—unless he be all too captious and severe—cannot but be struck with the easy and lively dramatic action, pretty melody, and graceful instrumentation.*

Auber was less successful with his later "*grands*" operas (*Gustave, ou le Bal masqué, Les Diamants de la Couronne, Le Lac des Fées*, &c.)— partly because a new composer had arisen—one who far surpassed him in clever adaptation of *all* possible stage effects, viz., Giacomo MEYERBEER [properly Jakob Meyer Beer, born at Berlin, Sept. 5th, 1791, died at Paris, May 2nd, 1864]. In opera composition Meyerbeer is the very caricature of the universal Mozart; he is the cosmopolitan Jew, who hawks his wares among all

---

* "For the rest, mediocre productions are not to be despised, so long as they are free from affectation. We must have something of all sorts—something wherewith to pass the time pleasantly and without intellectual exertion. Moreover, a large portion of the public can appreciate nothing but mediocre productions. For which reason, I would not be hard on a great many favourite songs and pieces, as is the case with too many connoisseurs. All we have a right to expect is, that those who can understand and appreciate nothing but second-rate music should abstain from passing judgment on grand and original compositions."—THIBAUT. *Ueber Reinheit der Tonkunst.* P. 103.

nations indifferently, and does his best to please customers of every kind. He endeavoured to conceal absence of originality, vigour, and style —all too apparent in his patch-work melodies— by indefatigable accumulation of every musical and non-musical means of effect within his reach; and, to do him justice, in his five-act monster operas, '*Robert le Diable*' [1831], '*Les Huguenots*' [1836], and '*Le Prophète*' [1849]— mainly written with a view to scenic effect—, he has succeeded only too well. In face of such meretricious advantages as these, it matters little to us whether Meyerbeer improved the opera in a *dramatic* sense; if so, the advantages are wholly *external*. The character of the Meyerbeer drama is, as compared with the weak, sentimental productions of his immediate predecessors (especially in Italy), energetic and vigorous, but overwhelmed by the splendour of the *mise-en-scène*. Music cannot maintain its concrete beauty and value with such elaborate and heavy theatrical decoration, and these overstrained exertions in search of effect are prejudicial to that which alone can give duration to a work of art, viz.—nature and sentiment. In spite of the intense exertions of musical abilities of a very high order, Meyerbeer produced nothing great, original, or of a novel kind; his operas leave on the mind of the more intelligent listeners an impression of mingled admiration and contempt.

There is no need to enter into the respective merits of these works; after 'Robert le Diable' and 'Les Huguenots' (both which to a certain extent and under certain conditions we admire), every opera of Meyerbeer's, ('*Ein Feldlager in Schlesien*' [1844], afterwards remodelled into '*Vielka*' for the Viennese, and '*L'Etoile du Nord*' for the Parisian stage; the music to his brother Michel Beer's tragedy of *Struensee* [1846]; '*Le Prophète*,' '*Dinorah, ou le Pardon de Ploërmel*,' [1859]) abounds more and more in studied effects and strange, unnatural combinations. Phantom nuns dancing, girls bathing, sunrise, skating, gunpowder explosions, a king playing the flute behind the scenes, the *prima donna* leading a goat, &c.—all this, and more to boot, has been dragged into his operas, and cost the composer himself no trifling sum. The apparently flourishing house of Scribe and Meyerbeer could not even await the selling off, but came to a sudden smash. "Meyerbeer's operas left the impression that it was impossible to keep going on in this manner without doing something for the higher requirements of art; for, notwithstanding the composer's remarkable talent for musical drama, his operas contain sometimes too much, sometimes too little,—too much in the subject-matter, external adornment, and effective 'situations,'— too little in the absence of poetry, ideality, and sentiment (which are essential to a work of art), as well as in the unnatural and constrained combinations of the plot."*

Whereas even the better part of the press considers the 'Huguenots' to be a superior and remarkable work, we can only reply that the several (and frequently considerable) beauties of this opera (the page's *cavatina*, Margareta's *aria*, her duet with Raoul, the finale of the second act, the grand duets in the third and fourth acts, and the benediction of the swords) cannot blind us to its defects. History **must not view the** subject she contemplates "from **the perspective of the**

---

* Vischer. *Aesthetik.* Vol. iii., p. 1149.

"All honour to great Meyerbeer!" is, of course, the watchword of his party; but Mendelssohn, who had no part with them, held a different opinion. Concerning *Robert le Diable* (of which, however, we cannot but admire the rich and masterly instrumentation), he wrote to Immermann (the poet), from Paris, as follows: "The subject is of the romantic order, *i.e.*, the devil appears in it (which suffices the Parisians for romance and imagination). Nevertheless **it** is very bad, and, were it not for two brilliant seduction scenes, **there** would not even **be** effect. The devil is altogether a poor **devil who** appears dressed **as** a knight in order to seduce his son—Robert, a Norman knight, and in love with a Sicilian princess; **he succeeds by persuading** him to gamble away all his money and personal **property,** *i.e.* his sword; after which, he causes him **to commit sacrilege,** gives him an enchanted twig, which takes him to the **chamber** of the aforesaid princess, and renders him irresistible. All **this the son does** willingly enough; but when, at last, he is to sell himself **to his father,** Scribe brings in a peasant girl, who has in her possession **the will of** Robert's deceased mother, which she reads to him, and thereby **places** him in such a state of indecision, that the devil has to disappear **below the boards** at midnight without having gained his point; whereupon Robert marries the princess, the peasant girl being **a** sort of guardian **angel**. The devil's name is Bertram. I cannot imagine any music **for such** a cool transaction as

present and immediate past;"* it is her duty to mete out judgment according to the true standard of beauty and fitness in art. 'Les Huguenots' and that far weaker production the 'Prophète,' are, we think, all the more reprehensible (now-a-days, especially, when too much stress is laid on the *subject* of a work, and, consequently, on the *libretto* of an opera) because the Jew has, in these pieces, ruthlessly dragged before the footlights two of the darkest pictures in the annals of Catholicism, nor has he scrupled to bring high mass and chorale on the boards. "He has the ballet on the proscenium, with the organ behind the scenes."†

---

this; and, accordingly, the opera does not please me; it is devoid of sentiment and feeling, and I do not even find it effective. People admire the music, but where there is no warmth and truth I cannot even form a standard of criticism." Mendelssohn wrote to his father about this opera as follows: "When, in *Robert le Diable*, nuns appear one after another and endeavour to seduce the hero, till at length the lady abbess succeeds; when the hero, aided by a magic branch, gains access to the sleeping apartment of his lady love, and throws her down, forming a *tableau* which is applauded here and will perhaps be applauded in Germany; and when, after that, she implores for mercy in an *aria*; when, in another opera, a girl undresses herself, singing all the while that she will be married at this time to-morrow—it may be effective, but I find no music in it. For it is vulgar, and if such is the taste of the day and therefore necessary, I prefer writing sacred music."

K. M. von Weber, Meyerbeer's fellow-pupil under Abbé Vogler, complained, in those days, that in his Italian Operas ('*Emma di Resburgo*,' '*Il Crociato in Egitto*,' &c.) "he prostituted his profound, admirable, and German talent for the applause of the crowd which he ought instead to have despised."

* *Berliner National-Zeitung.* † Riehl.

What Meyerbeer achieved on a large, Jacques OFFENBACH [from Cologne, but naturalized in Paris] attempted on a small scale; and he has done his very best to corrupt the taste of the masses to its core. Not content with the success which his charming operettas ('*Le Mariage aux Lanternes,*' '*La Fille d'Elizondo,*' &c.) met with, he started "burlesque operas" (written for his own opera company *Les Bouffes Parisiens*), such as '*Orphée aux Enfers,*' '*Geneviève de Brabant,*' '*Le Pont des Soupirs,*' &c.—a style, of which the object is to parody the Opera *seria*, whether "classical" or "romantic." When the mythological *Opera seria* was in its prime, satire—within due bounds—may have been in good taste; but now, it is nothing but a coarse mockery of the ideal in art. It is characteristic of this low-bred genus that the imitation of animals (Jupiter's "fly" song in 'Orphée,' the 'Miau' song in 'La Chatte métamorphosée en Femme,' cackling of hens in 'Genofeva,' &c.) always obtains the greatest applause—animals have become men, and men, animals. 'Orphée,' in especial, owes its chief popularity to the political and satirical allusions with which it abounds, as well as to its scenery and decorations; as for the music of this *opus*, nearly all of it is condensed into a set of quadrilles; it is made up almost entirely of commonplace dance tunes, and is, in short, the music of *casinos* and gin-palaces. We cannot but augur badly for the future of the drama, as well as for art in general, when we find this heterogeneous, silly stuff actually obtaining enthusiastic applause.

In comic opera (*L'Eclair, Les Mousquetaires de la Reine*, &c.) HALÉVY [properly Levy, 1799—1862] resembled Auber; but in the grand opera, his brother Israelite Meyerbeer. Riehl (who delights in comparisons) says he is a commentary on Meyerbeer, as Marschner is on Weber. We consider this opinion far too favourable to Halévy. His principal work, '*La Juive*,' is a tedious, heavy opera teeming with Marschner and Wagner recitative;—in a musical point of view, poor, and in moral, objectionable.

Not so much in Meyerbeer's style, though scarcely more original, is GOUNOD [born 1818] who has with true French frivolity, *operatized* Goethe's Faust for the delectation of the multitude. Margaret is a sentimental Parisian *grisette*; Faust, a wild *Quartier Latin* student; and so on to the end of the chapter. What would Goethe—who thought Mozart the man to compose his 'Faust' —have said to this! "And though the jaded opera *habitué*, thirsting for novelty, may smile at the pedantic litterateur who shakes his head at Gounod's 'Margareta' and Offenbach's 'Orphée,' and thinks of Beethoven's 'Fidelio' and Mozart's 'Figaro'—it is a disgrace that we should be continually importing such rubbish, while our good old native stores lie mouldering on dusty shelves."* Gounod's latest operas are 'La Reine de Saba' and 'Mireille,' of which the female choruses are the best part.

Giuseppe VERDI [born at Roncole in Lombardy, 1814]—far superior in musical ability to the above-named Frenchman—has resuscitated the "fearful and horrible" tales of Victor Hugo and Dumas *fils* in his operas, '*Ernani*' [1844], '*Rigoletto*' [1851], '*Il Trovatore,*' '*La Traviata*' [both in 1853], which now hold the stage in almost all the cities of Europe. If Verdi were as sound and conscientious as he is a prolific composer, he might have restored the Italian stage—sorely deteriorated since Rossini's time—to something of its pristine purity and excellence. As it is, he has, by his fatal connexion with France, rendered his country the worst possible service. Exquisite vocalisation—the pride and glory of the Italian stage—is absolutely threatened with annihilation in the noisy clamour of his operas. Verdi is—*i. e.* as far as an Italian can be—the successor of Meyerbeer, having all his defects and but few of his merits. Of Verdi's earlier operas ('*Nabucodonozor,*' '*I Lombardi,*' '*I due Foscari,*' &c.), and those whose subjects are taken from the dramas of Shakespeare and Schiller ('*Macbeth,*' '*I Masnadieri,*' '*Luisa Miller*')—the least said

---

* *Deutsche* **Musik-Zeitung.** This somewhat too severe verdict refers rather to Gounod's superficial treatment of Goethe's profound poem than to any defect in the music, which is not only beautiful, but, occasionally, even sublime.

the better. Nor are his latest productions, '*Un Ballo in Maschera,*' '*La Forza del Destino,*' &c. much to be commended.

As was the case in every other country, so also in Germany, did Rossini's operas hold the sovereignty of the stage; yet they exerted no influence whatever on musical art and artists in Germany. Even before Rossini had taken Vienna by storm, Weber's *Freischütz* created such a sensation at Berlin [June 18th, 1821] as could not fail to decide the tendency of the German Opera during the period that was to follow.

KARL MARIA von *WEBER** [born at Eutin in Holstein, December 18th, 1786, died in London a few weeks after the first performance of 'Oberon,' June 5th, 1826] is, above all, a thoroughly *German* composer. As his noble battle songs (from Körner's '*Leier und Schwert*') had been the means of spreading patriotic feeling, during the war of liberation, far and wide through Germany, so did his operas embody the spirit of the romantic school of poetry (which originated in those stirring times) in the brightest and most popular form imaginable. "Weber's music to *Preciosa* (the subject of which is taken from a novel of Cervantes) is an admirable rendering of

---

* *The Life of Carl Maria von Weber.* From the German of his son, Baron von WEBER. By J. PALGRAVE SIMPSON. 2 vols., post 8vo. Chapman and Hall.

the true spirit of Spanish romance—so much admired and so rarely attained by the romantic school of German literature. How genuine and expressive is Preciosa's song! how fascinating are those vigorous gipsy choruses, so hearty in their rendering of the joys of forest life—a favourite topic with the romance writers of the period!"*

Even more delightful is the spirit of romance in the natural and unseen world in 'Freischütz.' "I should never," said Beethoven, " have expected it of that quiet fellow. And now he must write operas, one after another, straight a-head, without beating about the bush. That wretch Caspar stands as firm as a house, and wherever the devil puts in his claw, he is felt at once." But not that alone—not Zamiel, the Wolfsschlucht, &c., but the gentle, tender, and expressive strain which, whether joyful or sorrowful, pervades the entire work wins all hearts to 'Freischütz.' In a natural, unconstrained manner, such as never before had been heard in a *prima donna*, Agathe —the huntsman's fair *fiancée*—tells, in dreamy soliloquy, of her true love, her joyous raptures, and overwhelming happiness at her lover's return. In scheme and design 'Freischütz' resembles not so much an opera as an enriched *Singspiel*; highly-finished *ensembles* and *finali* would not have suited the style of this thoroughly German and

* AMBROS. *K. M. von Weber in seinen Beziehungen zu den Romantikern der deutschen Literatur. Musikleben der Gegenwart*, p. 44.

popular opera—qualities which, probably, cause it to be looked down upon as " commonplace " by " men of the future."

Weber's reputation established of a sudden (" Freischütz has hit the mark," wrote he to Kind,* immediately after the first performance), he must of course write an opera for the Viennese, and the composer must go to Vienna to superintend the first performance of *'Euryanthe'* (October 25th, 1823). " The thing is good," said Beethoven ; but F. Schubert went with the public, who said it had too little melody, and ' Freischütz ' was quite another thing. Whatever the musical beauties of this opera (we refer to Euryanthe's song, "Glöcklein im Thale," her duet with Adolar, " Nimm hin die Seele mein," the great *aria*, " Zu ihm, zu ihm," the chorus of huntsmen, the first *finale*, and the first scenes of the third act), the dismally sentimental *libretto*, lengthy recitatives, and elaborate orchestration were not to the taste of the audience. Dramatically speaking, Euryanthe is an admirable, and historically, an important work ; the Marschner opera and Lohengrin (Wagner) are directly descended from ' Euryanthe.' Whatever is at all musical in the " musicdrama," which Wagner substitutes for the opera, appears to us to be nothing more than a very one-sided development of Weber's style in this opera.

Weber, however, did not sit down complaining

* The poet who wrote the *libretto* of ' Freischütz.'

that he was not appreciated ; he made no appeals from a present and ignorant to a future and more enlightened public ;* but, in his next work, he consulted, as far as was compatible with his art-theories, the requirements of the age and the audience to whom it was to be presented. His ' *Oberon*' has frequently been found fault with for want of completeness in the design, for the mixture of opera, play and *singspiel* it contains. The London public, however, would have it so ; and Weber (to whom the book, compiled from Shakespeare's ' Midsummer Night's Dream,' and Wieland's ' Oberon,' was sent act by act) had no other choice than to adapt himself to circumstances or give up the work. But how nobly and gracefully has the master acquitted himself of this somewhat difficult task, and even managed to invent quite a new and original style. We allude more especially to the fairy choruses, and also to the delicate, ethereal colouring of the whole piece.† Oberon and the real personages,

* In his *Hinterlassenen Schriften* (*Posthumous writings*, edited by Theodore HELL in three small volumes), Dresden and Leipzig, 1828, he does not even allude to his own works. They are merely simple jottings of his opinions on those works which most frequently came under his observation during the course of his practice—chiefly as Court chapel-master at Dresden—, and are delightful witnesses of the thoughtful artist, always ready to sympathize with the beautiful and the good whenever presented in the works of others. In 1861, a monument (by Rietschel) was erected to Weber's memory near the theatre at Dresden.

† The first of the fairy choruses in Oberon with the highly

it is true, are comparatively cast into the shade; while, again, the male characters are subordinate to the female ones. Taken altogether, we find that the airs (not excepting Rezia's, which bears a strong resemblance to Agatha's *scena ed* **aria**) savour of theatrical pathos, whereas all the smaller songs (Rezia's *cavatina*, Huon's *preghiera*, Fatima's *arietta*, and the quartet in the second act) are full of expression and significance.

Some **musicians detect in** Weber's *Overtures* **to** the aforesaid operas inequality **of workmanship** and want of coherence; but they are masterpieces of imagination and **expression,** and, accordingly, are admired and esteemed **by the discerning** connoisseur. Somewhat in the **manner of the** overture to Beethoven's 'Leonore,' they present a correct and complete outline—set as if in a jewelled frame—of the entire work to which they severally belong; not an *introduction* to an introduction, **to** which the overture has been reduced in modern **days** (by Meyerbeer, Wagner, Gounod, &c.). The *potpourri* kind of overture, formed out **of the** principal airs in the opera itself, we find generally prevalent *after* **Weber; as,** for instance,

---

effective bassoon, flute, and horn notes, the delicate, sprite-like progressions of wood and stringed instruments alternately, the mermaid's song with the charming horn figure, are the most ethereal of anything that has ever been composed in the "romantic" supernatural style—not even excepting Mendelssohn's music to 'A Midsummer Night's Dream,' which is, as it were, a description of the bustling activity of this miniature fairy-realm.

'Zampa,' and even the brilliant overture to 'Guillaume Tell,' and many of Auber's overtures, &c. If, as Marx and others maintain, this external manner of composing the overture was usual with Weber, it is singular that the Overtures to 'Freischütz' and 'Oberon' are, in every respect, far more complete, vigorous, and jubilant than the actual '*Jubilee Overture*' (a work independent of any opera) itself.

In a *dramatic* sense (*i.e.* in the so-called grand opera styles consisting in recitatives and *ensembles*), Marschner and Wagner trod in Weber's footsteps. We shall refer to them presently. Other composers who restricted themselves to productions within the range of their capabilities, especially KONRADIN KREUTZER [1782-1849] and FRANZ GLÄSER [1799-1861], copied Weber's lyrical tendency in 'Freischütz' and 'Oberon,' but almost entirely neglected dramatic expression. "Accordingly," as Riehl observes, "it is no small achievement that in Kreutzer's '*Nachtlager in Granada*,'—the best work of this style—he has managed to keep up the interest wholly by scenes of a lyrical nature, while the absence of dramatic action is made up for by the lyrical 'situations.'" We, ourselves, are by no means so infatuated with the *dramatic* element as to prefer the noisy, pretentious "music-drama" of our own day to the refreshing simplicity and tuneful melody of Kreutzer's opera songs. Likewise deserving of praise is Kreutzer's graceful music to Raimund's popular piece '*Der Verschwender*,' in which, in his time, Lortzing took the part of Valentine.

Foremost in the lyrical opera stands LUDWIG SPOHR, an admirable and accomplished, but of late years undeservedly neglected, composer. He has previously to, and contemporary with, though quite independently of Weber, treated the Opera in an original and graceful manner. *Faust*, with the splendid Polonaise [1813], and *Jessonda* [1823] are far superior, both in style and expression, to the would-be dramatic works of Weber's successors. In the last-named opera, the gifted musician has seized and rendered the spirit of oriental poetry in the happiest manner. The duet "*Schönes Mädchen, wirst mich hassen*" and the so-called 'flower duet' are the most perfect embodiment of dreamy yearning for a distant and beautiful land; both these pieces were, contrary to etiquette, encored at the first performance of the opera at Cassel [July 28th, 1823]. In his other operas, '*Zemire und Azor*,' '*Der Berggeist*,' &c., Spohr has not always steered clear of the shoals on which almost all succeeding opera composers grounded, viz., the lack of dramatic vigour and truthfulness;—lucky, indeed, if the overture (as for instance Reissiger's Overtures to 'Nero,' 'Die Felsenmühle,' 'Yelva') or, now and then, a song, survived the general wreck. The stage requires from those who devote themselves to it, whether in a creative or representative capacity, total abnegation of self; *egotism,* so much admired in the stage performance of some actors, is intolerable in the dramatic poet or composer. Accordingly, the operas of the best modern composers, such as LINDPAINTNER, FRANZ LACHNER, FERD. HILLER, WILH. TAUBERT, DORN, and others, have, with few exceptions (generally owing to local considerations), vanished from the stage.

Albert LORTZING [born at Berlin, October 23rd, 1803, died there, January 20th, 1851], who was formerly actor, singer, and opera-manager, has manifested superior judgment in combining the popular and tuneful element with the requirements of the modern stage; his comic operas and *Singspiele,* 'Czaar und Zimmermann,' 'Der Wildschütz,' &c., are excellent.* Lortzing is, indeed, the only composer who has, since Dittersdorf, successfully devoted himself to comic opera, and equalled him in the natural and unaffected delineation of mirth and joviality. Grotesque characters were his *forte,* but he also frequently rendered tender and gentle characters and scenes

* *Albert Lortzing,* sein Leben und Wirken. Von DÜRINGER. Leipzig, 1851.

in the happiest manner. The romantic opera, Lortzing himself admitted, was "not so much his style;" yet it may be questioned whether, since Weber, a downright "romantic" opera composer has ever written anything better than the charming and gracefully mysterious third *finale* to '*Undine.*'

Heinrich MARSCHNER [born at Zittau in Saxony, August 16th, 1795, died senior Court-chapel-master at Hanover, December 14th, 1861] is of the genuine romantic school (both in choice and treatment of his subjects), and the veritable successor of Weber. He was introduced to the Dresden public by Weber himself, but—he was no Weber. Though interesting to the musician, his gloomy and fatiguing operas have never become popular. Brendel, however, is of opinion that "Marschner writes in the true popular spirit, whereas Weber leaves the impression of having studiously adopted it." Certainly, Marschner is most successful in songs, and, above all, in comic pieces, where the *realistic* tendency in some measure acts as a counterpoise to the "romantic" and mysterious ('*Der Vampyr,*' 1828, '*Hans Heiling,*' 1833). Opera of the best kind, as well as genuine dramatic action, is not to be found in Marschner, although he frequently sacrifices to dramatic *effect* not only the characteristic of his personages but even the musical form

and vocalisation itself. We refer to the opera
'*Der Templer und die Jüdin*' [1829]—still occasionally performed—a work which, we think, partially resembles the Wagner style. According to modern notions, it is thoroughly dramatic, *i.e.*, constructed with a view to grand and effective scenes; but to the musical taste it is not so satisfactory as the two first-mentioned pieces; for the action, instead of resulting from the characters of the plot, is entirely linked to the story which forms the subject of the opera (Walter Scott's 'Ivanhoe'). Here again the comic parts are the best, viz., the fool's and the hermit's songs. Lighter in texture, but charming for its clear design and lively vigorous tone, is the opera '*The Merry Wives of Windsor*' by Otto NICOLAI [born at Königsberg 1809, died at Berlin 1849], of which the delightful Overture reminds one of Weber's exquisite style. Not long since, this opera was repeatedly performed in London, under the title of 'Falstaff,' with the greatest success.

"But there arose a colossal genius, a flaming spirit, to whom was decreed a crown of fire and gold; one who thought to aspire so high that, if art and society ever appreciated his ideal, it would be when the public taste was no longer &c., &c." The genius thus extolled by Liszt is no other than RICHARD WAGNER—the much-talked of poet-composer [born at Leipsic, May 22nd, 1813]. After having, like Meyerbeer (according to Wagner "The most despicable music-manufacturer of the period"), tried his hand on operas of the Italian-French stamp ('*Das Liebesverbot*,' after Shakespeare's 'Measure for Measure,' and '*Rienzi*,' after Bulwer), and vainly endeavoured to out-do Marschner's horrible romance in '*Der fliegende Holländer*' [Dresden, 1843], his vanity and ambition led him to protest against the degenerate Opera of the present day, —against Meyerbeer's show operas, the French and Italian dramatic and vocal opera, and, finally, into open and declared opposition to the Opera in general.

He begins by informing us* that the Opera—as hitherto practised—is radically a mistake; because (what is true only of inferior Italian operas) the means of expression (music) has become an aim, whereas the aim (drama) has been used as a means of expression. Accordingly, in '*Tannhäuser*' [Dresden, 1844] and yet more in '*Lohengrin*' [Weimar, 1850] and his subsequent opera-dramas, he has endeavoured to show us what the only genuine and veritable "art of the future" ought to be. His theory is that the sister arts, principally those of music and poetry, are no longer to act separately, but mutually combine and assist each other—opera, drama, and symphony

* See WAGNER's writings.

are no longer to be esteemed on their own account. Wagner's most successful work (judged by his own theories) is, we think, *Lohengrin*; for 'Tannhäuser,' with its dreary recitatives and paucity of melody, never was really popular notwithstanding the magnificent *mise-en-scène*. In 'Tristan und Isolde' and 'Das Rheingold' (first part of 'Die Nibelungen'), Wagner has arrived at that point which we should have supposed long since left behind when Lessing proved the necessity for the separation of the arts by unanswerable arguments. Thus, **Wagner's reforms are reduced to the idea (already advocated by Rochlitz*) of an intimate connection between drama and opera**; but the new form will never be able to assert itself if the opera is to lose all its special advantages and attractions, and become nothing more than a *finale*, and singing to be abandoned for continuous recitative.† "A down-

---

* *Für Freunde der Tonkunst.* Vol. ii., p. 270—275.

† Wagner, by rejecting the forms of air, duet, &c., only proves thereby that he has a thoroughly *realistic*, unimaginative—consequently unartistic—conception of the musical drama. "Introduce a new kind of opera which shall consist solely of recitative. It is more natural, for it certainly resembles speech more nearly than an air, a duet, or an *ensemble* do; because there can be nothing more unnatural than for two, three, or more persons to get up and sing at the same time. But naturalness in art is quite another from that in real life. If art is to be anything at all, it must, from its very nature, indulge in a great many things that are unnatural; and herein lies the charm of art that, notwithstanding its heterogeneous means, it can bring about an illusion that shall resemble real life." These are the words of the talented actor LORTZING; and Goethe—

right poet or musician is, after all, better than one who is half and half of each."*

The public has **never been over** favourable to 'Tannhäuser;' but, with its performance in Paris, Wagner appears to have completely played out the part he had undertaken so confidently—that of a would-be reformer. Amid unprecedented uproar, Tannhäuser was hissed off the stage at the Imperial Opera house [1861]; yet the composer, in the famous letter "to a Leipsic friend," pretended to have achieved a grand and complete triumph among the "real" public,—the "general opera-going public, as yet, not being sufficiently enlightened" to appreciate his music. We doubt if this will ever come to pass; for the "general opera-going public" has no taste for the mediæval romance to which Wagner is so partial, and will have nothing to say (and very properly too) to an opera without singing: "*Ce n'est point pour entendre du récitatif* que *l'on va à l'opéra.*†

---

who most certainly would have esteemed the sound judgment of the comedian far above the worm-eaten theories of "the man of the future"—held the same opinion, as we gather from the author of the '*Fliegende Blätter für Musik*,' who chronicled the poet's words on this subject. "Herein lies the dangerous demon for you youngsters. You are quick to create new ideas, but how about giving them shape and form? Every branch of art has its weak point in theory, but which must be retained in practice, because by suppressing it you come too near to nature, and art would be unartistic."

* CARRIERE. *Aesthetik.* Vol. ii., p. 440.
† ROUSSEAU.

Having given a slight sketch of the opera subsequent to Mozart, it remains for us to add a short chronicle of those by whose talent the above mentioned works have been rendered famous, viz., celebrated singers, both male and female. **First and** foremost come the Italian singers (more especially of the Rossini Opera): TAMBURINI [born 1800], RUBINI [born 1795], and LABLACHE, the famous bass singer [born at Naples 1794, died there 1858]. In Germany, likewise (which is far from being the case at the present day), the bass singers were the best. The masterly vocalisation of FISCHER [born 1745], STROMEYER [born 1779], Wilhelm HÄSER [born 1781], WÄCHTER [born 1796], SPITZEDER [born 1795], and others, is, of course, known **to the greater** number by tradition only; so that the few contemporary singers, Karl FORMES and A. KINDERMANN, are, in another sense, but to their own advantage, placed *hors de concours*. Especially deserving of notice are the **oratorio and concert** singers (particularly of Schubert's songs) J. M. VOGL [1768 - 1840], Joseph STAUDIGL [born 1807, died in a madhouse at Vienna, 1860], and Jules STOCKHAUSEN [born at Paris, 1826] (both of the two first were likewise admirable opera singers). Anton RAFF [1714—1797], whose singing cured the Princess Belmonte of hypochondria; Karl BADER [born 1789], WILD **[born** 1792], HAIZINGER [born 1796], MANTIUS [born 1808], **TICHATSCHEK** [born 1810] were celebrated tenors; to whom **may be added in** recent times SCHNORR V. CAROLSFELD, ANDER, NIEMANN. Of ROGER—the first of **French** singing actors or acting singers (*acteurs chantants*)—Riehl writes: "Roger is more than a singer—he is a dramatic poet. By his wonderful pantomimic action he invents new 'situations' and new phases of character, such as are found neither in the *libretto* or the **score.** He has such a fund of **individuality in his parts, that with him the opera** hero expands **into the sublime tragedy hero." Celebrated French singers are, also,** NOURRIT and DUPREZ. Nor must the English **singers be overlooked:** KELLY [born at Dublin 1764, died 1826], and the celebrated tenor BRAHAM [first appeared in public 1774, died 1856], were renowned **even on the** Continent. SIMS REEVES (tenor) and SANTLEY (baritone) now uphold **the fame of** English singing in oratorios and concerts.

Of female singers, who in accordance with the design of the modern Opera, **almost** monopolize its triumphs both in Italy and elsewhere, Angelica CATALANI ["*la prima cantatrice del mondo*," born at Sinigaglia 1783, died at Paris 1849] was the most renowned. Her magnificent voice was heard to the best advantage in Handel's music, or when in intoning, **in the** noblest and purest style imaginable, England's national hymns, 'God save the King,' and 'Rule Britannia,' on which occasions enthusiasm knew no bounds. "The last air had ended," writes Rellstab in 1827,* " when, amid thunders of applause, louder and louder the cry **arose for** 'God save the King!' Like a born queen, the great *cantatrice* stepped forward on the proscenium. The orchestra struck up the glorious melody; after which, Catalani sang her verse with such dignity, grandeur, and majesty as has never been equalled. The chorus joined in the solemn strain; when, with increasing power, the great songstress took up the second verse. Every gesture of her noble frame corresponded to the inflexions of her voice; her sparkling eyes denoted the ardour which inspired her and with which she inspired others. Once more her full rich tones soared, as if on eagle's wings, above the full-voiced chorus and orchestra." Others, **as** for instance Henriette SONTAG (in the execution of Rode's variations), the English singer Clara NOVELLO [born **1818**], **and** Pauline VIARDOT-GARCIA [born 1821], may have nearly equalled her in flexibility of voice, perhaps even **surpassed** her in executive skill; but the quality **of** her voice is such as probably has never been heard before or **since, unless it were in the** great concert singer MARA. The most remarkable opera singers were : Imperatrice [1783—1808] and Marianna SESSI, Giuditta PASTA [born at Como 1798; died there 1865] celebrated in 'Norma' and other tragic parts, Josephine FODOR [born at Paris 1793], the gifted and accomplished Maria Felicita MALIBRAN-GARCIA [eldest daughter of the Spanish tenor and singing-master Manuel Garcia, born at Paris 1808, died at Manchester 1836, shortly after her marriage with De Beriot], Giulia GRISI [born 1812, married 1856 the celebrated tenor MARIO], Giuditta GRISI [died 1840], for whom Bellini wrote the part of Romeo, and the renowned contralto Marietta ALBONI [born 1824].

It is, however, to the German *cantatrici* that the brightest laurels should be awarded; for, to our taste, they far surpassed the Italian singers in depth of expression and dramatic talent. Foremost among them stands Wilhelmina SCHRÖDER-DEVRIENT [born at Hamburg 1805, died at Coburg 1860].† She excelled, not so much

---

* On the occasion of a concert which took place at **the Berlin** Opera house.

† *Wilhelmine Schröder-Devrient*. Von Alfred Freiherrn von WOLZOGEN. Leipzig, 1863. *Erinnerungen an* **Wilhelmine** *Schröder-Devrient von* Claire **von** GLÜMER. Leipzig, **1862.**

in vocalisation, as in bold, original conception of her parts, and the artistic and poetic feeling with which she combined both the musical and dramatic element. The grandest and most gifted of women who ever trod the stage in modern days, she invested her parts (Fidelio, Donna Anna, Euryanthe, the Vestal, Norma, &c.,) with an individuality and grandeur never attained by any of her predecessors. Henriette SONTAG [born at Coblentz 1806, died in Mexico 1854] and Jenny LIND [born at Stockholm 1821], both of whom combined perfect vocalisation with exquisite feeling and charming dramatic action, achieved, however, greater popularity than the first-named artist. Then comes Nanette SCHECHNER [born at Munich 1806] " whose soul glowed in song." " Nanette Schechner is the grandest artist in my recollection, as far as singing goes ; but Jenny Lind is more intellectual, and her style more finished ; she is, indeed, the most perfect dramatic artist I have seen."*
Afterwards come: Anna MILDER-HAUPTMANN [born at Constantinople 1785, died at Berlin 1838], who was celebrated for her impersonation in Gluck's and Spontini's operas ; Sabine HEINEFETTER [born 1805], Karoline UNGHER [born 1800], Sophie SCHOBERLECHNER [born 1809], Wilhelmine STREIT [born 1806], Clara VESPERMANN [1800—1827], Pauline v. SCHÄTZEL [born 1812], Jenny LUTZER [born 1816], Agnes SCHEBEST [born 1815], Henriette CARL [born 1811], Sophie LÖWE [born 1815], and, recently, Louise KÖSTER—an artist whose noble conception of her parts (Fidelio, Donna Anna, &c.,) reminds one of the immortal Schröder-Devrient; Louise DUSTMANN-MEYER, Johanna WAGNER (niece of the composer), Jenny BÜRDE-NEY, Sophie CRUVELLI (properly Crüvell, born at Bielefeld in Westphalia), Therese TITIENS, Sophie STEHLE, Pauline LUCCA, and the latest Italian singers Adelina PATTI, Zelia TREBELLI, Désirée ARTOT, &c. England can boast exquisite dramatic as well as vocal talent in Mrs. BILLINGTON [born in London 1765, died at Venice 1818], Miss STEVENS, Adelaide KEMBLE (who quitted the stage 1843); and, at the present day, Mesd. LEMMENS-SHERRINGTON, PAREPA, and SAINTON-DOLBY (the well-known contralto and concert singer) share with the German Madme. RÜDERSDORF the honour of representing England's best oratorio and concert singers.

On the whole, to women is due the honour of maintaining (in our day when materialism obtains even in music) art in its highest and best sense ; in other respects, genuine vocalisation is sadly on the

---

* L. RELLSTAB.

decline, if not actually hastening to its fall. Voices have no longer the compass nor the *timbre* they formerly possessed; on the other hand, there is a plentiful supply of medium and mediocre voices. Those who have to answer for this deterioration are the composers, who have either forgotten or disdained to write in accordance with the capabilities of the human voice. In this respect, they are the exact opposite of the old *Opera seria*; whereas, formerly, the singers were in the habit of sacrificing truthfulness of dramatic expression to the display of their individual capabilities, the composers of our day subject singing to *their* caprices, to loud instrumentation and dramatic effect. "If this goes on, is there not," asks Riehl, "every probability that, with this 'dramatic' mania, music will go to the devil?" Meyerbeer's, Halévy's, Marschner's, Wagner's, and Verdi's operas have, in truth, been the ruin of many voices. It is no uncommon occurrence for the luckless singer to be so fatigued by the rehearsals as to be obliged to plead a "sudden attack of hoarseness" (the Postillon de Lonjumeau, TH. WACHTEL!) and leave his part to be taken by another. It must ultimately come to this: that it is no longer good style, finished vocalisation, or musical talent which is expected of a singer, but strong lungs, and great powers of endurance. For the future, the choice must lie between two alternatives, viz.—whether singers are really "to give up singing and accustom themselves more and more to grand recitative performances," or whether it would not be advisable to relinquish the grand and pretentious music-drama, and return to the unassuming but melodious opera of former days.

CHAPTER XV.

The later Musicians of Germany: Spohr, Mendelssohn, Schumann. Present and Future.

THE latest attempts in Germany, France, and Italy have proved only too clearly that, at the present day, not only drama in general, but the Opera in particular, is far from flourishing. In Germany, musical talent has, generally speaking, quitted the stage for the concert room; dramatic music has, to a great extent, made way for oratorio, instrumental, and song composition. The last of those who successfully cultivated *every* branch of musical art—the artist who stood, as it were, on the confines of "Past and Present,"* was the venerable LUDWIG *SPOHR* [born at Brunswick, April 5th, 1784, died, Court chapel-master at Cassel, October 22nd, 1859.]† We have already had occasion to remark‡ that,

* In his violin *concerto* "Past and Present" [1839], Spohr contrasted both the old and new styles with the express intention of ridiculing modern violinists who aped PAGANINI.

† *Spohr's Autobiography.* Translated from the German. Longman, Green and Co., 1864.

‡ See p. 295.

notwithstanding their manifold separate **beauties,** Spohr's operas fell short of perfection because the composer did not grasp the subjects he chose for dramatic representation with sufficient vigour and distinctness. The same may be said of his oratorios ' *Die letzten Dinge*' [first performed on Good Friday 1826], '*Des Heilands' letzte Stunden*' [1828], '*Der Fall Babylons*' [1840], in which tender and melancholy expression is too prevalent, and, consequently, individual characteristic wanting. Though greatly superior, especially in the choruses, to the effective, showy instrumentation observable in the works of Friedrich SCHNEIDER [born 1786, died at Dessau 1853, '*Das Weltgericht,*' &c.], and even to the sacred songs for male voices by Bernhard KLEIN [born at Cologne 1794, died at Berlin 1832], they could not fail to be cast into shade by Mendelssohn's oratorios, which are not only more popular, but also of a profounder calibre.

Of the pieces in 'Die letzten Dinge,' the quartet and chorus '*Selig sind die* **T***odten,*' the duet (for soprano and tenor) '*Sei mir nicht schrecklich in der Noth,*' and the chorus '*Gefallen ist Babylon*' will live in the recollection of those who have heard this highly attractive work—attractive both in a religious and musical **sense.** Of the above mentioned Klein, the oratorio '*Jephtha*' is a work of noble conception, and entirely free from adventitious effects; but compared with the Handel oratorio, it would seem to lack vigour and originality. A few of the choruses, in which rich instrumentation and polyphony conceal the absence of melodic invention, are alone of some merit,—indeed, it is in these points that ingenious and skilful musicians are most likely to succeed.

As is the case with almost all modern musicians, Spohr delighted more especially in instrumental composition. His songs have met with but little success; and that vocal composition was less congenial to him is evident in his celebrated instrumental work '*The Power of Sound.*'*
He tells us in his autobiography that he had originally intended to write a cantata on the poem which forms the subject of this work, but that he found "the words would not suit this genus." The work, which appeared as "a characteristic delineation in the form of a symphony" [1832],† is by no means free from defects; instead of a symphony, it presents a number of symphonic phrases. Taken by themselves, the first *allegro*, the cradle song, and military music are splendid pieces, whose distinct and complete form is not marred by any mysterious and poetical allusions or reminiscences; were the other phrases of the other movements equally perfect, we should be quite inclined to

---

* '*Die Weihe der Töne.*'
† Spohr's superscription to the piece.

admit the excellence as well as novelty of this kind of symphony, and assign it an honourable place beside the classical symphony—just as we recognize the merit of the Weber overture (which takes the opera for its programme) as well as that of the earlier thematically developed overture. Spohr's work contrasts favourably with the pretentious but shallow symphonies of recent days, from which it differs in this respect—that, instead of individualizing and describing a Francesca, a Tasso, or a Faust (Liszt), it contents itself with a general delineation of human life and emotion; and, after all, tells us even more than we find in the book. Similar to it in character is that ideal conception — the grand double symphony for two orchestras, entitled: '*Irdisches und Göttliches im Menschenleben;*' and inferior to this latter, though presenting points of interest in the detail, is the descriptive symphony '*Die Jahreszeiten.*'

But the magnificent *C minor Symphony* is, taken in its entirety, an admirable and complete work—one in which the composer's imagination (too frequently swayed by yearning, sentimental feelings and ideas) takes a vigorous and joyous flight. The wild, demonic, and enchanting *Scherzo* was encored on the occasion of its first performance at Vienna.

We think that the most sterling compositions of Spohr's—especially when compared with later works of the kind—are his *violin concertos*, among which is the well known one '*in modo di Scena cantante*;' it is exquisitely beautiful, and highly successful in its rendering of vocal recitative and *aria* on the violin. In the *quartet*, Spohr—like Weber in the sonata—adopted the brilliant concerted style, wherein the violin solo plays a prominent part. Of this style the double quartet is a development, of which the idea originated, as Spohr himself admitted, with Andreas Romberg. Finally, we must not omit to mention his rich and variously arranged *Nonet* (for stringed quartet, flute, hautboy, clarionet, horn, and bassoon), nor his graceful and melodious sonatas for violin and harp, which Spohr and his wife Dorette used to play at concerts.

Spohr's later works, especially his operas and quartets, are mere repetitions of his earlier ones; and that which formerly made him appear original degenerated into mannerism and affectation. These faults are only too evident (as, for instance, in the so-called 'Historical Symphony'), and have so warped the judgment of musicians on the subject of Spohr's music that not only have vigour and distinctness of expression been denied to him, but also depth, imagination, and sentiment. "Yet whoever," says Hand,* "maintains that Spohr's music is utterly wanting in depth, and resembles the modern

---
* *Aesthetik.* Vol. i., p. 320.

Italian style, judges wrongly and unfairly. Profundity is not wanting, but it is solely of sentiment—not that intellectual depth in which grand thoughts and ideas are gathered up and reflected by means of powerful imagination. The plastic —*objective*—element, so far as it obtains in music, is utterly foreign to Spohr; on the other hand, he is, like all artists who are prone to the "sentimental," apt to fall into monotony and mannerism. In the quartets, as also in the oratorios, we are aware of a great deal we have already heard in 'Jessonda.'" Nevertheless, though even the most favourable opinion may find much that is onesided or deficient in Spohr's compositions, he is greatly to be respected as a sterling German musician—one who made no attempts to appear that which he was not; but, so far as he went, was genuine and entire.

Of recent days, many admirable works of Spohr have in Germany been treated with undeserved neglect; but the best violinists of the period: Ferd. DAVID [born 1810], Jos. JOACHIM [born 1831], Ferd. LAUB, Heinr. ERNST, Aug. KÖMPEL, POTT, WIENIAWSKY, LAUTERBACH, STRAUSS, and, in England, BLAGROVE and SAINTON, &c.—all of them his pupils or educated by these—witness to the noble spirit which directed his efforts. Differing entirely from the clever fiddling accomplishments of NICOLO *PAGANINI* [born at Genoa 1784, died at Nice 1840] and his numerous imitators (BAZZINI, SIVORI, OLE BULL, and others, in Germany and France), the Spohr school—to whom may be reckoned the composers MAYSEDER [1789—1863], B. MOLIQUE [born 1803], MAURER, and LIPINSKY—aimed at full, rich tone, and expressive declamation on the violin. "Paganini is an extraordinary man," said Spohr; "but, besides several eccentricities in bad taste intended only for momentaneous display, he introduces impossibilities of such a nature as are thoroughly calculated to destroy good playing." His variations on the G string, his curious flageolet ('*Les clochettes*') and pizzicato playing, his extraordinary facility for double notes and all kinds of *bravura* passages—what was all that, compared to a fine bow, full tone, and *cantabile* execution? But because it was wonderfully effective, it found admirers, both among players and composers; since Paganini's time, the greater number of violinists—especially the French of recent days—are weak imitators of the great virtuoso, and '*Le Carnaval de Venise d'après Paganini*,' in endlessly varied transformations, is the stock piece of violin players at miscellaneous concerts.

Whereas the earlier French musicians (pupils of Viotti)—of whom RODE [1774—1830], Rudolph KREUTZER [born of German parents at Versailles 1767, died 1831], and BAILLOT [1771—1842], (authors of the famous violin *méthode*, adopted by the Paris *Conservatoire*)—maintained with Spohr that *tone* was "the source of all genuine instrumental music," the moderns: DE BERIOT [born at Louvain 1802, 'Tremolo' on the *Adagio* of Beethoven's 'Kreutzer Sonata'], and LAFONT [1781–1839] aimed almost exclusively at execution and effect. Far superior to the two last is de Beriot's pupil Henri VIEUXTEMPS [born at Verviers 1820], though even he has sacrificed too much to mere execution. His violin *concertos*, in particular, are crowded with difficult passages and continued to wearying lengths by the noisy unmeaning *tutti*; on the other hand, many of the movements, as well as his smaller pieces, are full of charming variety and imagination. The other Franco-Belgian composers: PRUME, LEONARD, &c., produced and reproduced whatever they could manage to attain of Paganini's and Vieuxtemps' skill and execution. Even the sisters MILANOLLO— Theresa [born 1827] and Maria [1832–1848], who created such a sensation from 1839–46, that they rarely needed to depend on other performances than their own to render their concerts attractive, found imitators; but speculating fathers and mothers could not bring about such another miracle as nature had produced in the artistic and finished execution of those two ingenuous and gifted children. A remarkable phenomenon is the repetition of the wonderful quartet performance of the brothers MÜLLER of

Brunswick [born between 1797 and 1809] in the Meininger quartet of the younger Müllers.

What Spohr was to violin, BERNHARD ROMBERG [born near Münster in Westphalia 1767, died at Hamburg 1841] was to violoncello playing He impressed one by his perfect command of the instrument and exquisite playing, which never gave the idea of difficulties sought and overcome. Romberg was not merely a travelling artist—he was, in truth, an original master, who, as Oulibicheff expresses it, has left something more than a name. His compositions (*concertos*, variations, *capriccios*, &c.) are, in the opinion of all good players, models of their kind, and far superior to the celebrated ones of GOLTERMANN, GRÜTZMACHER, &c., in our own day. SERVAIS [born at Brussels 1807], who might with propriety be styled a miniature Vieuxtemps on the violoncello, stands at the head of those who do violence to the grave, masculine nature of the instrument by playing violin on the violoncello. Of modern violoncellists, Alfred PIATTI [born 1823] is one of the most distinguished. HOWELL, and BOTTESINI [born 1823] are celebrated double bass players.

The other orchestral instruments likewise became transformed to meet the requirements of professional dexterity. Like the bowed instruments by a thinner quality of strings, so also the wind instruments by additional vents, lost in *tone* what they gained in compass. The "straightforward, masculine" tone which Leopold Mozart considered **essential** to violin playing is, owing to the high pitch now required, no longer to be found in the greater number of musicians. In later times the best players are: flute—Anton [died 1852] and Moritz Fürstenau, Berbiguier, Tulou, Drouet, Heineimeyer, Böhm, the English Richardson, Pratten; clarionet—Heinrich and Karl Bärmann, Hermstedt, Iwan Müller, Lazarus; hautboy—Nicholson; horn—Punto [properly Stich 1747–1803], the five brothers Schunke, König, the Distin family; trombone—Queisser [died 1846]; trumpet—Harper; harp—Nadermann [born at Paris 1773, died there 1835], Parish Alvars [1816–1849], Aptommas, Oberthur; guitar—Giuliani [1796–1820]. The compositions of many of these artists are, with few exceptions, trivial, and in direct opposition to old Haydn's maxim: "A piece of music must have flowing melody, connected ideas, and must be neither artificial nor overladen." Who does not shudder while thinking of the miserable, drawling, variations of Kummer, Drouet, and the like? Fortunately, the now prevailing custom of giving a series of concerts has done away with that **species** of music, written solely with **a view to** professional display, with which the migratory solo player called forth admiration and astonishment in all the cities of Europe; and only a few, really superior musicians venture to give concerts (in proportion to their means and abilities) on their own account.

From out the countless throng of public pianoforte players stands *FRANZ LISZT* [born at Raiding in Hungary, October 21st, 1811]—a marked and singular character. A clever woman once said that Thalberg was the *first* of pianists, but there was only *one* Liszt. Liszt's playing was distinguished not so much by the marvellous and brilliant execution which made light of seemingly insurmountable difficulties, as by the bold, original style which made his performances appear more like the inspiration of the moment than a matter of study and effect. For this reason, Liszt is entitled—though only in a partial degree—to the claim he put forth in Brendel's '*Neue Zeitschrift für Musik*,' viz., that equal merit is due both to creative and executive talent.* We repeat, only in a partial degree;

* To that species of professional skill which may be regarded in the light of genuine artistic inspiration, and of which Liszt was a brilliant example, Hegel even assigns a place in æsthetics. Speaking of another striking example of this power, he says: "The wonderful command of material means, the ease and freedom with which it makes light of apparently impracticable difficulties—delighting in elaborate flourishes, sudden interruptions, arch surprises—, its originality and invention lend a charm even to quaint caprices and effects. For, unless there be imagination, there can be no *artistic* performance; but the wonderful command which really talented musicians possess over their instrument, and with which they are enabled to increase its resources, and occasionally even counterfeit the sounds of other musical instruments, is a proof of this faculty.

for Liszt's own compositions (of **which more** hereafter) furnish the best proof of the **great** distance there **is** between clever playing and clever composing. Both these gifts were, however, united in one whom Liszt himself extols **in** a work* specially treating of

FREDERIC *CHOPIN* [born near Warsaw, March 1st, 1810]. An exile since the revolution of 1830, he lived—admired both professionally and in society (especially by women)—at Paris. In 1840, he was attacked with consumption, **and** died October 17th, 1849, and **was** buried, **by his own** desire, beside Bellini, at the cemetery **of** Père la Chaise. He was designated by the French "*Français du Nord,*" and admirably does this epithet describe the peculiar mixture of Polish character and French taste, which prevails in Chopin's compositions—more especially his Polonaises and Mazurkas. We think Chopin excels mostly in dance compositions, in which humble **branch of art** he displays **a** fund of poetical

In this species of execution we enjoy the greatest amount of musical variety; we are conscious of a strange mystery in that an **inanimate machine is transformed** into an organ of expression, and **are** impressed both with the conception and execution of a work of art in one and the same moment."

* *Frédéric Chopin*, par F. LISZT. Leipzig, 1852. **The most** interesting parts of this ingenious and highly **imaginative work are,** we think, the detailed and poetical description **of some of the musical** pieces,—more especially as denoting **the tendency of Liszt's** later productions.

sentiment clothed in elaborate ornamentation. His Polonaises, Waltzes, and Mazurkas are not, strictly speaking, dance music; they are, as Liszt expresses it, "*de petits drames amoureux de divers caractères*"—dreams of dance scenes, such as the sick and sad young man would picture to himself in a modern ball-room. These small imaginative pieces teem with fanciful scenes and pictures; it would, indeed, be a delightful, and by no means difficult task for "programme musicians" to invent superscriptions for them,—more especially as Liszt, in the work already alluded to, has intimated and sketched out much that would afford a clue to the reading of Chopin's music.

In all his compositions—in the dances, as well as in the looser form of *Etudes, Nocturnes, Impromptus*, &c., the elegiac strain prevails; his poetry is wholly *subjective*, and always tender, delicate, dreamy; no wonder, therefore, that women of a highly cultivated taste have a partiality for Chopin's music. But Chopin is by no means (as we have heard it asserted) "a thoroughly diseased, unwholesome nature;" of the sickly fancies and caprices, the morbid feeling, which possibly adhere to some of his later works, no traces are discoverable in his best and well-known compositions. "*Chez lui*," says Liszt—in reply to the further charge of artificialness and

---

* *Frédéric Chopin*, p. 7.

over-ornamentation—"*la hardiesse se justifie toujours; la richesse, l'exubérance même n'excluent pas la clarté; la singularité ne dégénère pas en bizarrerie baroque, les ciselures ne sont pas désordonnées, et le luxe de l'ornementation ne surcharge pas l'élégance des lignes principales.*" But Chopin—the classical drawing-room composer—is, of course, far inferior to the grand old masters in *concerto* and sonata composition; wherefore, the charm of novelty having subsided, only a few movements are still cherished—the *adagio* of the second *concerto*, and the Funeral March from the first sonata.

In Germany, ROBERT SCHUMANN endeavoured, previously even to Liszt, to obtain popularity and esteem for Chopin's imaginative creations; and CLARA SCHUMANN (*née* Wieck)—the most estimable of living female musicians—prefers the music of Chopin after that of Bach, Beethoven, and Schumann. To the ordinary pianist his wide stretches in the chords, his difficult and unusual cadences, &c., are troublesome—they would like something different. After Chopin, the best drawing-room composers are: Adolph HENSELT [born 1814, '*Concert Etudes*'], Stephen HELLER [born 1815, '*Nuits blanches*'], Alexander FESCA [1820-49], Jules SCHULHOFF [born 1825]. Spare us a careful enumeration of the whole of them: *Genus irritabile vatum!* They are synonymous with the downright technical "*pianistes compositeurs*"—DÖHLER, Alexander DREYSCHOCK,

Leopold DE MEYER, &c.; and are, moreover, well known to all pianoforte players. On the other hand, Ernst PAUER, Chas. HALLE, Mad. Arabella GODDARD, and Miss ZIMMERMANN are musicians of sterling merit, who devote themselves to genuine, classical pianoforte music.

We are about to enter on the most recent period, of which Mendelssohn and Schumann have determined the character in all essential details. FELIX *MENDELSSOHN-BARTHOLDY* was born at Hamburg, February 3rd, 1809. The prime of his artistic career was passed at Leipsic; but his education and first public success took place at Berlin, where his father (a wealthy banker, and son of the philosopher Moses Mendelssohn) had established himself about the year 1812. His mother (*née* Bartholdy) bestowed the utmost pains on the education of her son, who early gave promise of unusual talent. ZELTER, the founder, and for a number of years director, of the *Singakademie* at Berlin, instructed him in composition; L. BERGER and, subsequently, MOSCHELES taught him pianoforte playing. So early as his ninth year Mendelssohn appeared in public as a pianist, and, seven years afterwards, produced compositions (C minor Symphony, 1824, Overture to 'A Midsummer Night's Dream,' 1827, &c.) highly esteemed to this day. After visiting England, Italy, and France [1830—1833], and residing for some time in the capitals of those countries,* he was appointed music-director at Düsseldorf [1833—1835], "General music director of Church music" at Berlin [1843—1845], and, between whiles, as well as from the year 1845 till his death [November 4th, 1847], director of the *Gewandhaus* concerts and the conservatory of music at Leipsic.

Mendelssohn's historical importance will be best understood when we bear in mind that, no sooner did he appear than Spohr's influence and authority declined. Mendelssohn, though personally less gifted and profound than Spohr, had the faculty of employing his more active and plastic talent to such advantage that, during his comparatively brief **career, he overtook** and left **far** behind him the steady-going, old-fashioned **master.** Whereas in Spohr we frequently observe want of proportion between the elaborate form and comparatively inferior subject-matter, in Mendelssohn (who in this respect almost equals Mozart) we are aware of the innate relation of form and subject to **each other.** His delicate

* *Mendelssohn's Letters*, **translated by** LADY WALLACE. Longman and Co., 1863. They consist of letters to his family during his sojourn in foreign countries,—not "musical" letters addressed to an imaginary correspondent with a view to publication. The letters to Zelter contain a great deal of interesting information on art subjects **and** history (on the liturgy of the Holy Week at Rome), as well **as those** to Ed. Devrient (on the opera), to Frau v. Pereira at **Vienna** (on ballad composition and descriptive music), **to Immermann** (on Meyerbeer and 'Robert le Diable'), to his sister **Fanny** (on the recent composition of the 'Waldpurgis Night').

Y

perception and exquisite taste are the very embodiment of modern civilisation; invigorated by the study of the old masters, his productions yet breathe the soft, tender spirit which suits the taste of the day, and, accordingly, they have obtained universal admiration. "A new vein of genuine, original, and withal, exquisitely poetical music has cropped up in a reflective and intellectual age, unfitted for the production of works of a grand and majestic kind; salient characteristics, vigour, and vivacity, are, however, by no means wanting in the more remarkable compositions of this master." The works to which these latter words of Vischer* are most applicable are not so much Mendelssohn's great sacred compositions as the smaller ones in the "romantic" style: '*The first Waldpurgis Night*,' with its highly original spectral chorus ('Come with torches brightly flashing') and solemn conclusion—a unique and charming work [first performed at Leipsic, February 2nd, 1843]; the exquisite music to Shakespeare's *Midsummer Night's Dream*, of which the instrumental pieces—especially the *Scherzo* and *Wedding March*—are the finest [first performed at Potsdam, October 14th, 1843]; the descriptive concert overtures *Ruy Blas* [1839] and the *Hebrides* [1832], of which the first, written for Victor Hugo's drama of that name, is grand and noble in style, and the second (entitled 'Fingal's

* *Aesthetik.* Vol. iii., p. 1149.

cave' in the score) is a musical reminiscence of a visit to those remarkable islands.

The absence of innate vigour, masculine simplicity, and genuine feeling (commented on by Vischer and unjustly insisted on by Marx), is particularly felt in the *Symphonies* [C minor 1824, A major 1833, A minor 1842], in which either the dreamy song or the *scherzo* prevails. Of these, the A minor ('Scotch Symphony'), which is almost exclusively of a *scherzo* character, is the most spirited; in the A major Symphony, the *scherzo* and the *scherzo*-like *finale* are again the best parts. Although containing much beauty of detail, especially in the instrumentation, Mendelssohn's Symphonies lack the grand scheme and consistent character of Mozart's and Beethoven's; they are—what the French reviewer Pierre Scudo unfairly asserted of all Mendelssohn's works without exception—"*plus remarquables par les détails que par la pensée première.*" The hard trials and acute sorrows which alone could give emotion, pathos, and tragical grandeur to compositions of this kind never fell to the lot of happy *Felix*—and to counterfeit emotion and raging grief was utterly foreign to his upright, candid nature.

In the oratorios *St. Paul* [first performed at the Düsseldorf Musical Festival, May 22nd, 1836] and *Elijah* [first performed at the Birmingham Musical Festival, August 13, 1846] Mendelssohn has displayed such a fund of exquisite originality, and such dignity and solemnity (especially in St. Paul*) in the treatment of this previously almost neglected branch of composition, that his works may henceforward be regarded as models of modern oratorio composition. To our taste, the somewhat overstrained pietism of some of the solos in the (musically-speaking) far richer and more brilliant 'Elijah' is scarcely congenial, and we reserve our admiration for the noble choruses "Thanks be to God," "Woe to him," "Behold, God, he passed by," &c.

Similar in character to 'Elijah' is the music to Racine's biblical drama *Athalia* [written for the performance at Charlottenburg, November 12th, 1844]. We think the conception of this work is not sufficiently lyrical; in proportion to the number of choruses, choral dialogues, and

* "In this Oratorio, Mendelssohn has given us of his very own in the choruses, as for instance: 'Now this man ceaseth not'—'Stone him to death'—'Happy and blest are they'—(sung at Leipsic at his funeral)—'Is this he, who in Jerusalem'—'O great are the depths.' He has given us music of the *past* in his admirable adaptations of the chorale harmonized after the manner of Bach, as well as in the chorus 'But our God abideth in Heaven.' He has given us *modern* music intermixed with reminiscences of Handel in the solo pieces. Over the whole is thrown the charm of exquisite instrumentation; gracefully pleading in the chorus 'O be gracious,' humbly petitioning in the air 'O God! have mercy upon me,' infinitely touching in the *cavatina* 'Be thou faithful unto death.'" (F. M. Böhme, *The Oratorio*, p. 57). The same writer remarks that Mendelssohn—the reviver of oratorio after the Bach and Handel models—was the first who took the *unadorned words of Scripture* for his text, and who also revived the chorale, which had been neglected for a length of time past.

choral recitatives—so far as one can judge from a concert performance—the lyrical intervals are too few and far between. The solo pieces, viz., the duet "Ever blessed child, rejoice," and the trio "Hearts feel, that love Thee" (both combined with chorus), are among the noblest and most delightful of Mendelssohn's compositions.

The *Organ Sonatas, Motets,* and *Psalms,* for choir, *soli,* and orchestra ('When Israel out of Egypt came,' Ps. cxiv., 'As the hart pants,' Ps. xlii.) are a resuscitation of Bach's severe style in a modern—not would-be ancient—garb. A few contemporary critics are of opinion that Mendelssohn has too much secularized Bach's severe forms in St. Paul and other compositions, and leavened sacred art with "romantic" elements, &c.; whereas, at the time he produced these works, he had to defend himself against the charge of having copied Bach in a formal and too accurate manner. "If my sacred music bears any resemblance to that of Seb. Bach," writes he to Devrient, "I cannot help it; for I wrote as I felt, and if I have felt the words as old Bach did, I am all the more glad of it. For I do not suppose you mean that I have copied his forms without any reference to the substance; if such were the case, I could never have finished anything for sheer disgust and inanity."

In order to complete our description of Mendelssohn's versatile and prolific talent, we must specify: the *Pianoforte concerto in G minor* [1832]; the *Violin concerto* [1845]; the *D minor trio* [1840]; the brilliant *Sonatas for pianoforte and violoncello*; the *Ottet* for bowed instruments; the *finale* of the unfinished opera *Loreley*;* Schiller's ode *To the Sons of Art,* for male chorus and orchestra; the *Choral Songs* and *Duets*; and, finally, the *Capriccios* and highly popular *Songs without words* (in seven books) for pianoforte. We are inclined to regard the semi-religious, semi-secular Symphony-Cantata, the *Lobgesang* ('Song of praise'), as well as the choruses to Sophocles' tragedies *Antigone* and *Oedipus in Colonos* (written by desire of the late King of Prussia) as, on the whole, the least successful of his compositions. Mendelssohn had not Gluck's admirable conception of the antique; in lieu of a certain distinct tone pervading the whole work, he gives us only detached reminiscences in the vocal as well as the orchestral parts. But even Mendelssohn's inferior works, amongst which may be reckoned 'A calm sea' and 'Melusine,' display the true musician; in delightful combinations of sound, and well-defined form and proportion, he is a master indeed.

Nevertheless—and we trust without incurring

* The book, by Em. Geibel, has been adopted by Max. BRUCH [born at Cologne, 1838] in his opera of the same name, which has lately been performed at Mannheim, Cologne, Hamburg, and elsewhere in Germany, with great success.

the charge of inconsistency—we **are constrained
to admit** that in the musical world of our day
(**on** which female* and *dilettanti* influences are
brought to bear in **no** slight degree) Mendelssohn
plays an all too important part. Scarcely a
concert takes place without one or even more of
Mendelssohn's compositions. **Not** only do the
great models of Bach and Handel seem likely to
be cast into the shade by the very composer who
has **deferred to them** in so eminent a degree, but
even Schumann—the last musician of historical
importance—has had **to** make way for the
favourite of the day.

ROBERT *SCHUMANN* [born June 8th, 1810]†
—almost the same age as his contemporary Mendelssohn—was the youngest son of **a** bookseller
established at Zwickau, in Saxony. He did not
enjoy the advantages of a downright **musical**
education from early childhood — a few short
intervals between the hours of study at college

---

* NOTE BY THE TRANSLATOR. We are reminded of several talented women in private life. Foremost amongst them stands FANNY HENSEL, Mendelssohn's gifted sister [died at Berlin 1847]. Not to mention a host of others in Germany and elsewhere, we will content ourselves with distinguishing two of our countrywomen:—MRS. ARKWRIGHT, whose charming song 'Ruth' needs no commendation of ours, and VIRGINIA GABRIEL, the talented composer of the Cantatas 'Dreamland' and 'Graziella,' as well as **of a number** of songs ('The Forsaken,' &c.).

† *Robert Schumann. Eine Biographie* von Joseph v. WASIELEWSKY. Adorned with portraits of Robert and Clara Schumann and two facsimiles. Dresden, 1858. The *Hinterlassenen Schriften* (4 Bände, Leipzig, 1854) contains Schumann's critical essays.

was all he could **devote to** the pianoforte. From 1828 to 1830, however, when **he was** supposed to be studying jurisprudence at Leipsic and Heidelberg, he was enabled to give more time to the study of his favourite art, and finally resolved to give up the profession he was intended for, and devote himself entirely to music.* In the autumn of 1830 he returned to Leipsic in order to perfect himself **in** pianoforte playing under Friedrich Wieck's (Clara's father) tuition. **In** the fallacious hope of acquiring greater mechanical facility, he subjected his hands to a mode of treatment which ultimately lamed the middle finger of **the** right hand. He then applied himself to the study of harmony and composition under Heinrich Dorn.

Partly to pave the way for his compositions (widely deviating from **all** heretofore received maxims), Schumann, together with Wieck and others, edited the 'New Musical Journal'†—the organ of genuine, enthusiastic art-students *versus*

---

* Hereditary musical talent—so common in the **days of Haydn** and Mozart (*vide* the Bendas, Rombergs, Fescas, Pixis', Fürstenaus, &c.)—is unknown in our generation. Many of **our modern** musicians, indeed, have, like Schumann, begun their career **as** musicians after having **studied for the** learned professions, as: Berlioz, **Marschner,** Reissiger, **Curschmann,** Marx, Hans v. Bülow, **J. Raff.** Of these, the **history of art will probably take count of only a** few; the others are esteemed **at the present day for other** reasons. Some of the most recent musicians **appear to be totally** devoid of originality, and have little else to **recommend them;** but in lieu of this they have "**a high consciousness of art,**" **and know how to criticise** with pen and tongue what others knew **how to *write*.**

† '*Neue Zeitschrift für Musik.*'

the old-fashioned party—artisans and manufacturers all;—in short, the poetic-minded and *educated* section of the musical world *versus* that of mechanically-accomplished, time-serving, *vulgar* musicians. "The days are gone when a luscious *cadenza*, a languishing *appogiatura*, or an E flat run from one end of the keys to another delighted a whole audience; now-a-days we must have ideas, and those consequently carried out,— we must have poetical conception; everything must bear the impress of lively imagination, else the effect is merely momentary. What fingers do is simply mechanism, but what comes from the heart speaks to the hearts of all." Under the name of "Florestan," he attacks Meyerbeer's 'Huguenots,' saying that Meyerbeer is "no better than Franconi's *troupe*, &c.—a mere makeshift, full of shams and hypocrisy." Having given up the editorship of this journal [1844], Schumann settled at Dresden; which place he quitted in 1850 to succeed Ferd. Hiller as music-director at Düsseldorf. But, so early as 1853, he was compelled to withdraw from active life; and, not long after, the "nervous hypochondria," of which he had already complained at Dresden, resulted in confirmed insanity. He died at the asylum at Endenich, near Bonn, July 29th, 1856.

His works correspond to his career and education. He struggled through the "storm period" —as he himself called the period of preparation and transition from one career to another—and attained to maturity in an incredibly short space of time. The latter period of his active life, from about 1847, bears a general resemblance to the first; partly, in the restless, and occasionally fantastic, imagination, and partly, in the over-intellectual tendency which it displays. These characteristics are evident in his first pianoforte compositions: *Papillons, Davidsbündlertänze, Carneval,* and, to some extent, even in *Kreisleriana.* In these pieces, Schumann is as unartistic and devoid of form as his favourite poet Jean Paul; like him, he has an insurmountable antipathy to commonplace, every-day life; and, like him, is for ever taking refuge in the ideal. The *Kinderscenen, Fantasiestücke, Waldscenen,* &c. are carefully finished as regards form; and in their graceful characteristic superscriptions* we perceive the poetical mind of the composer—albeit this kind of poetic miniature-painting affords but little satisfaction to the real musician.

"In proportion as his apprehension of the nature and object of music became clearer and deeper, in proportion as he endeavoured to write good music without making wit, poetry, &c. his foremost aim, Schumann's music improved in

---

* "*Glückes genug*" ("Too happy to live") "*Träumendes Kind*" ("The child's dream"); "*In der Nacht*" ("In the night"); "*Herberge*" ("Asylum"); "*Verrufene Stelle*" ("Ill-omened spot"); "*Einsame Blumen*" ("Solitary flowers"); "*Vogel als Prophet*" ("The prophet-bird,") &c.

vigour and originality. The two *allegro* movements of his *First Symphony* in B flat [1841] teem with youthful vigour and vivacity; the terse, short rhythms in the first *allegro* of the *Second Symphony* in C remind one of the same kind of thing in Beethoven (the first *allegro* movements of the fifth and eighth Symphonies); and the *finale* of the splendid *Pianoforte Quartet* is as healthy and joyous as any (?) of old Sebastian Bach's quick, vigorous movements, (whose manner, indeed, Schumann occasionally reminds us of in this piece). In these and similar passages, Schumann rejoices in having attained the mastery after protracted struggles and many a backsliding."*

To this classical, but brief [1841—1846] period of Schumann's career belong likewise: the '*Overture, Scherzo, and Finale*' [1841]—a kind of small Symphony in three movements; to which the fantastically-constructed Symphony in E flat major, with its five movements, forms a curious contrast; the extremely difficult, but fine *Pianoforte Concerto* in A minor; the grand and brilliant *Pianoforte Quintet* in E flat; the *Quartets* for bowed instruments (op. 41), and the Cantata '*Das Paradies und die Peri*' (from Moore's 'Lalla Rookh,' 1843). It is highly probable that Mendelssohn's example, as well as the influence of his talented wife (whom he married in 1840), contributed to the wonderful improvement on

* AMBROS. *Musikleben der Gegenwart*, p. 85.

his earlier compositions observable in the above-mentioned pieces.

Latterly, Schumann evinced a partiality for the treatment of poetical subjects on an enlarged scale. These are: the gloomy, tragic music to Lord Byron's *Manfred*; the tender and lyrical opera *Genofeva*; and the '*Scenen aus Faust*' [first performed in its entirety at Cologne, January 14th, 1862], of which the *finale* of the second part (Faust's transfiguration) was especially admired. Similar in subject and treatment to the afore-mentioned Cantata is '*Die Pilgerfahrt der Rose*,' which Brendel does not even scruple to call a weak imitation of the same. In both these works, the entire effect is, notwithstanding considerable beauty of detail—particularly in the choruses—,unimposing; for nowhere does it appeal to the feelings, and its overstrained and doleful fairy-romance fails to arouse sympathy or interest.

In taking leave of Schumann, we cannot bestow too much praise on his *Songs*, which, though not equal in point of form to Schubert's, deserve to be ranked next to his, as for example: 'To the sunshine,' 'Go, roseate zephyr,' 'Devotion,' 'The lotus flower,' 'Thou art a beauteous flower,' '*Ich grolle nicht*,' '*Wass will die einsame Thräne*,' &c.; the collections of songs called '*Dichterliebe*' (of Heine, op. 24), and '*Frauenliebe und Leben*' (of Chamisso, op. 42); the charmingly graceful songs for choir without accompaniment: '*Schön Rohtraut*,' '*Das Dörfchen*,' &c., and for choir with pianoforte or small orchestra, '*Zigeunerleben*;' and the farewell song, '*Es ist bestimmt*' (likewise set by Mendelssohn), &c. Few of them have obtained absolute popularity; which is not to be wondered at when we consider that Schumann's melodies are not such as are readily seized by the ear and memory, nor easily separated from the context and "transcribed" for instrumental purposes in the manner of "Songs without words;" for they seek to follow the poet's thought with the utmost accuracy, even to the smallest minutiæ. Although at first sight this proceeding seems to indicate want of attention to musical form, in reality, it was the only way to get rid of the unmeaning vocal phraseology of Mendelssohn's imitators, and infuse new vigour into vocal composition.

Of Schumann's successors, the most distinguished is Robert FRANZ [born at Halle in Saxony, 1815], though he is not, for one moment, to be seriously compared with the former. The graceful conception and charming proportion observable in Franz's compositions distinguish them favourably from those of many modern vocal composers, who are in the habit of utterly disregarding, not only tuneful melody, but the metre of the verses they set to music; but as to healthy, vigorous, and characteristic melody—we seek for it in vain in the songs of Robert Franz. The vocal composer should be something better than an obedient interpreter to the poet; his highest, nay, his only object should be to invent a melody which appeals directly to the feelings, and reflects the poet's idea in every trait. Declamatory rendering of the words, be it ever so exact and true, correct conception of the poet's meaning, and melody aiming exclusively at a close affinity with the verse metre are far from answering to the idea of genuine vocal composition.

The case, however, is different in ballad composition; where, so long as the epic, narrating tone prevails, the plain recitative style of singing is in good keeping. But in how far even this is permissible, the talented Karl Löwe [born at Halle, November 30th, 1796], who is the first of ballad composers, has shown us in his numerous ballads after Herder, Goethe, Uhland, etc. He adopts a medium between simple recitative and *arioso*, which, however attractive it may seem when taken in connection with the words, becomes tedious after a time, because effective lyrical crises—"mere pleasing melody," as Wagner contemptuously calls it—is too much lost sight of. Thus his larger compositions, and particularly his ballad "groups"—not to mention his Oratorios: 'Die sieben Schläfer,' 'Die Apostel in Philippi,' 'Die eherne Schlange' (the two last for male choir only)—soon become monotonous; but, on the other hand, the smaller songs: '*Edward*,' '*Heinrich der Vogler*,' '*Der Wirthin Töchterlein*' ["Es zogen drei Burschen"], etc. are superior to almost anything we can recollect of the kind.

In the ballad for choir, *soli*, and orchestra, NIELS WILHELM GADE [born at Copenhagen, October 22nd, 1817] was far more successful than Löwe, or even Schumann ('*Vom Pagen und der Königstochter*,' four ballads of Geibel; '*Das Glück von Edenhall*,' by Uhland). '*Comala*' (after Ossian) and '*Erlkönigs Tochter*' (after a Danish legend) are, next to Ferd. Hiller's *Lorelei*, those works which, since Mendelssohn's 'Waldpurgis Night,' have deservedly obtained the greatest success. Though Hiller may have displayed more vigour and dramatic movement in the treatment of his '*Lorelei*' (similar in subject to Gade's '*Erlkönigs Tochter*,' but of greater pathos in the poetry), Gade has the, now-a-days inestimable, advantage of greater simplicity and naturalness. His charming melodies are thoroughly tuneful and easy to retain; and his characteristic, but never obtrusive, instrumentation harmonizes admirably with the feeling of the entire piece. Latterly, he has produced the graceful Cantatas: '*Frühlings-Fantasie*' (for four solo voices, orchestra, and pianoforte), '*Frühlings-Botschaft*' (for choir and orchestra), 'Die heilige Nacht' (for contralto solo, choir, and orchestra).

Likewise, his gracefully arranged and evenly elaborated *Symphonies* (1. C minor, 2. E major, 3. A minor, 4. B flat major, 5. D minor, with pianoforte *obligato*, 6. G minor) place Gade amongst the foremost of living musicians. Some would fain deny him all merit except what they call his "northern colouring," and maintain that his ideas are insignificant and poor; but we cannot help acknowledging that Gade has shown admirable judgment in refraining from conceptions of a grand order, and has managed to unite the ideal, though not profound, subject-matter with *motifs* of a *genre* or landscape kind. If we compare Gade's Symphonies with those of his predecessors, we find they most resemble those of Mendelssohn; but the gifted Dane is as much superior to Mendelssohn's imitators, as the English composers STERNDALE BENNETT, with his smooth concert Overtures ('Die Najaden,' 'The Wood-nymph,' etc.), and his Cantata 'The May Queen,' and Arthur SULLIVAN ('*The Tempest*' Cantata) is of their number. Gade's first Symphony (in C minor) as well as his concert Overtures '*Nachklänge von Ossian*' and '*Im Hochland*,' inspired both Mendelssohn and Schumann with the liveliest interest,—the latter even regarding it as a good omen for the young musician that the letters of his name corresponded to the four strings of the violin.

In regard to vocal composition (little cultivated by Gade and the best musicians since Schumann's time), we have lately had to put up with a great many weak and trivial productions; but should we disdain to admit a REISSIGER, ABT, KÜCKEN, ESSER, KREBS, &c., together with PROCH and GUMBERT ("genteel ballad-minstrels" as they are called) into good company, because they too have been guilty of some trivial, but highly popular, compositions? Excellent German vocal composers are Alex. FESCA, CURSCHMANN [born at Berlin 1805, died 1841, "Streamlet, cease thy constant flow," "The sailor draws near land," &c.], Karl BANCK [born 1804], W. TAUBERT, H. DORN, K. REINECKE, TRUHN, and others.

Genuine *ballad-singing*—to adopt Reissmann's* nomenclature—is found in those choirs for male voices, in which Karl ZÖLLNER, Aug. SCHÄFFER, and the journeyman patriarch Jul. OTTO are esteemed "classical." The better and more artistically disposed societies, like the Cologne Choral Society,† are sadly in want of good modern songs. Since Weber, Marschner, Mendelssohn, and Konradin Kreutzer, Friedrich SILCHER [died at Tübingen 1860] is the only one who by his "*Volkslieder*" (in twelve books) has given a

---

* *Das deutsche Lied in seiner historischen Entwickelung*. Dargestellt von August REISSMANN. Cassel, 1861.

† NOTE BY THE TRANSLATOR. Many of our readers will doubtless remember the visits of this Society to England in 1853 and 1854.

nobler impetus to popular musical art—already threatening to degenerate into wretched hum and dance tunes. How genuine and true was his conception of the popular song is evinced in his composition of '*Lorelei*' ("Ich weiss nicht, was soll es bedeuten,"), "*Zu Strassburg auf der Schanz*," "*Morgen muss ich fort von hier*," and a number of other well-known songs. SPOHR, **Franz LACHNER** ('*Sturmesmythe*'), Ferd. HILLER, GADE, Jul. RIETZ (Schiller's '*Dithyrambe*,' 'Old German war-song'), HAUPTMANN, TAUBERT, &c. did not consider it beneath their dignity to do something towards improving the despised, because neglected, male choir singing; but **the** majority of musicians are content to accept the present state of things, and abandon this branch of composition to the above-mentioned manufacturers.

In a greater degree even **than the "music-drama"** founded on the **old French recitative opera,** is the modern genus of composition **called** "*programme-music*" utterly foreign to German art **and feeling.** It owes its origin to BERLIOZ—a Frenchman; and LISZT (who writes his books in French) displays an affinity to French taste and feeling in his "symphonic poetry." Programme-music is **a degenerate species** of instrumental music, which **requires a** special explanation in **order to be understood;** consequently, while **setting at nought form** and proportion, which are absolutely essential to all true art, it ignores the first and most essential feature of German instrumental music, viz.—ideality. With what right the representatives of this style appeal to Beethoven's example in support of their theories we think we have already satisfactorily shown; and, with regard to Schumann, it is only his first attempts which they imitate. The Heidelberg student's '*Papillons*' (op. 2) are of such importance in Brendel's eyes that—though he bestows but little attention on Schumann's later compositions—he thinks it incumbent on him[*] to "allude to them more particularly." Schumann's later compositions are entirely free from the tendency to describe external events and occurrences. He protests against Berlioz' programmes, which he says "confined his view," and even the *few* superscriptions to his pieces he declares are not to be understood in a universal sense,—that which suited him individually ought not to be taken as a rule. "It is a bad sign for music when it needs a superscription; for it is a proof that it is not the result of genuine inspiration but of some outward suggestion. That our art is able to express a great many things, and even to follow the course of an event, who will deny? But those who are inclined to test the value of the images thus originated can do so easily—they need only erase the superscriptions."

[*] *Geschichte der Musik*, p. 506.

Indeed, the value of this would-be "characteristic" music is determined by the simple fact that the superscriptions are usually invented *after* the music is composed; but modern "tone-poets" are rarely as candid as the one who consulted us as to whether he should call his recently composed overture 'Minna von Barnhelm'* or 'Clavigo,'† or another—rather celebrated pianist—whom Ambros‡ describes as hesitating between 'Abd-el-Kader' and the 'Falls of Schaffhausen' for the title of a "*grande Etude*"! "*Une fille est-elle dépourvue de beauté, d'esprit et de dot, on nous vante son caractère.*"

HECTOR BERLIOZ—"the chief pillar of modern development"—, who endeavoured to replace absence of ideality and artistic perception by meretricious devices and "grandeur of detail" (!), and faulty design by enriched colouring, was born in a village of the Isère department, December 11th, 1803. His father intended him for the medical profession, to which he objected. All assistance from home being withdrawn in consequence of this decision, he hired himself out as chorist at a *vaudeville* theatre; afterwards he gave singing lessons, and ultimately made money enough to enable him to complete his studies at

* Comedy, by LESSING.
† Tragedy, by GOETHE.
‡ *Grenzen der Musik und Poesie*, p. 136.

the *Conservatoire* at Paris. For his Cantata 'Sardanapalus' [1830] he obtained a prize and allowances for a journey to Italy. After his return to Paris [1832], his Symphonies '*Sinfonie fantastique, Episode de la vie d'un artiste,*' and '*Harold en Italie*' were performed in public. Both of them purport to represent incidents in his own career; the first, a vision engendered by passionate admiration of an actress (terminating in the execution march, guillotine, and witches' revel); the second (with viola *obligato* [Harold!]) impressions of the country and people in Italy, viz.—Harold in the mountains, scenes of sadness, happiness and joy—pilgrimage—serenade in the Abruzzi mountains — bandits' orgies. This symphony has nothing whatever in common with the fourth Canto of Byron's 'Childe Harold;' he might, says Ambros,[*] with equal propriety have styled it '*Berlioz en Italie*' or, after the usual fashion, simply, '*Souvenirs d'Italie.*'

In his "dramatic Symphony," '*Roméo et Juliette,*' Berlioz attempted to render an entire poetical work (Shakespeare's 'Romeo and Juliet') by means of orchestra alone. To the introduction on the first scene of the tragedy, (the Dispute) and a 'Prologue' sung by the chorus with the interpolation of two songs (Song for a contralto voice in honour of love, Italy, and

---

[*] Compare *Grenzen der Musik*, &c., p. 156—178.

Shakespeare, and a tenor solo, "Story of Queen Mab"), succeed—likewise explained and connected by choral and instrumental movements—the principal scenes of the drama, viz.—Romeo's melancholy—the ball at Capulet's house—the balcony scene—Queen Mab (taken from Mercutio's narrative)—scene in the vault. Berlioz has not been successful in his endeavour to render Shakespeare's play in music; for he did not possess the secret of combining all the details of the poetry with artistic unity, *i.e.* to group the details according to the laws of composition and reduce them to an harmonious whole. On this account, he did right *not* to treat the '*Damnation de Faust*' in the form of a symphony, but to confine himself to the description of a few scenes:—Introduction, Rakocsky march (instead of the soldiers' song), rustic dance under the lime tree, Mephistopheles' rat song, &c.

As really original pieces, (though, as regards their relation to the rest, *hors d'œuvre* both of them), the Rakocsky march and the *Scherzo*, '*La Fée Mab*', are much admired though but little known. Berlioz calculated his instrumental effects for such a large orchestra (*at least* fifteen first and as many second violins, ten violas, &c.), that, apart from other considerations, his works could rarely be performed. After a time, "finding himself no longer appreciated" (*i.e.* when the French were tired of him), he made the tour of Germany, in

1843, but arrived—according to Brendel—too soon. "We were not yet prepared for Berlioz' innovations." The only thing for which Berlioz was admired was the brilliant, ethereal colouring* which he shed over his otherwise insignificant compositions. Among the few who stood up for him as a composer was Liszt, who even urged him to come to Weimar in 1852, when the 'Romeo' symphony, 'Faust' scenes, and his opera of '*Benvenuto Cellini*' (with the pleasing overture 'Le Carnaval Romain' in the second act) were performed under his own auspices. The only genuine, and really complete, work in the style of which Berlioz is the founder is the Symphony-ode '*Le Désert*,' by Félicien DAVID [born 1810]; his later Symphony-cantatas 'Moses on Mount Sinai' and 'Columbus,' as well as his operas, met with but little success.

Whereas in the compositions of Berlioz we may find somewhat to admire, LISZT's "symphonic poems" come very near to that which is no longer musical art; it consists in giving prominence to reflective, intellectual, "highly symbolical," ideas—consequently art defeats its own purpose ("*cogitat, ergo NON est*"). "Spiritual music," forsooth, which robs spirit of its thought, and music of its soul! When passing judgment on "symphonic poetry," we must, however, bear in mind that Liszt has, generally speaking, selected

---
* *Traité d'instrumentation et d'orchestration modernes*. Paris, 1844.

the most impracticable subjects* for musical treatment, and that the want of form they exhibit throughout is by no means characteristic of the style or necessitated by the subject. On a nearer view, "symphonic poetry" presents a strange contrast to the old-fashioned "*suite*;" it professes to mean something as a whole, without even expressing anything clearly and distinctly in detail. "As a matter of course, it goes on in the same strain without interruption; one part grows out of the other without resulting in any distinct, complete idea;—distinct, complete idea is only to be discerned in the symphonic poem in its entirety." Thus Ambros,† the partial admirer of Liszt; **his, also,** is the clever saying: "These works *are* not, they *signify!*"

That amongst his numerous symphonic poems (as for instance '**Tasso**' and '**Prometheus**'), we find musical passages of considerable merit, **is** only to be expected in a musician like Liszt; but

* They are as follows: 1. '*Ce qu'on entend sur la montagne*' (after V. Hugo); 2. '*Tasso: Lamento e Trionfo;*' 3. '*Les Préludes*' (after Lamartine); 4. '*Orphée;*' 5. '*Prométhée;*' 6. '*Mazeppa*' (after V. Hugo); 7. '*Festklänge;*' 8. '*Héroide funèbre;*' 9. '*Hungaria;*' 10. '*Hamlet*' 11. '*Hunnenschlacht*' (after Kaulbach); 12. '*Die Ideale*' (after Schiller). Besides these is the *Faust Symphony* (first movement — Faust; *Andante*—Margaret); *Scherzo*—Mephistopheles; concluding with the *chorus mysticus* ("*Alles Vergängliche ist nur ein Gleichniss;* . . . . *Das Unbeschreibliche hier ist es gethan!*"); and the Symphony to DANTE's '*Divina Commedia*' (*Inferno* and *Purgatorio*), with concluding chorus for soprano and contralto voices.

† *Musikleben der Gegenwart*, p. 159. Compare p. 153—173.

the general impression is **one of** blank, dreary discomfort. As a performer, Liszt is a phenomenon; as a writer, he is entitled to a high place in musical literature; **but as a composer, he has remained** what he was in his numerous "*Partitions de Piano*," "*Paraphrases*," "*Transcriptions*" (of Beethoven, Wagner, Meyerbeer, Verdi, &c.)—a translator.

That which Liszt vainly essayed in his **symphonic poems,** others (after the example of **Mendelssohn** and Beethoven) attempted **in the overture—a branch of composition which aims at** rendering a poem **in its general** character and with reference to a particular subject or event in a musical and agreeable form. Among the best of those which have appeared in recent times, we reckon those of F. RIES to 'Don Carlos;' SCHINDELMEISSER's to 'Uriel Acosta' (which, however, strongly reminds one of Meyerbeer); BARGIEL's to 'Medea;' W. TAUBERT's to Shakespeare's 'Tempest;' and K. REINECKE's to Calderon's 'Dame Kobold.' Unfortunately, a number of less gifted composers have followed in their footsteps, and, if it goes on much longer, we shall have an overture to every play.

Finally, we must mention the small **superscription** composers — the poetical pianoforte players who, in the amiable intention of describing a poetical or characteristic subject, torment **us with** nothing **but** their miserable **selves.** *Their* works exhibit the **tokens by which** Goethe **particularly** recognized the decay of poetry in our age, as well as the **sterility of our poets** :—extreme finish in the technical portion, and a tendency to *subjective* contemplation.* Even in works of a larger calibre, the much-talked of close **association** of music and poetry is of a purely *personal* **origin**; indeed, this latest achievement has **confused and** disturbed everything, and it is high time for it to be thoroughly understood that the limits of art are necessarily also the limits of the Beautiful.

Like Wagner in the opera, **Liszt** and Berlioz in instrumental music have ignored the proportion which should exist between **the subject-matter and form;** and **art** is left vacillating between the two extremes of vulgar realism and a too abstract idealism;—theory has got the start of practice. But it is not so much the *aim* that the artist strives at—not so much what his *idea* was when he set about producing **a work of art,** as what he *can* and really *does* produce, **which is** of consequence **to us;** he will **not meet with appreciation** and admiration unless his creations are carried out with legitimate methods of art. "The real intention of fine **art,"** says the greatest of art philosophers—Lessing, "**can be no other than that which** each art is competent to produce

* Compare Gervinus' *Geschichte der deutschen Dichtung*, vol. v., p. 659.

independently of another. With modern painters, the means is evidently an object. They paint history for the sake of painting history, without reflecting that they are thereby making their art merely accessory to other arts and sciences; or, at least, are so dependent on other arts and sciences that their own is entirely deprived of its value as a primitive art."

When we come, however, to copyists—the composers *à la* Liszt and Wagner—the case assumes a serious aspect. These gentlemen seem to think that they have nothing to do but to take things easily in order to appear original and in the modern taste; they do not even compose, they simply *concoct*, and expect that the programme or superscription will do the rest. "Whatever has already been done need not be done again, and what *can* be done *must* be done." Fortunately, however, the number of those who thus transgress against the beauty of form is small indeed; and, although they may boast that their admirers esteem their errors a proof of genius and devotion to the Beautiful and the True, and pursue to the death all who hold a different opinion with their newly-discovered theory, "the æsthetics of ugliness,"—[*] we need entertain no fears about the future. The "new German" school—as it now claims to be called—

[*] *Aesthetik des Hässlichen.* Von Karl ROSENKRANZ. Königsberg, 1853.

will doubtless exhaust itself in as short a space of time as did the "storm-period" of 1770—1780 and the Young Germany of literature; and we have greater reason to fear that whatever of a wholesome and genuine tendency is yet existing in the works of R. Wagner will remain undeveloped than that the recently proclaimed freedom and equality in art will ever be thought seriously of.

The taste of the present generation is decidedly in favour of music of a simple and sterling calibre; the works of the great masters are diffused among the multitude by means of cheap and excellent editions and well managed Festivals, societies, and Popular Concerts. Whereas, in the year 1815, Spohr wrote from Munich: "An entire symphony is performed at every concert," as of something unusual,—at the symphony-concerts established by Liebig at Berlin, by Pasdeloup at Paris, and at the Philharmonic and New Philharmonic Societies' and other concerts in London, the finest instrumental compositions are now constantly performed to hundreds and thousands of people. Likewise, in contemporary compositions we observe, with pleasure, a tendency to improve. A considerable number of, for the most part, sterling and admirable musicians, who do *not* follow the advice of Mephisto:

"A poet choose as thine ally."

have (as we gather from their much and deservedly admired compositions) withdrawn from the easy-going eclecticism of the day :—Franz LACHNER [born at Rain in Suabia, April 2nd, 1804, Symphonies, '*Suites*' for orchestra]; the celebrated thorough bass master (author of '*Die Natur der Harmonik und der Metrik*' 1853) Moritz HAUPT-MANN [born at Dresden 1792, Masses, Motets— among which the '*Salve Regina*,' called by Spohr "ravishingly beautiful," — ecclesiastical pieces for choir and orchestra]; NIELS GADE (whose admirable compositions have been already alluded to); Ferd. HILLER [born at Francfort-on-the-Maine 1811: '*Die Zerstörung Jerusalems*' and '*Saul*,' both oratorios—; '*Ver sacrum*' or '*Die Gründung Roms*,' a cantata;— Hebrew songs of Lord Byron, &c.]; Karl REINTHALER ['*Jephtha, und seine Tochter*,' an oratorio]; Bernh. MOLIQUE ['*Abraham*,' an oratorio]; Friedr. KIEL ['*Requiem*']; COSTA ['*Eli*,' '*Naaman*,' oratorios]; HESSE [died 1863], RITTER, and in England, Goss, ELVEY, and others [organ and choir compositions]; Wilh. TAUBERT [music to Shakespeare's '*Tempest*']; Karl REINECKE ['*Ave Maria*,' and other choral songs, pianoforte *concertos*, &c.]; Jul. RIETZ [overtures and symphonies]; J. JOACHIM [violin *concerto* in the Hungarian style]; also chamber and pianoforte music by a great many of the aforesaid, and Johannes BRAHMS [serenades in D and A for small orchestra, sestet, and pianoforte pieces: variations on airs of Handel, Schumann, &c.]; Ferd. DAVID [chamber music for violin]; Rob. VOLKMANN, A. RUBINSTEIN, J. RAFF and a number of others. Yet we are to believe that the field of art lies fallow and must be ploughed up before it can produce another crop? True, no one among living composers has been able to replace Mendelssohn; and, were *he* still living, we should most certainly never have heard all this talk about new theories in art.

We therefore await patiently the resurrection of real genius—genius, such as shall put to silence the disputes which distract the musical profession in Germany—genius, whose works shall proclaim a new ideal, and draw everything into its mighty vortex. Another spring-time of music—another classical epoch in music as well as poetry, we may scarcely hope to see. The tendency of the age is a different one; there is less scope for imagination in these scientific days; and instead of art,—political, national, and material interests principally employ the minds of men. For this reason, the artist who reveres the immortal Past will cherish the element in which its greatness consisted—the beautiful Ideal,—that it may continue to set forth all that is best and noblest in man. This is Schiller's injunction to the Sons of Art; and so long as the sublime words of the poet are not only sung, but understood and cherished, so long will—similar to Nature's inexhaustible resources—genuine love of art and creative power abide and continue :

> "O Sons of Art! into your hands consigned
> (That trust revere!)
> The liberal dignity of human kind!
> With you to sink, with you to reappear."*

* Sir E. Bulwer Lytton.

INDEX.

	PAGE
ABT, FRANZ	337
ADAM, Adolphe	279
ADAM de la Hale	19
ALBERT, Heinrich	74
ALBONI, Marietta	303
Albrechtsberger	196
Allegri	40
Amati	62
AMBROSE, St.	10
Ander	302
ANERIO, Felice	40
Aptommas	315
Arcadelt	25
ARKWRIGHT, Mrs.	327 n.
ARNE, Dr.	100
Arnold	100
ARTÔT, Désirée	304
Astorga	63
Auber	277
BACH, Joh. Seb.	78
——, Phil. Em.	79, 92, 114, 148
——, Wilh. Friedemann	92
——, Joh. Christian	92
Bader	302
Baillot	312
Bai	41
Balfe	279
BANCK, Karl	337
BARGIEL, Woldemar	345

	PAGE
BARMANN, Heinr. and Karl	315
Bazzini	311
Beethoven	188 n., 195
Bellini	234 n., 269
BENDA, Georg	145
BENEDICT, Julius	280
Benevoli	42
BENNET, John	100
BENNETT, William Sterndale	336
Berbiguier	315
BERGER, Ludwig	258, 320
BERLIOZ, Hector	340
Bernabei	42
Bernacchi	61
BERNHARD the German	44
Berton	125
BILLINGTON, Mrs.	304
BIRD, William	100
Bishop	100
Blagrove	311
BLOW, John	100
Böhm	315
Boieldieu	126, 250, 276
BORDONI, Faustina	62
Bottesini	314
Braham	302
Brahms	349
BROSCHI, Carlo (Farinelli)	62
BRUCH, Max	326 n.
BULL, Ole	311

2 A

354 INDEX.

	PAGE
Bülow, Hans v.	93
Bürde-Ney, Jenny	304
Caffarelli	62
Caldara	45
Callcott	100
Calzabigi	128
Cambert	117
Carafa	270
Carissimi	55
Carl, Henriette	304
Carpentras	25
Catalani, Angelica	302
Catel	125
Cherubini	234 n., 250, 274
Chopin	317
Cimarosa	122, 171 n., 263
Clemens non Papa	25
Clementi	257
Corelli	61
Costa	340
Cramer, J. B.	258
Crescentini	62
Crüger	74
Cruvelli, Sophie	304
Curschmann	337
Cuzzoni, Francesca	62
Czerny	258
D'Alayrac	125
Danzi	253
Da Ponte	177
D'Auvergne, Antoine	123
David, Félicien	343
——, Ferd.	311
De Beriot, Louis	313
De Meyer, Leopold	320
Dibdin	100
Distin, family of	315
Dittersdorf	259
Döhler	320
Doles	92

	PAGE
Donizetti	234 n., 269
Dorn	296, 337
Dowland, John	100
Dreyschock	320
Drouet	315
Dufay	22
Duni	59, 123
Duprez	302
Durante	57
Dussek	255
Dultmann-Meyer, Louise	304
Ebeling	74
Eccard	73
Elvey	349
Ernst	311
Esser	337
Farinelli	62
Faustina	62
Feo, Francesco	57
Fesca, Alexander	319
——, Friedr. Ernst	254
Festa, Costanzo	25
Field, John	258
Fioravanti	263
Fischer, Mich. Gotthard	87
——, Ludwig	302
Flotow	280
Fodor, Josephine	303
Formes, Karl	302
Franco of Cologne	18
Franz, Robert	333
Frescobaldi	87
Froberger	87
Fürstenau, Anton and Moritz	315
Fux	151
Gabriel, Virginia	327 n.
Gabrieli, Francesca	62

INDEX.

	PAGE
GABRIELI, Giovanni	43
GADE, Niels Wilh.	335, 338
GALLUS, Jacobus	46
Galuppi	59, 122
Geminiani	61
GIBBONS, Orlando	100
Giuliani	315
Gläser	294
Glover	100
Gluck	127, 147, 168, 250
GODDARD, Mdme Arabella	320
Goltermann	313
Goss	349
Gossec	125
Goudimel	25, 70
Gounod	287
Graun	113
GREGORY the Great	11
Grétry	124
GRISI, Giuditta	303
——, Giulietta	303
Grützmacher	314
Guarneri	62
Guglielmi	59
GUIDO of Arezzo	17
Gumbert	337
Gungl	267
Haizinger	302
Halévy	287
HALLÉ, Charles	94 n., 320
Handel	95
Harper	315
HÄSER, Wilh.	302
Hasse	59, 64, 112
HASSLER, Hans Leo	72
Hassler	87
HAUPTMANN, Moritz	338
HAYDN, Joseph	150
——, Michael	164
HEINEFETTER, Sabine	304

	PAGE
Heinemeyer	315
HELLER, Stephen	319
HENSEL, Fanny	327 n.
Henselt	319
Hermstedt	315
Hérold	279
HERZ, Henri	259
HESSE, A. F.	349
HILLER, Joh. Adam	143
——, Ferdinand	296, 338
Himmel	144
Homilius	92
Horsley	100
Howell	314
Hucbald	16
Hummel	255
HUMPHREYS, Pelham	100
Hünten	259
Isouard	125
Joachim	311
Jomelli	59
Josquin des Près	23
Kalkbrenner	257
Kalliwoda	254
Kauer	260
Keiser	96
Kelly	302
KEMBLE, Adelaide	304
Kerl	87
KIEL, Friedr.	349
Kindermann	302
Kirnberger	93
Kittel	87
KLEIN, Bernh.	307
Kömpel	311
König	315
KÖSTER, Louise	304
KREBS, Joh. Ludwig	92

356 INDEX.

	PAGE
KREBS, Karl Aug.	337
KREUTZER, Konradin	294
———, Rudolph	312
Kücken	337
Kummer	315
Labitzky	267
Lablache	302
LACHNER, Franz	296, 338
Lafont	313
Lagroscino	122
Lanner	267
LASOS of Hermione	3
LASSUS, Orlandus	27
LAUB, Ferdinand	311
Lauterbach	311
Lazarus	315
LEMMENS - SHERRINGTON, Madame	304
LEO, Leonardo	58
Leonard	313
LIND, Jenny	304
Lindpaintner	296
Lipinsky	312
Liszt	316, 343
Lolli	61
Lortzing	296
Lotti	44
LÖWE, Karl	334
———, Sophie	304
LUCCA, Pauline	304
Lully	117
Lumbye	267
Luther	68
LUTZER, Jenny	304
Macfarren	280
MAJO, Ciccio di	59
Malibran-Garcia	303
Mantius	302
MARA, Gertrud Elisabeth	144

	PAGE
Marcello	45
Marchesi	62
MARCHETTUS of Padua	18
MARENZIO, Luca	48
Mario	303
Marschner	297
Martin	262
Mattheson	97
Maurer	312
MAYER, Simon	264
Mayseder	312
Méhul	126, 271
Mendelssohn	2, 239, 320
Mercadante	270
Metastasio	60
Meyerbeer	281
MILANOLLO, Theresa and Maria	313
MILDER-HAUPTMANN, Anna	304
Molique	312
Monsigny	123
Monteverde	51
Morales	25
MORLEY, Thomas	100
Moscheles	257, 320
Mosel	107, 111
MOUTON, Jean	25
MOZART, Leopold	148, 111, 165
———, Wolfg. Amadeus	60, 110, 165, 237 n.
MULLER, the brothers	313
———, Iwan	315
———, Wenzel	260
MURIS, Johannes de	18
Musard	267
Nadermann	315
Nanini	40
Nardini	61
NAUMANN, Jos. G.	114
NEANDER, Joachim	74

	PAGE
Neukomm	256
Neumark	74
Nicolai, Otto	298
Nicholson	315
Niemann	302
Nourrit	302
Novello, Clara	303
Oberthür	315
Ockenheim	22
Offenbach	286
Olympos	4
Onslow	253
Osiander	72
Otto, Jul.	337
Pacchiarotti	62
Pachelbel	87
Paër	264
Paesiello	122, 263
Paganini	311
Palestrina	33
Parepa, Madame	304
Parish-Alvars	315
Pasta, Giuditta	303
Patti, Adelina	304
Pauer, Ernst	320
Pergolese	63, 121
Peri, Jacopo	51
Petrucci	25
Philidor	123
Piatti	314
Piccini	59, 122, 136
Pistocchi	62
Pitoni	42
Pleyel	255
Porpora	62, 151
Pott, Aug.	311
Prätorius, Michael	74
Pratten	315
Proch	337

	PAGE
Prume	313
Pugnani	61
Punto	315
Purcell, Henry	99
Pythagoras	3
Quanz	148
Queisser	315
Quinault	117
Radziwill	238
Raff, Anton	302
———, Joachim	350
Rameau	119
Reichardt, Joh. Friedr.	141
Reinecke, J. A.	87
———, Karl	337, 345
Reinthaler	349
Reissiger	337
Richardson	315
Ries, Ferdinand	253, 345
Rietz, Julius	338
Righini	262
Rink	87
Ritter, A. G.	349
Rode, Pierre	312
Roger	302
Rollet, Bailly du	135
Romberg, Andr.	254, 259
———, Bernh.	314
Roeb, Cyprian de	27
Rossini	250, 264
Rousseau, J. J.	121
Rubini	302
Rubinstein	350
Rudersdorff, Madame	304
Sacchini	59, 262
Sainton	311
Sainton-Dolby, Madame	304
Salieri	139, 262

INDEX.

Salomon, John Peter .. 153
Santley 302
Scarlatti, Alessandro .. 56
———, Domenico .. 98
Schäffer, Aug. 337
Schätzel, Pauline v. .. 304
Schebest, Agnes 304
Schechner-Waagen, Nannette 304
Scheidt 87
Schenk 260
Schicht 92
Schikaneder .. .. 172 n.
Schindelmeisser 345
Schneider, Friedrich .. 307
Schnorr v. Carolsfeld .. 302
Schoberlechner, Sophie 304
Schröder-Devrient, Wilhelmine 303
Schröter, Corona 144
Schubert 241
Schulhoff 319
Schumann, Clara 319
———, Robert 319, 327
Schunke, the brothers .. 315
Schütz, Heinr. 74
Schweitzer 142
Scribe 60
Senesino 61
Senfl, Ludwig .. .. 71 n.
Servais 314
Sessi, Imp. and Marianne 303
Seyfried 196
Silcher 337
Sims Reeves 302
Sivori 311
Sontag, Henriette 304
Spitzeder, Joseph 302
Spohr 295, 306, 338
Spontini 271
Staudigl 302

Steffani 96
Stehle, Sophie 304
Steibelt 255
Stevens, Miss 304
Stobäus, Joh. 74
Stockhausen, Jules .. 302
Stölzel 92
Storace 100
Stradella 57
Straduari 62
Strauss, Joh. 267
———, Ludwig 311
Streit, Wilhelmine .. 304
Stromeyer 302
Sullivan, Arthur 336
Süssmaier 181, 188
Sylvester, Pope 10

Tallis 99
Tamburini 302
Tartini 61
Taubert, Wilh. .. 296, 338
Telemann 92, 97
Terpander 3
Terradeglias 59
Tesi, Vittoria 62
Thalberg 257
Tichatschek 302
Tietjens, Therese 304
Traetta 59
Trebelli, Zelia 304
Truhn 337
Tulou 315

Ungher, Karoline 304
Umbreit 87

Velluti 62
Venosa, Gesualdo di .. 48
Verdi 288
Vespermann, Clara .. 304

	PAGE
Viadana	53
VIARDOT-GARCIA, Pauline	303
Vieuxtemps	313
Viotti	61
Vittoria	40
Vivaldi	89
VOGL, J. M.	302
VOGLER, Joh. Caspar	92
——, Abbé	285 n.
VOLKMANN, **Robert**	350
WACHTEL, **Th.**	305
WÄCHTER, **J. M.**	302
WAGNER, Johanna	304
——, Richard	118, 299

	PAGE
Wallace	280
Walther	71
WEBER, K. M. von	257, 289
Weigl	261
WIECK, Friedr.	328
Wieniawsky	311
Wild	302
Willaert	27
Winter	261
Zarlino	27
Zelter	320
ZIMMERMANN, Miss	320
ZÖLLNER, Karl	337
Zumsteeg	259

FINIS.

www.ingramcontent.com/pod-product-compliance
Lightning Source LLC
Chambersburg PA
CBHW031423230426
43668CB00007B/415